Catholic Economics

Catholic Economics

Alternatives to the Jungle

Angus Sibley

LITURGICAL PRESS

Collegeville, Minnesota

www.litpress.org

© 2015 by Angus Sibley
Published by Liturgical Press, Collegeville, Minnesota. All rights reserved. No part of this book may be reproduced in any form, by print, microfilm, microfiche, mechanical recording, photocopying, translation, or by any other means, known or yet unknown, for any purpose except brief quotations in reviews, without the previous written permission of Liturgical Press, Saint John's Abbey, PO Box 7500, Collegeville, Minnesota 56321-7500. Printed in the United States of America.

1   2   3   4   5   6   7   8   9

Library of Congress Cataloging-in-Publication Data

Sibley, Angus.
    Catholic economics : alternatives to the jungle / Angus Sibley.
        pages cm
    Includes bibliographical references.
    ISBN 978-0-8146-4868-1 — ISBN 978-0-8146-4893-3
    1. Economics—Religious aspects—Christianity.   2. Wealth—Moral and ethical aspects.   I. Title.
    BR115.E3S4735   2015
    261.8'5088282—dc23   2015006944

To my ever lovely Aurora

Contents

Acknowledgments

Excerpt from Adair Turner, "Economics, Conventional Wisdom and Public Policy," INET (April 2010). Used by permission.

Excerpt from John Kay, "Business Lessons from the Sporting World," © *The Financial Times Limited* (1996). All Rights Reserved.

Excerpt from "Pour se démarquer, les magasins de l'Archipel . . ." from *Le Monde*, April 9, 2009. Used by permission.

Table from *Demography: Analysis and Synthesis* by Graziella, Vallin & Wunsch, vol. 3, Jean-Noël Biraben, "The History of the Human Population," 13. Copyright Elsevier (2006). Used by permission.

Excerpt from Alan Avery-Peck, "Charity in Judaism," in *The Encyclopedia of Judaism*, vol. 1. Used by permission of Koninklijke BRILL NV.

Preface

Our present economic systems and policies are not working well. The American economy suffers from exorbitant, and still widening, inequalities. It consumes resources wastefully; it degrades and pollutes the environment. Despite some recent improvement, America still has clearly too much unemployment and too many workers who are underemployed, underpaid, and badly treated. These problems are not just American; similar troubles afflict many countries all over the world.

Concerning economic and social matters, the Catholic Church has much to say. She has indeed a large body of teachings, based on fundamental Catholic doctrine and greatly developed over the past century and a half, to address the particular economic and social problems of the modern capitalist world. Yet this branch of the Church's teaching, generally known as *Catholic Social Teaching*, is often neglected and too little known, even among practicing Catholics.

Catholic Social Teaching radically challenges orthodox economic thought and practice. It explains what is wrong with the exaggerated individualism of our times: how this leads to economic behavior based narrowly on self-interest and heedless of the common good. It condemns one of the worst errors of standard economic thought: the tendency to treat human labor as just another commodity to be bought and sold in the market. It shows up the amoral character of modern economics: the view that we must blindly pursue economic efficiency, whether or not this means doing what is morally acceptable. It takes issue with the conventional view that we have to pursue endless economic growth, even though our consumption of the earth's resources is already running at unsustainable levels. And it proposes a higher and richer understanding of human freedom than the "negative freedom" promoted by orthodox economists.

This book examines our pressing economic problems in a practical manner, avoiding so far as possible the technical jargon of economics. It shows how Catholic economic thought points to ways out of the self-destructive jungle in which we are living.

CHAPTER 1

Introduction

The conviction that the economy must be autonomous, that it must be shielded from "influences" of a moral character, has led man to abuse the economic process in a thoroughly destructive way.

—Pope Benedict XVI, *Caritas in Veritate*, par. 34

This imbalance [between the very rich minority and the rest] is the result of ideologies which defend the absolute autonomy of the marketplace and financial speculation . . . behind this attitude lurks a rejection of ethics and a rejection of God.

—Pope Francis, *Evangelii Gaudium*, pars. 56, 57

Important though justice is, many economists deny that justice has any bearing on economic transactions.

—Michael R. Griffiths and John R. Lucas[1]

There is also a strong belief, which I share, that bad economics— or rather oversimplistic and overconfident economics—helped create the crisis.

—Adair Turner[2]

Economics without Ethics

We can trace many of our economic and social woes to a fact that lies hidden beneath the mountain of theories, statistics, arguments, and ideologies that the science of economics generates. That hidden fact is that economics, as it is generally understood, taught and practiced today, has by and large lost contact with ethics.

1

The "autonomy" (Greek *autó* = itself, *nómos* = law) of the economy and the markets simply means that the economy, nowadays dominated by the markets, is allowed to be a law unto itself. Many economists—and these economists have been all too influential for several decades—think that the economy should not be regulated by our laws, but rather that we should submit to its "laws." The political world, they say, should leave the economic world alone. But without democratic supervision and regulation, the economy becomes our master rather than our servant.

Today's highly competitive economies leave little place for ethics or morality. In our markets, producers and consumers, employers and workers, investors and borrowers act for their own private advantage. They too seldom ask themselves whether or not their actions are advantageous for others. And that "ethical negligence" does not happen only when people who trade in the markets make mistakes or deliberately misbehave. It is part of the normal functioning of autonomous markets.

This takes us all the way back to Adam Smith, but we cannot put all the blame on him. He argued that the individual "by pursuing his own interest frequently promotes that of the society more effectually than when he really intends to promote it."[3] But we have overlooked the word *frequently*. Instead, ever since the late eighteenth century, Smith's followers seem to have assumed that he wrote *normally*, or even *always*. We have favored the view that it is best simply to let everyone do what suits one's own interest without bothering about the interests of others, since the self-interested actions of us individuals will normally, or even always, combine to yield the best outcomes for us all. If that were so, then in economics, ethics would hardly be necessary. But in practice, the economy frequently does not work like that.

The distinguished Indian economist Amartya Sen, professor at Harvard and past Master of Trinity College, Cambridge (England), complains that the typical modern economist "in his economic models . . . keeps the motivations of human beings pure, simple and hard-headed, and not messed up by such things as goodwill or moral sentiments."[4] But, in the real world, we all depend on the goodwill of others, so we have a corresponding obligation to show goodwill toward them. And we can hardly have a healthy economy if our economic behavior is immoral. Economic theory, if it is to encourage decent and humane economic behavior, ought surely to recognize these facts. At the beginning of Mass, we sing: "Glory to God in the highest, and on earth peace to people of goodwill." Without goodwill, how can we hope to have peace, or prosperity, or happiness?

Free-market economics claims to offer a guarantee against tyrannical government: the markets, rather than the state, should rule our lives. The twentieth-century revival of this nineteenth-century ideology was inspired largely by reaction against fascism, Nazism, and communism. But it has become clear in recent years that markets too, given excessive power, can become oppressive tyrants. We need urgently to develop a more civilized economics than that of the free-market "jungle" in which the "fittest" not only survive but grow inordinately rich and powerful, while others (at least in mature economies) grow generally poorer or even struggle to survive at all. The aim of this book is to show how the tradition and teaching of the Catholic Church can guide us into better economic ways.

The Catholic Alternative

The Catholic Church has a substantial body of doctrine on economic and social matters, generally known as Catholic Social Teaching (CST). This is a practical, contemporary expression of Catholic theology. It is firmly based on Scripture and tradition. We can trace its roots back through the philosophy of St. Thomas Aquinas in the Middle Ages to the New Testament, and to the Old Testament too.

CST as we know it today, however, has been greatly enriched and updated by its vigorous development from the mid-nineteenth century onward. This began as a response to the pressing social and economic problems arising in the new world of the "industrial revolution," the great transition from rural to urban society and economy. Today, CST continues to develop to meet the challenges of our new age of information technology and globalization.

Yet, though CST carries vital messages for our times, it is not as well-known as it should be. Indeed, many Catholics, both laity and clergy, seem to know little about it, despite the fact that almost every pope from Leo XIII in the nineteenth century to Francis today has pronounced on this subject. The only exceptions were John Paul I, who reigned for only a month, and Benedict XV, whose short reign spanned the period of the First World War; he was preoccupied with diplomatic efforts to find a peace settlement and with humanitarian projects to help war victims.

What is worse, some Catholics deliberately reject CST. They argue that, because CST does not conform with the prevailing opinions of professional economists, there must be something wrong with it. Economists, they say, must surely know more about economics than priests, bishops, theologians, or popes. Therefore, religious thinkers and teachers should admit that "economics is not their subject" and leave it to the "experts."

That is an error. Economics is about human behavior, and the Church has always seen it as a major part of her mission to offer guidance to us wayward human beings on how to behave rightly. Christianity has inherited the tradition of the biblical prophets and lawgivers from Moses onward who have acted as guides to our worldly conduct as well as to our spiritual aspirations. The Bible is full of instructions on how we should behave toward one another, and many of these commandments are specific rules concerning economic transactions.

Some of those rules, of course, are not directly relevant to us today, who live in a very different world from that of the Bible. In any case, Christians do not consider themselves bound by all the detailed regulations of Jewish religious law. But the basic principles underlying those ancient rules are still relevant for us. It is the task of the Church to consider and explain how those principles can be applied in practice by us today.

Misguided Experts

Economic "experts" have often given advice that flies in the face of Christian teachings, not to mention common sense or basic human decency. For example, one highly regarded economist, of whom we shall have more to say later, argued that we should "gain from *not* treating one another as neighbors."[5] When notions like that are propagated by people who claim to be authoritative experts on economics, should the Church remain silent, saying, in effect: *no comment, that is not our subject*?

Furthermore, since the beginnings of modern economic science in the eighteenth century, economists have put forward a variety of differing and conflicting views. How do nonexperts discriminate between the good and the bad options? We need guidance as to which of these views are realistic, practical, and morally acceptable. The Church is surely entitled to point out to us that, while some economists' theories and practical recommendations are compatible with Church teaching, many others are definitely not.

The Vatican does not remain silent. But too many Catholics pay little attention to what the magisterium has to say about economics.

In the past few decades, the world has given the ideology of *laissez-faire* an extensive trial and has found it gravely wanting—and not for the first time. Very similar ideology prevailed in the nineteenth century; it threw up so many horrible social problems that it was largely abandoned in the first half of the twentieth. The ugly consequences of *laissez-faire* provoked the rise of communism, socialism, and other economic theories that did not rely on leaving the markets to their own devices. Today, our neo–free marketeers, or *libertarians*, obsessed by their hatred of communism and socialism, yearn to re-create the conditions that gave them birth! That is one indication of the basic fallacy of their stance.

Libertarian "Freedom"

There is a more profound explanation of why the libertarians are mistaken: their philosophy is based on a gravely defective understanding of freedom. In Catholic teaching, "there is no true freedom except in the service of what is good and just," as the *Catechism* (par. 1733) tells us; or, as Leo XIII put it, in striking words (*Libertas Praestantissimum*, par. 6): "The possibility of sinning is not freedom, but slavery." This saying, and others like it, is based on the words of Jesus (John 8:34): "Truly, truly, I say to you, everyone who commits sin is a slave to sin."

Thus, in Christian theology, sin is likened to slavery, the opposite of freedom. So freedom is fundamentally tied to virtue and justice. We can be free only in God's service. To borrow a memorable phrase from our Jewish friends, "to choose evil is to fail to be free."[6]

On the contrary, say the libertarians and proponents of *laissez-faire*, freedom is not about virtue and justice; it is about *absence of constraint*. Milton Friedman, doyen of the "Chicago school" of "neoclassical" free-market economists, put this very clearly in his best seller *Capitalism and Freedom*. In the very first chapter, he sets out one of his basic beliefs: "Economic freedom is an end in itself. . . . Freedom has nothing to say about what an individual does with his freedom."[7] Though Friedman was a Jew born and bred (but he turned atheist), his view fundamentally contradicts both Jewish and Christian philosophies of freedom.

Another prominent free-market economist, Friedrich von Hayek (it was he who disparaged neighborly behavior), was a leader of the "Austrian school" of economics. This is somewhat different from Friedman's "Chicago school," but both have in common a commitment to "negative freedom" (absence of constraints). Hayek argued that "the freedom of action that is the condition of moral merit includes the freedom to act wrongly."[8] If that is so, then there is no freedom in the kingdom of Heaven, where there is no possibility of sinning. Hayek was a Catholic born and bred, but like Friedman he became an atheist, or at least an agnostic.

Exaggerated Individualism

Thus, according to many libertarians, *freedom is amoral*. Driven by their belief in an exaggerated individualism, they say we find our freedom not in doing good but in doing whatever we think is in our own individual best interest. It follows that they abhor regulation. Should we have rules (or generally respected customs) to prevent us from paying our employees too little, from ruining our competitors by predatory competition, from borrowing our way into crippling debt, or from cutting our costs in ways that damage our environment? No, all such constraints are ruled out since they would allegedly destroy our "freedom." The policies taught by these economists, by dismantling necessary constraints, have permitted us to wreck our economies, abandon the pursuit of social justice, and gravely endanger the health of our planet.

Social Injustice

The more extreme libertarians reject the entire notion of social justice. It is a cardinal point of their thinking that *the market knows best*. Therefore, if our actions in the market system lead to a society of glaring inequalities, such as we see in America today, it is not for us to try to reform or regulate the system in order to achieve a more equitable outcome. "A just society must be the achievement of politics," wrote Benedict XVI (*Deus Caritas Est*, par. 28), but libertarians, even if they are Catholics, are not listening. According to John Paul II, a just society "is not directed against the market, but demands that the market be appropriately controlled" (*Centesimus Annus*, par. 35), but they are not listening to him either. They believe that the market is sacrosanct, that we must not tamper with it. This follows from their notion of freedom as merely noninterference or absence of constraint. We see here how a philosophical error is far from being a purely academic matter; it can have very serious practical consequences.

Hayek likened the free market to a game in which "there is no sense in calling the result just or unjust."[9] He even wrote that he would love to see the phrase *social justice* expunged from the English language.[10] And he paid Catholics a pleasing but wholly unintended compliment: he complained bitterly that "the Roman Catholic Church especially has made the aim of social justice part of its official doctrine."[11]

A Science in Poor Shape

Politicians have little time to think about economic theories; quite naturally, they prefer to leave that to the specialists of the economics profession, who should, logically, know far more about the subject than politicians know. But the science of economics, as we have known it in recent decades, is in poor shape. Indeed, some eminent members of the economics profession have had the courage and the good sense to say so in public.

Thus Paul Krugman, professor at Princeton and a leading *New York Times* columnist, has famously claimed that we are living in a "Dark Age of macroeconomics," having forgotten much wisdom acquired through hard experience in the past.[12]

Amartya Sen complains that "suspicion of the use of ethics in economics has grown" and deplores the "extremely narrow assumption of self-interested behavior."[13] He blames mainstream economists for assuming that people act solely from self-interested motives; in his more generous view, people often act from unselfish or altruistic motives. Therefore, he says, we should be skeptical about conventional economic theories that are based on that cynical and unrealistic assumption of orthodox economics.

Joseph Stiglitz, professor at Princeton and a renowned writer on economics, has severely criticized the ideology of the dogmatic free marketeers: he insists that "the problem is not just with the implementation of the ideas, but with the ideas themselves," and that "the intellectual foundation of *laissez-faire* economics, the idea that markets by themselves will lead to efficient, let alone fair, outcomes has been stripped away."[14]

So politicians who rely on economists for advice are often badly advised. This phenomenon may be described as the *misguided experts effect*.

The Error of Anti-Statism

Free-market economists have gone astray because, in their praiseworthy desire to promote freedom from oppressive governments, they assume that we can solve this problem by drastically cutting back the state and handing most of its duties over to the markets. Governments, they say, should give up trying to regulate our economic behavior. The markets can regulate themselves and our conduct too—just let them do so! Then, hey presto! We shall all be freer, richer, and happier. That, in a nutshell, is the philosophy of the free-market libertarians.

But this anti-statist attitude diverts attention from the age-old and vital question of how to establish and maintain a state that works effectively for the benefit of all its citizens. The founders of the American republic took great pains to devise a political regime that would serve American citizens well. Today, it is not working very well; reforms are needed. But libertarians in general are not much interested in reforming the state. Hayek did indeed propose an ingenious, if eccentric, constitutional reform: every year, voters aged forty-five should elect some of their number to a "legislative assembly" where they would sit for fifteen years.[15] For this assembly, each citizen would vote only once in a lifetime!

Most libertarians, however, just want to castrate the state; they think, with Ludwig von Mises, another dominant Austrian economist, that "liberty is always freedom from the government."[16] As Pope Francis complains (*Evangelii Gaudium*, par. 56), their ideologies "reject the right of states, charged with vigilance for the common good, to exercise any control." Those who basically despise the state are unlikely to be able or willing to endeavor to make it work better.

The market is not a substitute for the state. Free-market theories claim that markets naturally correct their own excesses before these become disastrous; even the brilliant Alan Greenspan, chairman of the US Federal Reserve from 1987 to 2006, was seduced by such arguments. So he refrained from restraining the grossly imprudent behavior of many banks in the years up to 2008. When the banking system exploded, however, Greenspan honorably and with much embarrassment admitted his error.

Distributive Justice

Catholic social teaching emphasizes the doctrine of the *universal destination of goods*, which means that God wishes every human being to have at least a basic sufficiency of this world's goods. Markets alone, however, do not assure this outcome. That fact has been recognized since ancient times; the Law of Moses prescribes obligatory (not voluntary) tithes and other measures to provide for the poor. Today the state is responsible for social security systems to protect our more vulnerable citizens. But many libertarians would like to abolish these systems, or most of them. Hayek grudgingly tolerated "some provision for those threatened by the extremes of indigence or starvation, be it only in the interest of those who require protection against acts of desperation on the part of the needy."[17]

The polity of a democratic state works on the basis of *one person, one vote*. But the market's basis is *one dollar, one vote*. Mises tells us, with emphatic approval, that "the capitalist system is a democracy in which every penny represents a ballot paper."[18] But that is plutocracy, not democracy. Today, the richest 10 percent of Americans receive around 50 percent of total personal incomes (including capital gains) and hold more than 70 percent of total personal wealth.[19] In the markets, therefore, affluent minorities hold the majority of penny "ballot papers"; so they rule. That is a good reason why the markets should not be allowed too much dominance. Hayek was suspicious of political democracy; he feared that it could lead to oppression of minorities by the ruling majority. With Mises and his plutocracy, we have the opposite problem.

Today, the majority of Americans are suffering a kind of oppression by a minority group, the very rich, who contrive to capture most of the benefits of American growth, leaving the rest to put up with static or declining incomes, high unemployment or underemployment, and increasingly precarious, frustrating, and overstressful jobs.

We need to recognize that market and state have quite distinct functions; both are necessary. We should distrust arguments that treat the state with contempt, that propose to abandon most of its functions to unhampered markets. Such a strategy expects the markets to shoulder responsibilities that are beyond their competence and outside their purpose.

The Excesses of Individualism

The dark side of individualism is a centering on the self, which both flattens and narrows our lives, makes them poorer in meaning, and less concerned with others or society.

—Charles Taylor[1]

Individualism, a Phenomenon of Modern Times

Individualism is the principle of priority for the aims of the individual over the claims of the community.

No doubt there has always been, and will always be, contention between, on the one hand, what we as individuals want to be and to do and, on the other hand, what is expected of us by the community that surrounds us. For human nature contains both the desire to act independently and the need to be part of a society, which inevitably imposes obligations and puts limits on independence.

We shall see later how Aristotle criticized certain Greek democracies where individuals felt free to do just as they fancied without regard to the constitution of their state or to the common good. "Man is by nature a political animal,"[2] wrote the philosopher, implying that the human being naturally dwells in a *pólis*; that is, in a village, town, city, country, or state, wherein one is part of a community. Therefore, one has a duty to consider the needs and wishes of one's community of neighbors, often in priority to one's own personal desires or ambitions. The famous statesman Pericles observed that "we [Athenians] are prevented from doing wrong by respect for the authorities and for the laws, having an especial regard to those which are ordained for the protection of the injured, *as well as to those unwritten laws which bring upon the transgressors of them the reprobation of the general sentiment.*"[3]

Ancient civilizations and religions have generally emphasized duty to one's community—one's country, religion, tribe, class, city, profession, or trade—as having at least as much importance as any right to pursue one's own preferences and make one's own choices. Confucius, for example, made much use of the word *li*, which may be translated, depending on its context, as ritual, rites, customs, etiquette, propriety, morals, rules of proper behavior, or worship. Two modern translators of Confucius, Roger Ames and Henry Rosemont, comment:

> *Li* are those meaning-invested roles, relationships and institutions which facilitate communication, and which foster a sense of community. The compass is broad; all formal conduct, from table-manners to patterns of greeting and leave-taking, to graduations, weddings, funerals, from gestures of deference to ancestral sacrifices—all of these, and more, are *li*. They are a social grammar that provides each member with a defined place within the family, community, and polity.[4]

In the Bible, the Ten Commandments are entirely concerned with duties to God and to neighbor or family; they do not mention any kind of "duty to be oneself." Nor do the 613 *mitzvoth* (rules or commandments) in the Torah.[5] Indeed, the Jewish tradition has always been profoundly concerned with the duties of every Jew to the Jewish community. This tradition continues into our own times; hear leading political scientist Daniel Elazar:

> In Western civilization the Bible is considered the foundation of democratic republicanism and has been so treated by democratic reformers throughout the history of the Western world. . . . The Bible emphasizes communal liberty . . . [which] stands in contrast to atomistic individualism as the highest good. The Jews, like the Swiss, have emphasized individual liberty within the community, not apart from it. This approach differs from the radical individualism espoused by many in the contemporary Western world.[6]

Medieval Europe was arguably less advanced than classical Greece in terms of individual liberty. As the eminent Cambridge (England) medievalist Walter Ullmann tells us, "One may well say that for the larger part of the Middle Ages it was the individual as a subject [of the king] that dominated the scene, while in the later Middle Ages the subject was gradually supplanted by the citizen."[7] The individual Christian was incorporated by baptism into society, "subjected, as far as his social and public life went, to the law as it was *given* to him, not to the law as it was made by him."[8] We may compare this with Aristotle's conception of the democratic republic, where "all the citizens alike should take their turn of governing and being governed."[9]

So little was there of individual self-promotion that the names of even the most brilliantly creative individuals—writers, craftsmen, architects of the great Gothic cathedrals—often went unrecorded. Ullmann comments: "I can only testify to my own annoyance . . . when I come across a work of art or of literature or of documentation which so successfully hides its author. . . . Today, when a new apartment house goes up, the name of its architect is splashed all over the papers, but in coming years neither the architect nor his building will be remembered, while after so many centuries medieval productions still evoke justifiably great admiration."[10]

Individualism as we know it has traditionally been traced back to the era of the Renaissance; it developed in diverse ways with the Reformation, the Enlightenment, and the period of Romanticism. These great movements, as we commonly define them, cover five centuries or more, from the close of the Middle Ages to the mid-nineteenth century, the opening of our modern industrial, commercial, and capitalistic era.

The Renaissance: The First Age of Individualism?

The Renaissance is reckoned to have begun in fourteenth-century Italy and to have run till the early seventeenth century, thus for some three hundred years. The Swiss historian Jacob Burckhardt (1818–1897), in his classic book on the Italian Renaissance, argued that this was the period when, for the first time, people became aware of their individuality.[11] "In the Middle Ages . . . Man was conscious of himself only as a member of a race, people, party, family or corporation."[12] But, in the fourteenth century, people began to think and act as distinct individuals. For example, "by the year 1390 there was no longer any prevailing fashion of dress for men at Florence, each preferring to clothe himself in his own way."[13] That sounds remarkably like our own times!

Moving on to the sixteenth century, "when the civilization of the Renaissance had reached its highest pitch," Burckhardt observes that "the fundamental vice of this [Italian] character was at the same time a condition of its greatness, namely, excessive individualism. . . . The sight of the victorious egotism in others drives [the individual] to defend his own right by his own arm. . . . He falls, by the vengeance which he executes, into the hands of the powers of darkness."[14]

Paradoxically, an age of violent, vindictive, egotistic, and immoral behavior was also an age that saw an amazing outburst of brilliant cultural and creative activity. Here we see a striking example of the double-edged nature of individualism; it can be highly productive, but it can also lead to gross misconduct. In our own times, individualistic economic behavior has given us not beautiful works of art but spectacular technological development and considerable economic growth. It has also given us hugely destructive financial disorders and glaring inequalities.

It is not surprising that many concerned thinkers have been ambivalent about individualism and even inclined to disparage it. Pope Francis uses the word often, usually with disapproval.

The Reformation Strengthens Individualist Claims

The traumatic religious upheavals of the Reformation began in the early sixteenth century, when Martin Luther published his ninety-five "theses" (mainly objections to the practice of selling indulgences) in 1517; the Treaty of Westphalia (1648), which ended the Thirty Years' War, may be seen as marking the close of this period.

The Reformation was individualist in the sense that it promoted the idea that the individual can and should have a direct relationship with God without depending on the Church as an intermediary. Reformers saw the organized church as a useful focus of community rather than as a prerequisite for salvation. Moreover, they argued that individuals are entitled to adopt their own interpretations of Holy Scripture, in contrast with the principle that Catholics should accept the interpretations propounded by the Roman magisterium. Not surprisingly, the Reformation led to the proliferation of a vast variety of doctrines. Protestants faced, and they face still, a potentially bewildering range of choices between different interpretations of the Bible.

All this contributes to the notion that it is up to individuals to make their own personal choices in this as in all matters. Emphasis on the *power to choose* is clearly a key feature of individualism, both in religion and in economics.

In practice, Protestant churches, like other religious groups, do indeed prescribe norms of acceptable belief and conduct, and many of them adhere to the ancient Apostles' and Nicene Creeds. But the theory of individual interpretation of Scripture points logically toward the belief that "you can make your own rules" by interpreting the texts in your own way.

Ultimately, this can mean that morality becomes "privatized." Instead of a *shared* system of ethics, with society broadly in agreement about what is morally acceptable and what is not, we move toward a state of moral confusion in which there is no such agreement. Everyone has one's own private and personal view; and some may have very odd views! That is in fact where much of the world stands today. There is, as Rabbi Jonathan Sacks vividly put it, "our new consensus-that-there-is-no-consensus."[15] Reaction against such ethical chaos can lead to the harsh and intolerant behavior of, for example, today's Islamic extremists, who endeavor to close down the chaos by forcing their adherents to follow regimes of extraordinary rigidity.

The Enlightenment: Reaction against Religious Turmoil

The Enlightenment, or *Age of Reason*, dates roughly from the mid-seventeenth century to the end of the eighteenth. The keynote of this period was rationalistic or scientific thought. Truth was to be discovered by experimental investigation and logical reasoning rather than through revelation and faith. Unlike the Reformation, the Enlightenment challenged not just Catholicism but religion in general.

This did not mean that "enlightened" thinkers were all atheists. Many of them called themselves *Deists*; they believed in a God but did not accept the supernatural aspects of religion. They held that no teaching should be accepted unless it appeared scientifically "reasonable." Thus Thomas Jefferson, who firmly asserted that he believed in God, compiled an abridged New Testament, known as the *Jefferson Bible*, which excludes all references to miracles and to the divinity of Jesus. The Deists believed in a remote God who created the world but who leaves it to run without further intervention and shows little or no personal interest in the affairs of us human beings.

The German philosopher Immanuel Kant (1724–1804) was one of the leading figures of the Enlightenment, and he gave us a simple definition of this word. Enlightenment, he wrote, "is man's emergence from self-incurred immaturity. Immaturity is the inability to use one's own understanding without the guidance of another. . . . Have courage to use your own understanding!"[16] Kant's conception of enlightenment is thus highly individualistic. We must think for ourselves rather than rely on the theories or precepts of others. Thus Kant, who was brought up in the Lutheran tradition, extended the Reformation principle from religion to philosophy in general. He held that ethical questions concerning our behavior in this world could be resolved by human reason alone, without any need for divine revelation. But he accepted that matters of which we have here no knowledge or experience, such as the ultimate destiny of the human soul, belonged properly to the domain of faith.

We are indeed well advised to think for ourselves; but if we try to do so *without any external guidance*, we are in the position of the person who "tries to reinvent the wheel." St. Thomas Aquinas, arguably the greatest of all Christian theologians, refers constantly to earlier sources of wisdom; to Holy Scripture of course, but also to Aristotle, St. Augustine, Boethius, St. Gregory the Great, occasionally Maimonides, and many other authoritative writers. Who are we to imagine that we can dispense with the guidance of others?

The Enlightenment can be seen as a phase of reaction against the terrible religious wars, controversies, and intolerances of the Reformation and its aftermath. Weary of the destructive passions of endlessly quarrelling sects, people sought relief in calmer philosophies based on cool reason rather than ardent faith. Thus the eighteenth century saw a rise in agnostic, rationalistic, and scientific thinking, and a decline in traditional religious practice.

Romanticism: Individualism in Full Bloom

The age of Romanticism, which can be dated from the late eighteenth century to the mid-nineteenth, was, in turn, a reaction against the chilly rationalism of the Enlightenment. Yet in this movement, individualism developed still further, reflecting the Romantic concern with the primacy of individual feeling. One may indeed argue that Romanticism in the arts is individualism *par excellence*, as the philosopher Isaiah Berlin explains: the "aesthetics of romanticism" involve "the self-expression of the artist's own unique, inner vision, to set aside which, in response to some 'external' voice—church, state, public opinion, family, friends, arbiters of taste—is an act of betrayal of what alone justifies their existence for those who are in any sense creative."[17]

In earlier times, many—perhaps most—of the great artists were *master craftsmen* in the literal sense of those words; they served apprenticeships in the studios of established masters and became in due course masters themselves, i.e., fully qualified members of artists' guilds. This was still the custom in the Renaissance period. Thus Leonardo da Vinci (1452–1519) was a master in the guild of St. Luke in Florence; likewise Diego Velázquez (1599–1660), in the corporation of painters of Seville; and Peter Paul Rubens (1577–1640), in another guild of St. Luke in Antwerp.[18] As master craftsmen, they worked to the orders of noblemen or rich merchants or ecclesiastics, so they had to provide what their patrons wanted. Though they were certainly more individualist than their medieval predecessors, self-expression was not their top priority.

By contrast, in the Romantic era we see the origins of the modern idea that a creative artist (painter, sculptor, composer, poet, architect, designer, etc.) is *not* a master craftsperson, trained in a tradition of creating good things for the use or enjoyment of one's fellow human beings. On the contrary, an artist is a self-expressionist who claims that one's own artistic notions, be they beautiful or horrible, realistic or grotesque, relevant or unintelligible, have intrinsic value just because they emanate from one's individual self. Thus art becomes primarily *individual self-expression* rather than *creation of what other people enjoy* or, if I may so put it, contribution to the common good. There are, of course, still many artists who work in traditional styles and create enjoyable works of art, but they are not seen as being in the mainstream of contemporary art.

Romantic writers, artists, and composers showed a strong tendency to glorify the lone individual who sets himself up in opposition to the society around him. In Wagner's earlier operas, Tannhäuser shocks his peers by frequenting orgies of debauchery in the Venusberg, while another minstrel, Walther von Stolzing, carries off the Mastersingers' prize, and the guildmaster's daughter Eva, with a song that flouts the guild's rules of musical composition. Robert Burns, the great Scottish romantic poet, writes:

> The Kirk an' State may join, an' tell
> To do sic things I maunna:

The Kirk an' State may gae to hell,
And I'll gae to my Anna.[19]

Reaction against Individualism Emerges

It was during the Romantic period that the word *individualism* was invented, apparently by the French counterrevolutionary Catholic writer Joseph de Maistre (1753–1821). He used it in a totally pejorative sense, for he was appalled by the social, political, and moral chaos that followed the French Revolution. The word first appears in a brief note recording a conversation in 1820 between de Maistre and an army officer, Charles de Lavau. De Maistre worried that "France was losing her way, Europe was following her in her errors . . . this limitless fragmentation of all doctrines, political Protestantism carried to the most absolute individualism." A little later, in 1821, he complained that "we have seen the social order shattered to its foundations, because there was too much liberty in Europe, and no longer enough religion."[20]

De Maistre's contemporary, the traditionalist (but later heterodox) priest Félicité de Lamennais (1782–1854), castigated "*individualism* which destroys the very idea of obedience and duty, thereby destroying both power and law; and what remains but a terrifying confusion of interests, passions, and diverse opinions?"[21] That was in 1829. As I write this (in October 2014), French Catholics and others are organizing a big demonstration, a protest primarily against surrogate motherhood for the benefit of homosexual couples, but also more generally against the conditions of social and economic upheaval under which we live. It is reported that, among the demonstrators, "individualism is a dirty word."[22]

It is reassuring to note that there is nothing novel about the disorders of society, the confusion of morality, and the neglect of religion that distress us today. These things have happened before, and history shows that the disease is not incurable. After all, the later nineteenth century was an age of religious revival, a great age of church building, an age which, particularly in Victorian Britain, has often been seen as a time when moral propriety was pursued to prudish extremes. It was also an age when new solidarities such as labor unions, cooperative movements, and friendly societies (mutual benefit associations) developed strongly as antidotes to the pains of harshly competitive capitalism.

Another nineteenth-century French Catholic who denounced individualism was the influential journalist Louis Veuillot (1813–1883).

Like de Maistre, he was a staunch traditionalist of somewhat extreme views, but he is worth quoting because he put the case against individualistic excesses with great vigor and clarity. Writing in 1843 in a letter to the French minister of education, demanding for Catholics the right to establish their own schools, he asserted:

> The evil that is gnawing at France is not unknown; everybody agrees to give it the same name: *individualism.*
>
> It is not difficult to understand that a country where *individualism* reigns is no longer under the normal conditions of society, since society is the union of minds and interests, while individualism is division pursued to infinity!
>
> All for each, each for all, that is society; each for himself, and consequently each against all, that is individualism.

All for each, each for all: Pope John Paul II affirmed this principle with a warning against "a distorted individualism that exalts self-fulfillment as the primary purpose of human life and regards society only as a means to pursue this self-interest." This, he said, "contradicts the call to exist 'for others' that God has inscribed in the hearts of his creatures."[23] Joseph Ratzinger, long before he became Pope Benedict XVI, was even more emphatic: "Hell is wanting-only-to-be-oneself."[24]

The Common Good

Catholic teaching stresses the vital importance of "the common good—the good of all persons and of the whole person" and insists that "the common good does not consist in the simple sum of the particular goods" of individuals. That is because "the human person cannot find fulfilment in himself. . . . [H]e exists 'with' others and 'for' others" (*Compendium of the Social Doctrine of the Church* [hereafter *Compendium*], pars. 164–65). Thus, the "atomistic" thought of the more extreme individualists, which sees each individual as a completely separate, independent "atom," is definitely not Catholic.

On the contrary, the common good "is indivisible and . . . only together is it possible to attain it" (*Compendium*, pars. 164–65). This principle is well expressed in the *Catechism* (par. 1879): "[T]he human person needs to live in society. Society is not for him an extraneous addition but a requirement of his nature. Through the exchange with others, mutual service and dialogue with his brethren, man develops his potential; he thus responds to his vocation."

On the Catholic view, the common good is a guarantee of personal good. Individualists have turned this principle upside down, arguing that the only good that matters is the good of each and every individual. If there is such a thing as a common good, they say, it can only be the result of each person getting what he or she wants out of life.

To see how the Catholic principle works out in practice, consider the design of a city. If the city council takes care to see that the development of the city is well planned, with good design and architecture providing a harmonious ensemble of buildings and green spaces, then every citizen will benefit from living in beautiful surroundings. That is what happened in Paris in the nineteenth century, when Baron Haussmann's[25] administration directed a huge reconstruction of much of the city center. Congested, squalid, decrepit streets were replaced by fine, spacious avenues and boulevards with elegant buildings and often lined with trees. The result was, and still is, one of the most beautiful cities in the world, one of the best loved and most visited. One cannot hope to achieve a city like that by allowing every individual property owner to look after his own good by building whatever he fancies. Good planning and coordination are essential.

Reconciling Individualism with Society

Society is the union of minds and interests, wrote Veuillot: here one seems to catch an echo, perhaps intended by him, of what is today the opening prayer at Mass for the Twenty-First Sunday in Ordinary Time: "O God, who cause the minds of the faithful to unite in a single purpose." That is a quite accurate translation of the first words of this ancient and beautiful Latin prayer. But other translations have altered the text; for example, the old Anglican prayer book has "O God, who alone canst order the unruly wills and affections of sinful men."[26] Some translators, it seems, have shied away from the original text, perhaps fearing that there is something totalitarian about everyone being "united in one same will" (*Dios, que unes a todos los fieles en una misma volontad*), as a good translation in an old Spanish missal has it.

And there we have a difficulty with the case against excessive individualism: how do we find unity sufficient for community, peace, and order without suppressing individuality? It seems that the wills of God's faithful people should be united in the sense that they should all be directed toward the "one single purpose" of God's service. The same prayer, as it continues, suggests an answer: "grant your people to love what you command and to desire what you promise." That does not, in my view, mean that everyone has to will the same objectives; for there are as many ways of serving God as there are individuals. What God commands and promises may be different for each one of us. Thus we can have unity in diversity.

But what if people's diverse objectives clash against each other, as too often they do? To achieve harmony, we need both tolerance and restraint. We need to be respectful and tolerant of other peoples' ways (insofar as they are not evidently and fundamentally unacceptable), even if we do not agree with them. But equally, we must avoid pushing forward our own ways to the point where they seriously offend other people and disrupt the harmony of society.

In a free society, people are entitled to have their own opinions and their own ways of life. Taketoshi Nojiri, a former professor at the Pontifical Academy of Social Sciences, explains: "Every individual must be equal in his status as a person, but his way of living must diverge from that of others. . . . Any attempt to equalize men's ways of living is incompatible with human liberty."[27] Yet while we can accept many, even innumerable, different ways of living, we should not accept ways that are incompatible with the basic values of the divine order. We need, therefore, a consensus about what are those basic values.

We cannot hope for a total consensus; there will always be disagreement, and hence the need for continuing debate. For, in this world, no one has complete knowledge of the divine order; as St. Paul affirms (1 Cor 13:12): "[N]ow we see in a mirror dimly . . . now I know in part." Here on earth, our knowledge is always imperfect.

But to quote Nojiri again, "To be imperfect is not to be false. And it often happens that a truth only vaguely known in the beginning comes to be clarified. Given this possibility, dialogue becomes possible and meaningful."[28]

American Individualism

Our preoccupation with negative freedom (absence of constraints) reflects the modern exaggeration of individualism, the notion that the individual should forge his own way with a bare minimum of social, religious, or political constraint. This idea developed strongly in nine-teenth-century America, encouraged by the pioneering spirit of those who struck out for the Western frontiers. It has been renewed and rein-forced in the twentieth century as a reaction against repressive tyrannies abroad that, among other things, have propelled waves of refugees into America. Yet contrasting philosophies of concern for good citizenship, solidarity, and the common weal have been prominent at various times in American history, notably in the early years of the republic, at the end of the nineteenth century, and in the age of the New Deal.

The early American republic seems not to have been dominated by the highly individualistic attitudes that are so widespread today. His-torian Barry Shain observes that eighteenth-century Americans "were pulled in one direction by the demands of a two-millennia-old ethical vision in which communal life was to limit the range of individual freedom and human selfishness and thereby shape the ethical existence of each individual. They were also pulled in the opposite direction by material and social forces and certain intellectual currents that de-manded higher levels of unstructured freedom and a greater tolerance of human selfishness."[29]

Tocqueville Describes Nascent Individualism

By the early nineteenth century, those more individualist attitudes were coming to the fore. The French aristocrat Alexis de Tocqueville, brilliant author of *Democracy in America* (1835), warned that concen-tration on individual interests could militate against good citizenship. He drew a striking contrast between aristocratic and democratic societies.[30]

In traditional, highly stratified, aristocratic societies, he argued, the social classes are separate and more or less static; and, within each class, families remain rooted in particular places for centuries. Thus, "all generations are therefore in a sense contemporaneous.[31] A man almost always knows and respects his forebears. In his mind's eye he can already see his great-grandsons, and he loves them." Moreover, each social class "becomes for its members a sort of homeland within a homeland." Thus, individuals are very conscious of their close links with fellow members—past, present, and future—of their own families and social or professional groups.

By contrast, in a democracy where there is little class structure and much mobility, the individual is more isolated; he tends to "withdraw into the circle of family and friends . . . [and] leaves the larger society to take care of itself." The ideal of self-sufficiency outweighs that of participation in the wider society. "These people owe nothing to anyone, and in a sense they expect nothing from anyone. They become accustomed to thinking of themselves always in isolation and are pleased to think that their fate lies entirely in their own hands."

Tocqueville was concerned that this individualist tendency might undermine democracy through a growing unwillingness of citizens to involve themselves in public affairs. He recognized, however, offsetting factors: the vitality of participatory local government (of towns and counties) and the prominence of voluntary associations, set up for countless purposes ranging from building inns to sending out missionaries.

Emerson Celebrates the Lone Individual

Soon the intellectual currents mentioned by Shain were pushing the development of individualism far beyond the stage that worried Tocqueville. In his famous essay *Self-Reliance* (1841), Ralph Waldo Emerson argues (par. 1) that one must trust in the rightness of one's own private intuition, "that gleam of light that flashes across his mind from within." He continues (par. 7): "No law can be sacred to me but that of my nature. Good and bad are but names very readily transferable to that or this: the only right is what is after [i.e., in accordance with] my constitution, the only wrong what is against it." These words imply the dangerous notion that there can be no clear distinction between right and wrong. And the assumption that whatever one intuitively feels to be right, must be right, is surely questionable.

It is recorded that in his youth Alfred Rosenberg, later one of Hitler's key henchmen, glanced at a copy of Houston Stewart Chamberlain's book *The Foundations of the Nineteenth Century*, whereupon, he declared, "I felt electrified. I wrote down the title and went straight to the bookshop. . . . Another world opened before me—Hellas, Judah, Rome. And to everything I assented inwardly—again, and yet again."[32] Surely one of those flashing gleams of light! But Chamberlain was another of Hitler's heroes; his book, published in 1899, propounded the notorious theory that the Germanic peoples were superior to all other races, while the Jews ranked among the lowest of the low. The success of this book, which sold more than a quarter of a million copies, suggests that a good many other people may have intuitively felt that Chamberlain was right. Intuitive feelings can be sound and true; they can also lead us badly astray.

According to Msgr. John Ryan, "Individualism . . . means that the individual conscience, or the individual reason, is not merely the decisive subjective rule, but that it is the only rule; that there is no objective authority or standard which it is bound to take into account."[33] That sums up well much of what is wrong with undiluted individualism. To avoid falling into serious error, we need standards or norms outside of ourselves, against which to evaluate our own personal feelings. We must not be so arrogant as to assume that, through our inmost feelings or intuitions, we always know best.

William Sumner's Uncompromising Stance

A notable proponent of *laissez-faire* individualism was William G. Sumner (1840–1910), who began his career as a clergyman in the Episcopal Church but later turned to academia and became professor of political and social science at Yale. He propounded individualism of a starkness that foreshadowed the work of Ayn Rand, pointing up Tocqueville's contrast between traditional aristocratic or feudal societies and modern democratic societies. In the old system, your duties to other people, and their duties to you, were based on the social positions (status) into which you and the others were born. Now you acquire rights and duties through voluntary, time-limited agreements (contracts) with other people.

The duty of the rich to help the poor, Sumner argued, is a relic of the feudal past, when the lord of the manor had an obligation to look after his servants and followers; such a duty has no place in modern contractual society. Democracy "must oppose . . . any claims to favor on the ground of poverty, as on the ground of birth and rank." He ridiculed the "old ecclesiastical prejudice in favor of the poor and against the rich,"[34] which Catholics today call the *preferential option for the poor*. "The 'weak,' as defined by humanitarians and philanthropists," he thundered, "are a dead weight on society."[35] This kind of thinking was recently the target of a precisely aimed attack by Pope Francis, who castigated "rampant individualism . . . fueling that 'throw away' mentality which leads to contempt for, and abandonment of, the weakest and those considered 'useless.'"[36]

Individual civil liberty, as Sumner defined it, meant "a status created for the individual by laws and institutions, the effect of which is that each man is guaranteed the use of all his own powers exclusively for his own welfare. . . . He should be left free to do the most for himself that he can, and should be guaranteed the exclusive enjoyment of all that he does."[37] No question, then, of requiring anyone to contribute from his personal resources to the common good, or to the relief of distress. Sumner offered a bleak vision of a "lone ranger" way of life with few, if any, real ties to anyone; with everyone living and working for oneself (and one's immediate family) alone; with only contractual obligations, rather than relations of loyalty or comradeship or community, toward other people.

Reaction against Individualism

"Individualism is democratic in origin, and it threatens to develop as conditions equalize": that was Tocqueville's view. But what will happen to it as conditions disequalize, as is happening today? We know what happened toward the end of the nineteenth century. As inequalities grew exorbitant, a reaction against individualism set in. It was so strong that some people even feared that America was going socialist.

In 1888, Edward Bellamy published *Looking Backward*, a fantasy novel that was unashamedly socialist, indeed communist, though he was careful to avoid using those words. It described a utopian America in which money had been abolished, production and distribution were entirely nationalized and centrally planned, and everyone had the same income. Yet, believe it or not, this book was a best-seller in late nineteenth-century America, and many people formed groups for the express purpose of studying, disseminating, and promoting Bellamy's ideas.

In the 1880s, the *Knights of Labor*, a trades union that favored cooperative enterprise, grew rapidly to a membership of some 700,000; and though this movement did not last, the American Federation of Labor (AFL), founded in 1886, developed strongly in the late nineteenth and early twentieth centuries and is still a major force today.

The "institutional school" of American economic thought (Thorstein Veblen, John R. Commons, Richard T. Ely, and others) was influenced by the German "historical school" of economics, which favored a mixed economy with robust social welfare provisions. This "institutionalism" became the American orthodoxy in the early twentieth century, partially displacing "classical" free-market economics.

Individualism in the Twentieth Century

The return to free-wheeling markets after the 1914–1918 war culminated in the 1929 crash and the subsequent Great Depression. Franklin Roosevelt's New Deal marked a more durable anti-individualist reaction. Again, this aroused the anger of the libertarians, who developed a paranoid fear of an insidious trend toward socialism or even communism. The most forceful interpreter of this mood was doubtless Ayn Rand, who drove individualism to preposterous extremes. We note an example of this in chapter 9. Two others: the steelmaker Hank Rearden in *Atlas Shrugged* claims that "I held it as my honor that I would never need anyone";[38] the architect Howard Roark in *The Fountainhead* asserts that nothing matters to him but "my work my way. A private, personal, selfish, egotistical motivation. That's the only way I function. That's all I am."[39]

From the 1970s onward, the cult of individualism has swept the world. Collective bargaining in the workplace has largely given way to flexible individual employment contracts. Uniform, fixed salaries have been replaced by compensation linked to individual performance. The outcomes are better for some workers but worse for many others; hence, we have widening inequalities. Many businesses are dominated by arrogant individuals who demand exorbitant rewards on the ground that their individual efforts are highly profitable; there is too little recognition that business success depends heavily on teamwork.

Our sense of community, of the "common good," has weakened under the influence of a philosophy that overemphasizes individual, self-centered aspirations. We need self-reliance, yet it is in our nature also to need each other. The pseudofreedom of total self-determination is impossible, and if we could achieve it we would hardly enjoy it. The itch of our times for complete personal independence is arrogant and futile.

Yet as we have seen, reaction against excessive individualism has happened before. The time is ripe for it to happen again.

CHAPTER 3

Libertarians Misunderstand Liberty

The power to sin is not freedom, nor is it a part of freedom.
—St. Anselm of Canterbury (1033–1109)
On the Freedom of the Will, chap. 1.

A Word with Many Meanings

Freedom, or liberty, is among the most potent of rallying calls. We all want to be "free," and we tend to think that "freedom" is a simple matter. But it is not, for the word "freedom" can mean so many different things. And some of its commonly accepted meanings are deceptive. The pursuit of misleading notions of freedom can get us into deep trouble. There we find one of the roots of our present-day economic and social woes.

In ancient philosophy and theology, the word "free," as a rule, simply means not enslaved or imprisoned. In times when slavery was a normal and accepted part of the social structure, a free person was one who was not a slave. When Aristotle wrote that "constitutional rule is a government of freemen and equals,"[1] he had in mind a republic governed by those men (not women) who were not slaves. Alternatively, a free person could mean one who was not detained as a convict, suspect, hostage, or prisoner of war.

In the modern world, we have abolished slavery in its classical sense (one person being the legal property of another), and we recognize many kinds of freedom apart from simply not being locked up in jail. So the meanings of freedom have become more varied and complex. We talk of national freedom, religious freedom, political freedom, individual freedom, commercial freedom, freedom from hunger, freedom from discrimination, freedom of speech, freedom of conscience, freedom from regulations, freedom from addictions, free markets, etc.

For many years now, we have seen in economics, in politics, in the academic world, and in public opinion a massive emphasis on one particular element of freedom (*negative freedom* or absence of constraints), and very often on a perverted form of it. Meanwhile, other aspects of freedom, equally or even more important, have been neglected.

Negative Freedom

What is this element of freedom that has been exaggerated, distorted, and given disproportionate importance? It is *the individual's freedom from constraints imposed by other people* (especially the people who govern us). This is the particular freedom demanded by the libertarians who make so much noise in American politics, in the literature of Ayn Rand and others of her kind, in the countless websites of the zealots of Herbert Hoover's *rugged individualism*. They yearn for a world where everyone is totally independent and self-sufficient. Each of us, they say, should be free to do as one chooses without constraint by state or professional regulation, by social convention, by the needs or aspirations of the community as a whole, or by cooperative agreements with other people. This is called *negative freedom* because it means that, so far as possible, we are *not* prohibited from doing things and *not* obliged to do things.

Although the libertarian cult of negative freedom has developed largely as a reaction or defense against oppressive regimes, it is interesting to note that the totalitarian society of George Orwell's *Nineteen Eighty-Four* also imposed a negative conception of freedom. In *Newspeak*, the language of Orwell's fantasy world, "The word *free . . .* could only be used in such statements as 'This dog is free from lice' or 'This field is free from weeds.'"[2] Orwell's negative freedom means absence only of *impersonal* (nonhuman) constraints or nuisances: the lice on the dog, the weeds in the field. The negative freedom of the libertarians means the opposite: absence only of constraints imposed by other people. In libertarian economics, the market is regarded as an impersonal force; therefore libertarians argue that *market forces, however constrictive they may be, cannot diminish our freedom*.

In the economy, libertarian negative freedom implies unregulated markets, absence of central planning, minimal controls on finance, unrestricted cross-border trade, and full international capital mobility. You can invest wherever you wish, you can borrow wherever you wish, you can buy or sell where and what you fancy, and you can employ people on whatever terms you can persuade them to accept.

Many libertarians reject also any constraint by religious precept; this is hardly surprising, since many of them are nonreligious or atheist. Yet there are also libertarians who claim to be devout, orthodox Catholics. Their attitude would seem to be seriously misguided; for, as we shall see, the Catholic Church's teaching about freedom is very different from the philosophy of the libertarians.

Amoral Freedom

For strict libertarians, freedom is divorced from virtue and morality. Thus the Austrian economist Friedrich von Hayek, who was brought up a Catholic but turned agnostic at an early age, wrote that "liberty is an opportunity for doing good, but this is so only if it is also an opportunity for doing wrong."[3] The anarchist Murray Rothbard, a nonobservant Jew, was even more explicit; according to him, "Libertarians . . . would in short accord every person the right to be either moral or immoral as he saw fit."[4] That was because, for Rothbard, liberty was quite separate from morality; it meant, in practical terms, absence of government. Elsewhere, he insisted that "the libertarian stands foursquare for the freedom . . . to engage in such 'victimless crimes' as pornography, sexual deviation and prostitution."[5] Milton Friedman, likewise Jewish but atheist, held that "freedom has nothing to say about what an individual does with his freedom."[6]

This notion of *amoral freedom* flatly contradicts longstanding and diverse traditions of thought and belief, in which it is held that freedom and virtue necessarily belong together: "Only a virtuous people is capable of freedom," as Benjamin Franklin neatly put it. Even in the pre-Christian era, when freedom was often understood simply as not being enslaved or imprisoned, we can find the idea of freedom as living virtuously, in a law-abiding manner, with regard to the good of the community.

Aristotle, writing around 350 BC in *Politics*, tackles a misunderstanding of the meaning of freedom that is hardly uncommon today: "In democracies of the more extreme type there has arisen a false idea of freedom. . . . Men think . . . that freedom means the doing what a man likes. In such democracies everyone lives as he pleases, or in the words of Euripides, 'according to his fancy.' But this is all wrong;

men should not think it slavery to live according to the rule of the constitution; for it is their salvation."[7]

Aristotle's term *politeía*, translated here as *the rule of the constitution*, can also mean *the way of life of a citizen*. If we read it that way, we have the idea that we find our freedom in being good citizens, in devotion to the common good.

Freedom in Christianity

The New Testament speaks of the *slavery*, or *bondage*, or *captivity* of sin.[8] Wrongdoing is likened to slavery; therefore forgiveness is like buying a slave out of bondage, a transaction called *redemption*. This Latin-based word basically means buying back or buying out; today, in the world of finance, it is still used in that original sense. Bankers and stockbrokers habitually talk about *redemption* (repayment) of government bonds and other debts. The debtor pays off (redeems) his debt and becomes free of it.

There you have the basis of the Christian concept of *forgiveness as redemption*, release from the bondage of sin, which pervades the New Testament and indeed all Christian theology. It is found in the Old Testament too (Ps 130:7-8):

> For with the LORD there is steadfast love,
> and with him is plenteous redemption.
> And he will redeem Israel
> from all his iniquities.

If sin is equated with slavery, it follows that sin is the opposite of freedom. So the libertarian notion that freedom means being "free to do wrong" is self-contradictory. It is like saying that the right to sell oneself into slavery (historically, it was possible and legal to do that, often in order to pay off debts) was a kind of freedom. In fact, we develop our freedom by strengthening good dispositions and habits, thus becoming *less capable of sinning*; the truly free (and holy) person is one who "cannot bring himself" to commit any sin. Needless to say, that is a perfection that is not fully attainable in this world, but only in heaven. Yet even here on earth, "the more we share the life of Christ and progress in his friendship, the more difficult it is to break away from him by mortal sin" (*Catechism*, par. 1395).

In the fifth century, St. Augustine wrote that, in heaven, "one shall not be able to will anything evil, yet one shall not therefore lack free will. In fact, the will shall be much freer, since it will in no way be able to be the slave of sin."[9] In the thirteenth century, St. Thomas Aquinas wrote that "inability to sin does not diminish our freedom."[10] In the mid-twentieth century, the Catholic theologian Bernard Häring stated that "in essence freedom is the power to do good. . . . The power to do evil is not of its essence."[11] The *Catechism* (par. 1733) insists that "there is no true freedom except in the service of what is good and just." Thus, the libertarians' amoral notion of freedom is clearly rejected by Catholic teaching, and so it has been since the beginnings of Christianity.

The idea that freedom is inextricably bound up with moral virtue is not a Catholic peculiarity. It is shared by most Christians and can be found in Judaism too. The Presbyterian churches base their doctrines and practices on the *Westminster Confession* of 1646, a document which sets out the basic principles of Calvinist Christianity, each of them backed up by numerous biblical quotations. In chapter 20, "Of Christian Liberty and Liberty of Conscience," we find a clear and concise statement on freedom:

> The liberty which Christ hath purchased for believers under the gospel consists in their freedom from the guilt of sin. . . . They who, upon pretense of Christian liberty, do practice any sin . . . do thereby destroy the end [purpose] of Christian liberty, which is, that being delivered out of the hands of our enemies, we might serve the Lord without fear, in holiness and righteousness before him, all the days of our life.

Clearly, this is far removed from any notion of amoral freedom. In our own times, theologians Laurent Gagnebin and Raphael Picon of the French Reformed Church, which follows the Calvinist/Presbyterian tradition, have written eloquently on liberty. They explain that "true liberty is not independence; I am not free against or without the other, but for and with him. Freedom triumphs in communion and love. . . . The grace of God liberates us from ourselves to engage us in the service of others. . . . While Protestantism is a form of liberation from ecclesiastical authority, it calls for and values the regulatory function of the community."[12]

The Anglican clergyman Jonathan Boucher, a famous preacher in eighteenth-century America, stated that "true liberty . . . is a liberty to do everything that is right, and being restrained from doing anything that is wrong."[13]

Freedom in Judaism

In Judaism there is a very strong tradition of respect for the law; in particular, of course, for the Jews' own legal system, the *Law of Moses* or Torah. This is recorded in the first five books of the Old Testament. There, as we have already noted, the word *freedom* generally means the opposite of slavery or imprisonment. What preoccupies the Old Testament writers is not so much the need for free individuals to have scope to "do their own thing," but rather the need for them to behave decently and fairly toward each other; in other words, the need for justice. Many of the detailed rules and regulations of the Torah are designed expressly to further this purpose.

In Psalm 119, the great hymn in praise of the sacred law, we find a more developed conception of freedom (v. 45):

> And I will walk at liberty,
> for I seek thy commandments.[14]

Some translations have *I will walk in a wide path*, or words to that effect. Liberty is clearly tied to respect for God's law. For a law-abiding way of life can actually make us freer—can give us a wider path to follow—by restraining us from the misbehavior that can so easily derange our lives and ultimately reduce our freedom (power to do good). Do you hear a resonance with Aristotle's remark, that living according to the constitution is our salvation?

Rabbi Joshua ben Levi, early in the third century AD, used a curious play on Hebrew words to make the same point: "The tablets were the work of God, and the writing was the writing of God, graven upon the tablets. Read not *Haruth* (= graven) but *Heruth* (= freedom), for there is no free man for thee but he who occupies himself with the study of the Torah."[15] Thus, you cannot expect to be free unless you learn God's laws and strive to abide by them. Freedom is anything but amoral.

In our own times, the distinguished American rabbi and theologian Abraham Heschel has given us some illuminating comments on freedom as it is understood in Jewish thought and tradition:

Freedom is the liberation from the tyranny of the self-centered ego.[16]

Man is free in doing good; he is not free in doing evil. To choose evil is to fail to be free.[17]

Freedom is not a continual state of man. . . . It *is* not, it *happens*. Freedom is an act, an event. We are all endowed with the potentiality of freedom. In actuality, however, we only act freely in rare creative moments.[18]

The second of these remarks seems to echo St. Thomas, who wrote that "if the will sins by choosing some action that deviates from its ultimate purpose, the freedom of the will is defective."[19] Heschel's third remark is especially interesting, for it highlights a fundamental error in the position of the libertarians. Their idea is to establish a *continual state* of freedom by abolishing the constraints imposed by state law, by religious commandment, by social or cultural convention, or by mutual solidarity. But if Heschel is right, permanent or continual freedom is (at least in this world) not possible, since clearly one cannot be acting creatively all the time.

Artistic Freedom

If we are to express our freedom, from time to time, by acting creatively, then clearly we should not be bound by excessive or unsuitable constraints, which might seriously impede our creative activity. Yet history suggests that the best creativity often occurs within constraints, in spite of constraints, even with the help of constraints.

From the French essayist André Gide, we have the striking observation that "art is born of constraints, lives by struggle, dies of liberty."[20] This reminds us of another famous French writer, the nineteenth-century poet Charles Baudelaire. He wrote many sonnets, poems in an ancient fourteen-line format originally devised in twelfth-century Sicily, later used by many great poets such as Petrarch (1304–1374), Joachim du Bellay (1522–1560), and Shakespeare, who wrote a series of 154 sonnets near the end of the sixteenth century. Baudelaire valued the strict constraints of this tried and tested poetic convention. In his view, "because the form is constrictive, the idea emerges more intense."[21]

In the twentieth century, however, the French painter Marcel Duchamp got "modern art" off to an unsavory start by attempting to exhibit, in

1917, an ordinary urinal lying on its back, signed by himself with a pseudonym. Nothing else. This could be enjoyed simply as an amusing example of crude tendencies in French humor, but many in the artistic world do not see it that way at all. For them, Duchamp's *pissoir*, named *Fontaine*, is no joke. It is a "paradigm of 'ready-made' artwork," according to art historian Thierry de Duve.[22] Biographer and essayist Louise Varèse (wife of the avant-garde composer Edgard Varèse) called it *the Buddha of the Bathroom* and "the 'pure' example of an art of the future."[23] In 1999, the Greek collector Dimitri Daskalapoulos paid $1,762,500 for one of the several replicas approved by Duchamp, the original object having been lost.[24] Daskalapoulos declared that "for me, this represents the origins of contemporary art."

Duchamp, it is said, has "set artists free" by showing that they can achieve artistic fame and fortune without going through the long, hard disciplines of the academy and without abiding by any of the traditional artistic forms and conventions. *Anything* can be a work of art, just because a free, unconstrained "artist" says it is! That's the message; a fine example of the "negative freedom" that seems to have inspired economists and financiers as well as artists. If a urinal can be a work of art, just because Duchamp has said it is, why shouldn't a crappy bond be a sound investment, just because Lehman Brothers, or Standard & Poor's, has said it is?

Abuses of Freedom

It is painfully obvious that (in this world, not in heaven) freedom can be abused. Libertarians say that we must not try to prevent people from abusing it; that if we do try, we destroy their freedom. Hayek argued that "the freedom of action that is the condition of moral merit includes the freedom to do wrong."[25] There would, he argues, be no merit in doing good if we could not do evil. But that is bad logic. If we could do no wrong, we would still have the option of doing nothing.[26] Merit is earned by doing good works, not simply by not doing anything wrong (see *Catechism*, pars. 2008–11).

The libertarian concept clashes with the more traditional religious and philosophical view that freedom is inextricably tied up with goodness and righteousness; freedom is the power to do good and not the power to do wrong. As Aristotle wrote, criticizing the libertarians of his day: "They have a false idea of freedom." They think liberty means the right to do whatever they fancy, without regard to the constitution of the republic or the good of their fellow-citizens.

Clearly, we all have the temptation or inclination, and often the power, to do wrong. But to call this power *freedom* is a misuse of the word. It is not laws, rules, or customs aiming to prevent abuses that destroy freedom; it is the abuses themselves that destroy freedom.

To be fair, libertarians (unless they are outright anarchists) do not normally say that we should feel free to break the laws. But they do argue that the laws themselves should be no more than a basic framework of fundamental principles and should never be allowed to expand into a mass of detailed regulations. In practice, however, in this fallen world where we are all born with tendencies to misbehave, detailed rules are often necessary to keep us on the right lines and prevent harmful misbehavior.

Libertarians, horrified by tyrants' abuse of political power, want to get rid of political power, replacing (so far as possible) the government by the market. Hayek regarded political power itself as "the arch-evil."[27] Yet in reality, it is abuse of power that is evil, not power in itself. Any form of power can be abused or mishandled, generally with nasty consequences. Electricity can be very dangerous unless it is carefully controlled and the live wires are well insulated. But electricity is not evil in itself. And it does not lose its power because we control and regulate it to make sure, so far as possible, that it is beneficial and not harmful. On the contrary, it is lack of proper control that diminishes electrical power or makes it dangerous. Defective insulation or regulation can cause injury to people, damage to equipment, and loss of power (leakages). This is a well-known problem on electrified railroads, where the overhead cables that supply the traction current, if in poor condition, are said to be "leaky."

The amoral libertarian conception of freedom as merely absence of constraints is very far from adequate; it is indeed gravely defective and a cause of serious harm in practice. Why then is this notion of negative freedom apparently so popular? One reason, as we have noted, is that it appeals to people who follow an excessively individualistic philosophy, who are too much concerned with doing what suits themselves rather than with contributing to the common good. Another reason is that the notion of "positive freedom" (power to do good) has sometimes been perverted by totalitarian regimes which have claimed that they were liberating their peoples by forcing them to cooperate with allegedly "good" state policies. This has given libertarian thinkers an excuse for disparaging positive freedom and for promoting negative freedom as a better alternative.

But positive freedom, as it is understood in Catholic theology and elsewhere, means the power to do good by one's own choice, not under compulsion. It makes little sense to reject the good concept of positive freedom on the ground that certain political leaders have twisted it for their own evil ends. We should reject the bad leaders, not the good concept.

Freedom Is Social, Not Just Individual

If we separate freedom from morality and virtue, then we have an amoral "freedom" that includes Hayek's "opportunity for doing wrong." But doing wrong is very likely to damage other people's freedom. Your real freedom or *power to do good* may be drastically reduced if I exercise my pseudofreedom or *power to do wrong* by driving home after a hard-drinking party and knocking you down in the street.

Thus we see that true freedom is not simply an *individual* quality; it is also a *social* quality. To achieve true freedom, one must pursue, in one's own conduct, goodness and justice. One must not be the slave of one's own vices. Yet the good and just person may be injured or oppressed—may have one's own freedom curtailed—by the wrongdoing of others.

So, to be truly free, it is not enough to pursue goodness and justice oneself; one must also be surrounded by others who do likewise. Freedom is social and communal, not purely individual. The nineteenth-century English philosopher Thomas Hill Green expressed this idea well: "Freedom is a positive power or capacity of doing or enjoying something worth doing or enjoying, and that too, something that we do or enjoy in common with others."[28]

Thus, true freedom is about positive power and opportunity to do good things. It is far more than simply being left "free" to do whatever we please, right or wrong. And true freedom is something we achieve together rather than alone.

Freedom in Cooperation

Libertarians believe that agreements between individuals diminish freedom. Once you enter into any agreement or association with one or more others, you are under certain constraints; you are not "free" to act just as you please. You have to cooperate with your associates; to some degree, at least, you have to fall in with their wishes. If you refuse to do so and insist on going your own individual way, the agreement will probably break down. Hayek argued that free individuals can enter into associations, so long as these are strictly voluntary. You can join if you wish, you can leave if you wish. But that clearly does not work for marriage and family life as Catholics understand it.

It does not work too well for other kinds of association either. Once upon a time, a certain stability in employment was not unusual. A good business built a team of people who felt a strong commitment to stay together. Employees tended to stay with the same firm for long periods, even for life. The boss was reluctant to fire anyone unless it was absolutely necessary; one understood the value of a continuing team of loyal, experienced staff. Today, by contrast, we believe in "flexibility"; a firm should feel free to fire anyone at the drop of a hat, and its employees should not hesitate to quit if some other firm offers a few dollars more. So we have the *precarity of employment* of which so many people, with good reason, complain. Freedom from constraints kills stability.

If we think of freedom as Fr. Häring's *power to do good*, then we have a conception of freedom that is association friendly. For there are plenty of good things that we cannot do alone but can do in cooperation with others.

The musician who thinks that *negative freedom* is supremely important will, if she is strictly logical, prefer to perform alone, without even a pianist or guitarist to accompany her. She will feel that the need to cooperate with a fellow musician constrains her and thus destroys her "freedom." For two or more musicians performing together are obliged to keep in time, and in harmony, with each other. There is indeed a fair amount of music that can be performed by a soloist alone; but there is far more that cannot. Operas, symphonies, music for band or chorus, all call for a number of musicians cooperating as a team. Cooperation doubtless reduces their individual "freedom from constraint," but hear what it makes possible: the opportunity to make wonderful music together! An example of the "power to do good," is it not?

It is no accident that, since libertarianism became intellectually and socially fashionable, most forms of association or partnership or solidarity have weakened. Surely there is something very wrong with a concept of freedom that tends to undermine every form of human association, from matrimony to trade unions. The human being is a *social animal* with a basic need to associate with others. If we cannot find freedom as we imagine it, except by isolating ourselves, by "going it alone," surely that strongly suggests that the freedom we imagine is not the real thing.

The Need for Constraints

Since libertarians define freedom as *absence of constraint*, it follows that they want to eliminate as many constraints as possible. But experience shows that removing too many constraints can lead to intolerable levels of misbehavior. We see striking examples of this in economic and financial history, as described in chapter 4.

Far from being a desirable "freedom," *absence of constraints* is what has got us into horrible trouble today. Absence of constraints on bank lending has permitted the buildup of disastrously inflated debts. Absence of constraints on international capital movements has allowed countries like Ireland, Iceland, Greece, and Cyprus to import vast amounts of capital, far beyond the needs of their own economies, by accepting large bank deposits from foreigners, some of them tax evaders. Absence of limits on international trade has allowed multinational corporations to buy huge quantities of cheap goods from developing countries and to sell them very profitably in America and Europe, thereby destroying whole industries in those regions, leaving them with unbalanced economies and chronic high unemployment.

Here we have a problem that extends far beyond the world of economics and finance. Through most of the last century, the prevalent feeling has been that, in order to be "free," we must get rid of as many constraints as possible. It has become normal to believe that neither the Church, nor the law, nor social convention should oblige us to go to Mass every Sunday, to treat marriage as a lifelong commitment, to run our businesses in a socially responsible fashion, to dress decently, or to write our own language correctly. In big matters and small, we have indulged in a wholesale rejection of constraints.

That was a fundamental error. In our quest for true freedom, the real challenge is not to abolish constraints. It is to eliminate harmful constraints but also—and this is equally important—to establish and maintain constraints that help us live better.

CHAPTER 4

Abuses of Financial Capitalism

We require two safeguards against a return of the evils of the old order; there must be a strict supervision of all banking and credits and investments; there must be an end to speculation with other people's money, and there must be provision for an adequate but sound money supply.

—Franklin D. Roosevelt[1]

Growthmanship has long been imposed on [the banks] by their transformation from national utilities to deregulated profit-maximizers, fearful of losing business to the competition. Banks have thus become a destabilizing influence in the world economy.

—John Plender[2]

An Electrical Analogy

To better understand the latest financial crisis, come and spend a few minutes with me in an electrical engineering workshop. To grieve over the plight of yet another business stricken by the recent downturn? Not at all. Rather, to study a machine which strikingly illustrates what is wrong with capitalism as it has recently been practiced.

Here in the workshop is a *series-wound DC motor*, a type of electric motor traditionally used to power subway trains and streetcars. We have just completed an overhaul of this train motor, and the time has come to give it a test run. Take care! In this situation, there is a golden rule that we must follow. On no account must we allow the motor to run free on full power. For if we do so, it will spin faster and faster till its rotating center flies to pieces. With a traction motor weighing a ton or two, that would not be amusing.

Surely, you will say, if the motor behaves like that, there must be something seriously wrong with it, even though it has just been overhauled. We must have done our work very badly! No, we have not. There is nothing wrong with the machine. This very useful type of motor has a peculiar characteristic, as you can verify in any basic textbook on electrical engineering. Unless it is attached to a load (in this case, a train) whose inertia constrains it, the motor will accelerate without limit until it destroys itself.

That may seem strange to nonengineers. Motors like this have been widely used in transport and in industry for more than a century and have never caused disasters so long as they have been run under proper constraints. But it is in the nature of this kind of motor to run amok if it is allowed to run unconstrained.

The machine of capitalism is very like that motor. It needs constraint or inertia—otherwise it will spin out of control and go to pieces, as we observed in 2008 when for a time it seemed as though the world's banking systems might collapse. Such a collapse happened in America after the 1929 Wall Street crash, when more than nine thousand banks failed without rescue. This time, the banks were saved *in extremis* through resolute action by governments, the very organizations that libertarians and free marketeers most despise.

Finance and Capitalism

Today we hear much about the problems thrown up by *financial capitalism*. But if you are not an expert on these matters, you may perhaps find this phrase puzzling. Surely, you may say, capitalism is about finance, so all capitalism must be financial. Or is there such a thing as *nonfinancial* capitalism? What exactly do we mean when we talk about the abuses of *financial* capitalism?

Finance, properly speaking, is not just another word for money or capital. Finance is essentially *the process whereby one person or organization supplies funds to another*. Thus, for example, Harry turns to his richer friend Tom for funds to help him develop his business. Tom may respond by simply lending money to Harry; alternatively, he may buy a share in Harry's business. Either way, Tom *finances* Harry's business. Likewise, on a larger scale, banks finance businesses big and small by various forms of lending; savings & loan associations finance house purchases; investors finance businesses by buying shares listed on the New York Stock Exchange or on NASDAQ.

Thus, capitalism as we know it depends very largely on finance. On this topic, the *Compendium* (par. 368) speaks with approval in principle: "[T]he experience of history teaches that, without adequate financial systems, economic growth would not have taken place."

Nonfinancial Capitalism

But can there be such a thing as capitalism without finance? If by *capitalism* we mean simply an economic system in which capital assets are privately, not communally, owned, then the answer is yes. Indeed, such an economy seems to have existed in biblical Israel. The Old Testament prohibits the payment of interest on loans between Jews but not on loans between Jews and foreigners. Thus in Deuteronomy 23:20 we read: "To a foreigner you may lend upon interest, but to your brother you shall not lend upon interest," and the word *brother* is taken to mean fellow Jew; in Exodus 22:25 we read: "If you lend money to any of my people with you who is poor . . . you shall not exact interest from him."

Jewish historians explain that, in ancient Israel, there was very little commercial moneylending; a loan to a fellow Jew was generally a charitable act, helping out someone in difficulties. So it was considered wrong to make the borrower pay interest, especially since prevailing interest rates in biblical times were usually high, often in the region of 20 percent. Foreign borrowers, however, were generally merchants who borrowed for commercial purposes; moreover, the Gentiles did not have prohibitions on interest and charged it on any loans they made to Jews; so it was reasonable for Jews to charge them interest.

The economy of ancient Israel was predominantly agricultural; the main capital asset was land, which in general was privately owned. Other assets were buildings, farm equipment, livestock, and, to some extent, slaves. When the Jews settled in the land of Canaan, the land was divided among their various families (Josh 18ff.). Families lived by farming their land—generally, it appears, using little or no monetary finance from outside sources (though they often lent each other goods, rather than money). So, we may say, biblical Israel was an economy that came close to being a form of *nonfinancial capitalism*.

In the earlier centuries of the Middle Ages, rather similar conditions prevailed in Europe, where the Church, taking a harder line than Moses, declined to authorize interest on any kind of lending. MIT economist Charles Kindleberger, discussing the economies of early medieval Europe, observes that "the basis for the prohibition against charging interest is found in the ethical prescription . . . against taking advantage of the misfortunes of others. When a crop fails and a family goes hungry, brotherhood exacts a charitable response, not an exploitative one."[3]

Medieval European banking "owed its origins not to moneylenders or pawnbrokers, but to money-changers,"[4] generally merchants who had to handle diverse currencies in the course of their business. Early European banks were thus mainly concerned with currency exchange and with safekeeping of customers' deposits. They seldom provided credit; not only because the Church prohibited interest-bearing loans but also because bank credit normally means that part of the money deposited by bank customers is lent out to other customers. This practice was "illegal in most towns, being regarded as an abuse of public trust. Recent data indicate that, relative to the scale of total activity, the availability of bank deposits as credit was modest in Venice and miniscule in Florence, and did little to expand the money supply until the late Middle Ages."[5]

Banking and Its Errors

Even today, some people still hold that banks ought to keep in their vaults sufficient cash so that all customers could simultaneously withdraw all their deposits (or, at the very least, all deposits that are withdrawable on demand, without notice). It is argued that depositing money in a bank should be somewhat like leaving your coat in the cloakroom at the theater; the cloakroom attendant has no right to lend your coat to somebody else, trusting that it will be returned before the end of the play! A bank that followed this principle would not be able to provide much credit.

Today, this medieval view is heterodox. A bank can, in practice, safely lend out a prudent proportion of the money deposited with it. For, save in extraordinary circumstances, customers never all want to withdraw all their money at once. That can happen in the event of a panic, when customers suspect (perhaps wrongly) that their bank is going broke. But the modern practice of *deposit insurance* ensures that failing banks are "rescued," in the sense that depositors (other than those with very large deposits) do get their money back; so there is no need to panic.

If banks gave up lending to customers, some other way of providing credit would have to be found. Though there are historical examples of economies using little finance, bank credit has nonetheless a very long history. The more advanced civilizations have always felt the need for credit, or finance. Money began simply as a means of exchange, more convenient than the cumbersome practice of barter. Once it became customary for stocks of money in banks, instead of lying idle in vaults, to be lent out to people who wished to use it in business, money became a driver of economic growth and prosperity. One concludes that nonfinancial capitalism is relevant only to a very basic, undeveloped economy. But that does not mean that we in the developed world should tolerate overblown and exorbitant levels of financial activity.

In America, since the mid-twentieth century, the volume of credit has expanded far faster than the economy as a whole. According to World Bank figures, private credit in the United States rose from 75 percent of GDP in 1961 to a peak of 203 percent in 2008.[6]

Fundamentalist opponents of bank lending would seem to be misguided, yet they highlight a real problem: if it is allowed to get out of hand, bank credit can become very dangerous. If there are no restrictions on banking activities and none on competition between banks either, then aggressive bankers can compete with each other to attract more and more deposits. The more deposits they attract, the more they will be able to lend. The more they lend, the more money will be in circulation. And this money will find its way back to the banks in the shape of bigger deposits.

Here we have a circular, self-feeding process in which more and more money is created, borrowed, and lent. The quantity of money circulating in the economy expands faster than the real economy itself, as we see in the figures quoted above. This involves increasing debts and accelerating inflation in prices of consumer goods, and/or in prices of capital assets (real estate, stocks, bonds). Ultimately, something cracks and the boom collapses.

Does this remind you of the unrestrained electric motor that spins faster and faster until it disintegrates? To avoid disasters, financial systems, like that motor, need constraint and inertia. What went wrong in recent decades was that constraints on these systems were deliberately dismantled in the name of a false ideology of freedom, which proclaims that "liberty [is] the absence of restraint and constraint," as Hayek put it.[7] Bad philosophical theories can lead to bad practical policies.

We may also compare the financial system with a nuclear power station. Whatever we may feel about the rights and wrongs of nuclear power, we cannot deny that it is a great source of electrical energy. At the same time, we all recognize that a nuclear power station needs unremitting careful supervision and strict control, lest it run amok with catastrophic consequences. Likewise, the bank credit system and related financial systems form a potent but potentially perilous source of economic energy. Yet for too long we have been unwilling to acknowledge the need for strict supervision and control of financial activities. We have imagined that these systems could be self-regulating and self-correcting. That was a huge error.

The US economy, like many others around the world, became seriously *overfinanced* in the late twentieth century. Too much finance—too much credit granted by lenders—means too much debt taken on by borrowers. Once again we have learned, the hard way, that this is a gravely unhealthy situation. Finance, like other good and useful things, works best when used in moderation.

Abuses in Financial Markets

Unfortunately, finance is by its very nature prone to various ethical problems. One of most troublesome of these is called *asymmetry of information*: whoever receives funds usually knows more than whoever supplies them about how those funds are actually used (or misused). The people who run a business (the insiders) naturally know more about that business than do the outsiders, the external lenders or stockholders who finance it. Hence, unless the people concerned are strictly honest, there is always the risk of misrepresentation.

A sour old joke among mining investors has it that "a mine is a hole in the ground with a liar standing at the top." The promoters of the mine assure investors that "there's gold in them thar hills," though they may be well aware that the amount of gold is highly uncertain, and that the cost of winning it may be too high for the mine to be viable.

On the London Stock Exchange they say, "where there's a tip, there's a tap." A *tap* is a person who has a large line of stock to sell and is quietly dripping it out into the market. He may *tip off* potential buyers in the hope that they will buy what he is selling and thus keep the price high enough for his liking. But his tips may be misleading.

Practices like these take advantage of the fact that, in any market, information is very often asymmetrical; the seller knows more than the buyer. Or, rather less frequently, the buyer knows more than the seller. A landowner who is unaware that there is a valuable mineral deposit under his land might sell the land cheaply to someone who knows more about the local geology.

A related abuse springs from the fact that some investors have privileged information that is not available to the general public. They have *inside information*, either because they are themselves insiders (for example, directors of a public company) or because they have obtained it from insiders by devious means. They accumulate stock before some unexpected good news is announced; or they sell stock before some problem within the business is revealed. This is *insider trading*, and it is generally considered to be unethical.

Not everyone agrees. The economist Milton Friedman argued that "you should have more insider trading, not less";[8] his reasoning was that dealings by knowledgeable insiders help to bring prices into line with reality. This argument has a certain merit. Nevertheless, the prevailing view today is that insiders, if they trade on significant information that is not publicly available, profit from an unfair advantage over other investors. Therefore, such trading has been made a criminal offense in America and in many other countries too.

St. Thomas's view is relevant here: "If defects are hidden, and the seller does not reveal them, the sale is illicit and deceitful, and the seller will be liable to compensate the buyer for any loss."[9] Thus if an insider sells stock while knowing that the company has a problem that is unknown to the buyer, he is acting unjustly if he does not disclose the problem. But if he is a director of the company, he may be obliged to keep quiet about it until the board decides to make a public statement. Therefore, pending such a statement, he should refrain from selling.

Yet another well-known problem in financial markets is the temptation to manipulate prices. Since markets are gossip-ridden places, it is not difficult for an unscrupulous trader to start a rumor: for example, Anycorp Inc. is going to be bid for by Megacorp Inc. at a price well above the current price. The stock of Anycorp will then rise, so the trader, who has bought it before starting the rumor, can sell out at a profit. Of course, once it turns out that the rumor was unfounded, the price will fall back and investors (or speculators) who bought on the strength of the rumor will suffer losses. One may argue that they have only themselves to blame; one should buy on hard information, not on unsubstantiated rumor! But the fact remains that those who spread false stories for their own personal advantage are guilty of dishonesty.

Why Have Abuses Increased?

Abuses in financial markets are as old as the markets themselves. But there can be little doubt that they have become more prevalent, and more serious, in recent times. I recall that, back in the 1960s, someone wrote a striking comment about the City of London: "The City is not lily-white, but it is constantly becoming a paler shade of grey." Clearly, those words could not have been written recently. But in those earlier days, banking, investment management, and stockbroking were respected professions; today they are blamed, with some justice, for having grievously harmed our economies and societies. Why has the financial world deteriorated so horribly?

After the debacle of the early 1930s, when some nine thousand American banks failed without rescue, the surviving banks were put under very strict controls. As a result, for several decades there were no serious banking problems. In 1963 a famous old Democratic congressman, Wright Patman, even *complained* about this financial tranquility! Speaking as chairman of the House Banking and Currency Committee, he said: "I think we should have more bank failures. The record of the last several years of almost no bank failures, and, finally last year, no bank failure at all, is to me a danger signal that we have gone too far in the direction of bank safety."[10]

He should have known better. After all, this Texan was born in 1893 and so had lived through the Great Depression. His comment demonstrates how people tend to grow bored with stability, even if they are aware that the alternatives can be horrid. Patman died in 1976, without living to see the consequences of the attitude he had unwisely encouraged.

A decade later, his odd attitude had become fashionable. Banking regulations were progressively dismantled in the name of "freedom"; that, of course, meant libertarian "freedom," with minimum constraints. Released from their old restrictions, expected to compete fiercely with each other, and expected also to maximize their profits despite competitive pressures, bankers went mad. Even many long-established, respected banking houses indulged in large-scale, high-risk speculative trading and imprudent lending. And the prevailing view that *freedom includes the power to do wrong* was understood all too literally; many banks acted fraudulently. The result of all that was the financial crisis, whose aftereffects still plague us.

Bank Regulation Follows the 1930s Crash

The banking crisis of 1933 was even more dramatic than that of 2008. To calm the chaos, President Roosevelt declared a complete closure of American banks (the *Great Bank Holiday*) during the week beginning Monday, March 6. But 1933 was more effective than 2008 in triggering prompt, much-needed reforms. The crash demolished the political opposition that until then had blocked necessary changes. Congress, horrified by the consequences of financial indiscipline, rapidly passed the Banking Act of 1933, also known as the Glass-Steagall Act after its sponsors, Senator Carter Glass (D-VA) and Representative Henry Steagall (R-AL). This law set the tone of American banking policy for the next four decades.

The act deliberately restricted competition between banks. It prohibited interest on checking accounts, and it authorized the Federal Reserve Board to regulate the rates of interest on savings accounts. Older readers may recall *Regulation Q* which imposed this discipline. The idea was to stop banks from competing aggressively to attract deposits and thus acquire the means to boost their lending to excess.

Moreover, the act required investment banking to be kept strictly separate from retail banking; no bank was allowed to do both. Only the retail banks were permitted to accept deposits from the public. This wise and famous "Glass-Steagall rule" aimed to avoid conflicts of interest and to limit speculation. Investment banks hold and trade investments for their own account; if they also provide retail banking services, they may be tempted to use their retail customer base as a dumping ground for investments that they want to sell. They may also be tempted to use customers' deposits to finance speculative trading.

Reaction against Regulation

Under this strict regime, the American banking system enjoyed some forty years of stability. But by the late 1970s, libertarian ideas were widespread and free-market economists had gained influence in high places on both sides of the Republican/Democrat divide. In 1980, President Carter's *Depositary Institutions Deregulation and Monetary Control Act* set off a prolonged banking revolution that overturned most of the 1930s regulatory structure. It phased out interest rate ceilings and permitted banks to offer NOW (interest-bearing checking) accounts.

The Banking Act of 1933 had left in place earlier rules which prevented American banks from extending their activities beyond the borders of their home states. But the 1980s and 1990s saw the removal of most impediments to "interstate banking" and most of the restrictions, in some states, on opening local branches. Thus banks were enabled grow bigger. And the excessive size of some banks today is one of our problems. They are too powerful, and too big to manage effectively.

Meanwhile, London was moving in the same direction. The practice (seldom used in America) of directly restricting bank lending was abandoned. In the 1950s and 1960s, it was not unusual for the Bank of England to instruct the commercial banks to keep their lending to customers within specified "ceilings." In the 1970s, another method, known as the "corset," was tried; this involved penalties on banks that attracted deposits beyond pre-set limits.

The corset was abolished in 1980, shortly after Margaret Thatcher had become prime minister in 1979, and thereafter the Bank of England relied on changes in interest rates to regulate the supply of credit. It was thought that credit could be restrained simply by making it expensive, by raising Bank Rate and other interest rates. This policy was followed by Thatcher's finance minister Nigel Lawson, and it was hardly effective. Former prime minister Edward Heath, a keen golfer, accused Lawson of trying to *play golf with one club* by relying on interest rate policy alone. In the 1980s, during a period when, despite high interest rates and a sluggish economy, inflation was still rampant, I asked Lawson why he did not revert to more traditional credit controls. He replied very angrily that such a strategy was hopelessly out of date and impracticable: "No way am I going to reinstate it."

The Fall of the "Glass-Steagall Wall"

The Glass-Steagall rule on segregation of banking activities was for many years a bankers' bugbear; they spent much effort on finding ways of circumventing it. Finally, at the instigation of Senator Phil Gramm (R-TX), a famous deregulation enthusiast, the rule was almost completely abolished by the *Gramm-Leach-Bliley Act* of 1999, which was signed by President Clinton, having passed both chambers of Congress with overwhelming majorities. This success illustrates the prevailing feeling at the time: everyone, Democrats and Republicans alike, had caught the deregulation virus.

More recently, however, the demise of the Glass-Steagall rule has been seen as a factor contributing to the banking crisis. In 2013, proposals were tabled in Congress to reinstate strict segregation of different financial activities. These proposals also have bipartisan support, with Senators Elizabeth Warren (D-MA) and John McCain (R-AZ) promoting them. The tide, it seems, is at last turning against the perverse notions of the late twentieth century, and for that we must be thankful.

Loss of Specialization

The death of Glass-Steagall is an example of a wider problem, the *decline of specialization* both in Wall Street and in the City of London. During the long period of financial stability, from the mid-1930s to the late 1970s, both these financial centers had separate, specialist firms for distinct types of business. Thus, stockbrokers in London bought and sold investments on behalf of their clients, acting purely as agents; they were not permitted to trade, or even to hold, investments on their own books.

Own-account trading in stocks and bonds was, in London, mainly the preserve of stockjobbers, whose firms, like those of stockbrokers, were independent private partnerships with unlimited liability. Their capital was provided by small numbers of partners from their own personal resources and was therefore relatively small; moreover, the partners risked personal bankruptcy if things went wrong. So they were careful; they traded on a restrained scale and avoided excessive risks. But London's "big bang" of 1986, when a swathe of traditional rules disappeared, allowed jobbing and broking firms to be acquired by banks and to be combined. This made conflicts of interest more likely; it also meant that far more capital was available to support speculative trading activities, which expanded to exorbitant levels.

Specialization, together with restraints on competition, meant that each firm "stuck to its knitting," performing a limited range of activities in which it had long experience and acquired competence. This checked the tendency toward gigantism, with excessive concentration both of power and of risk. And it minimized conflicts of interest.

Specialization by independent firms might indeed be described as a form of *subsidiarity*. The *Compendium* (par. 186) describes the benefits of subsidiarity: "[I]ntermediate social entities can properly perform the functions that fall to them without being required to hand them over unjustly to other social entities of a higher level, by which they would end up being absorbed and substituted, in the end seeing themselves denied their dignity and essential place." In the "reforms" of our financial centers since the 1970s, how many good specialist firms—stockbrokers, stockjobbers, merchant banks, thrifts, building societies, and others—have found themselves "absorbed and substituted" on being acquired by megabanks? Many indeed. To the advantage, no doubt, of the people at the top of the megabanks; but to the disadvantage of many others.

High-Frequency Trading

A major ground for concern in our present financial world is the growth, since around the year 2000, of *high-frequency trading* (HFT). This technique exploits the fact that most trading today in stock, bond, commodity, and currency markets is done on computers, not in face-to-face dealing on traditional market floors. Electronic transactions can be put through in milliseconds (thousandths of a second), and experts have designed algorithms (computer programs) that can execute transactions automatically. These respond almost instantaneously to market movements and to price-sensitive announcements, such as company results or economic growth statistics. The ability to trade in this way enables professional investors equipped with specialized computer systems to trade much more quickly than anyone else. They may well be considered to be "insider traders" with unfair advantages over other investors.

There are other problems. Because in many markets there are now very large volumes of high-frequency trades, adequate supervision of market activities has become almost impossible; traders' computers are generally a few steps ahead of those of the supervisors. And there is always the risk of a major market disruption caused by accident or by deliberate malfeasance.

Jean-François Gayraud, a senior official in the French police who has studied organized crime in depth, remarks that HFT algorithms "are designed to be *autonomous*. They are equipped with a real ability to make independent decisions. . . . By definition, such algorithms are thus to some extent unpredictable. . . . Moreover, they are designed to *learn*, thus to develop and 'progress.' . . . Hence no one can know how they will behave."[11] An alarming situation, is it not? Gayraud argues that there is little point in trying to regulate this type of activity, since the practitioners will always find ways of outwitting the regulators. He believes, therefore, that HFT should be outlawed. He is probably right.

Excessive Emoluments

The gigantic salaries and bonuses of certain bankers, financial traders, and fund managers are a major scandal of our times. Estimates of average Wall Street bonuses, published by the office of the New York State Comptroller, show that the average was merely $13,970 in 1985 but had increased nearly fourteenfold to $191,360 by 2006, though the US consumer price index less than doubled over that period. Bonuses thus rose more than sevenfold in real terms. Although they fell back sharply after the crisis of 2008, by 2013 they had largely recovered, reaching $164,530. These figures, of course, are just averages. Many "ace traders" and top bankers continue to receive bonuses running into millions.

Such extravagance is not confined to the financial world; huge payments to top executives are widespread in the private sector. In the *Equilar* list of two hundred highest-paid CEOs in 2013, Charif Souki of Cheniere Energy tops the list with $141.9 million, while average pay among the two hundred was $20.7 million. Yet, in the public sector, people still work in highly responsible positions for much more moderate rewards. President Obama himself earns some $400,000, while the top rate in the US civil service general schedule is just over $130,000.

There are various reasons for the sharp increase in top revenues in recent decades. One is that tax rates on high incomes have been cut drastically. In the United States, the top rate of federal income tax was still 70 percent in 1981, and it had been 70 percent or more ever since 1934; it even hit 94 percent in 1944! Not to mention additional income taxes in most states. So there was little point in paying huge salaries or bonuses; most of the top slice would go to the Treasury. But in 1982 President Reagan cut the top rate to 50 percent; by 1988 it had come down to 28 percent. The way was open for greedy executives to award themselves increasingly portly compensation packages.

The high tax rates of earlier years had the effect of keeping top-level remuneration down to more or less reasonable levels. Few executives earned enough to have to pay the highest rates. The famous French economist Thomas Piketty, writing in 2009, comments on American experience during that era: "The lesson of this piece of history is that high tax rates did not kill capitalism, nor did they interfere with human rights . . . [we lived through] a half-century in which capitalism and democracy fared no worse than at other times. Quite the opposite."[12]

The remuneration explosion reflects also the greater mobility of executives between firms. On the London Stock Exchange, before the upheavals of the 1980s, "redundancies and sackings were rare events and then only in the most dire economic circumstances or for high crimes or misdemeanors . . . such loyalty to staff was generally reciprocated . . . as late as the 1970s, it was rare for people to change firms in stockbroking."[13] This traditional stability has crumbled. City banks, which now own most of the Stock Exchange firms, have no inhibitions about "poaching" each other's staff; they bid against each other to attract the cleverer traders; thus pay is driven up, often to crazy levels. In America we have seen the same change of climate, and not only in finance. Up till the 1980s, it was usual for top corporate executives to be appointed by promotion from within. They were long-serving officials who belonged with the company; as members of an ongoing team, they could not decently expect to be paid vastly more than their colleagues. But today, it is common for large firms to compete for the services of "stars" from outside, sometimes at astronomic expense.

A third factor is, of course, greed, exacerbated by envy. The greed manifested by executives and traders, who bully their employers into grossly overpaying them, often stems from an obsession with money as an end in itself, a *wealth addiction*. This is linked to the current free-market obsession with competitively *maximizing* profits, rather than being content with *adequate* profits. It provokes extreme rivalry between colleagues in trading rooms and envy of the most successful. The trader who works among people who "earn" up to ten million dollars a year feels mortified if he doesn't make at least five. Compare the description of envy in *The Catholic Encyclopedia* (it appears under the heading *Jealousy*): "The envious man tortures himself without cause, morbidly holding, as he does, the success of another to constitute an evil for himself."[14]

Preserving the Power to Do Good

The object of sound regulation is to inhibit misbehavior without preventing good behavior; to restrain the power to do evil while preserving the power to do good. In the banking world, this means strongly discouraging careless lending and speculation while encouraging banks to make a valuable contribution to the economy by providing credit in reasonable amounts to sound businesses.

Since 2008, many banks have lacked sufficient ability to do this, having gravely weakened themselves through their own follies. They have had to give priority to rebuilding their reserves and minimizing their risks. Their former "negative freedom" (lack of constraint) has damaged their present "positive freedom" (power to do good business). That is one reason for persistent business sluggishness and high unemployment in many countries.

But regulation of financial firms and markets will not by itself restore a civilized financial system. Misbehavior will persist so long as bankers and traders believe that "greed is good"; so long as they see the markets as zones of "freedom" where you can do as you please, so long as you avoid doing what is expressly forbidden; so long as any ingenious innovation is considered praiseworthy if it enhances profits. For bankers and traders have shown themselves to be very clever at getting round the rules. Whatever may be prohibited in the public interest, someone who does not care about the public interest will devise a crafty way of doing it while staying within the law.

What the financial world needs, therefore, is a change of heart. We must get back to the idea that the best banker is the one who serves one's clients honestly and well; not the one who makes the fattest profits for oneself or for one's bank. We must get back to the idea that working in finance is not just a way of earning a good living; it must also be a way of contributing to the common good.

CHAPTER 5

Competition and Consumption

Competition is always desirable and must always be defended.

—Pascal Salin[1]

The right ordering of economic life cannot be left to a free competition of forces . . .

—Pius XI, *Quadragesimo Anno*, par. 88

We are multiple players, but we are engaged in a single game—a game that must be cooperative, not simply competitive.

—Christine Lagarde[2]

An Obsession of Our Times

Competition is an obsession of our times, especially among economists. What is worse, governments share this obsession, largely because of the "misguided experts effect" that I have described in chapter 1. Most of us have, to some degree at least, caught the virus. Economists have succeeded in persuading us that any restraint of competition is inherently unethical, immoral, or corrupt. So we think we are virtuous if we tolerate unlimited competition, however nasty its consequences, and if we crack down hard on any attempt to moderate competition. It has become customary to believe that competition, or competitiveness, is such a good thing that we cannot have too much of it.

But if that were so, competition would be a very strange "good thing." Normally, as we well know, anything that is good in moderation is harmful if we take it to excess. Can it really be true that competition is an exception to that rule? I think not.

Moreover, not all the things for which people and organizations compete are good. Individuals rival one another in vanity and ostentation.

Businesses compete to be the biggest, growing oversized, overpowerful, and unmanageable. Nations, competing for territory or imperial power, go to war. Even if they avoid hostilities, they may squander their resources in striving to outdo each other in their power to destroy each other—or to prevent each other from destroying each other. The theory that *competition is always desirable* is unconvincing.

Why Competition?

Before examining in some detail the excesses and abuses of competition, let us begin by asking a basic question: Why are economists so obsessed with competition, and why have we let them persuade us to adopt their view? There are three main reasons. First, many economists are devotees of the pseudoreligion of the free market, one of whose "commandments" is that there should, in theory, be no man-made restraints on competition. Another, more practical reason is that competition leads to more efficient, therefore cheaper, production, and thus lower prices. A third reason is that competition stimulates innovation.

Competition does indeed drive us to cut costs and so to make things (or provide services) more and more cheaply. Why do we want to do that? Clearly, because if goods and services are cheaper, we can buy more of them. The basic aim of modern economics, ever since its beginnings in the eighteenth century, has been to raise standards of living; to enable us to consume more.

But this strategy has succeeded all too well. Today, we have an emperor-sized problem: we (the human race as a whole) are consuming too much. Competitive economic behavior has driven us to overgrow our overall consumption until it is too big for our planet. We are exploiting the Earth's natural resources too rapidly; we are generating more garbage than we know what to do with. We face an urgent need to learn to *consume less quantity but better quality* and also to *spread our consumption more evenly* so that everyone can at least enjoy a decent basic standard of living.

This means that the science of economics needs to turn a sharp corner. It must stop trying to motivate us to produce and consume ever more and more of everything. It must turn its attention to a quite different question: *how can we be motivated to produce and consume in a sustainable and equitable manner?*

Innovation and Change

Another alleged virtue of competition is that it stimulates innovation. Every business today is constantly told: *you must innovate or die.* For unrestrained competition forces you to sell your existing products more and more cheaply, until they are no longer profitable. So, to stay profitable, you must come up with new products whose novelty will command higher prices; just until your competitors get around to copying them, driving down their prices in turn to barely profitable levels. Then you will need another round of innovations to keep you in business.

Is all this good for us? Clearly, most of us appreciate a certain amount of novelty and change. And innovations can bring real progress. Yet change is not good in itself; there are good changes and bad changes. Today, everywhere we hear of the problems thrown up by yesterday's innovations. Modern farming methods have brought us pollution by pesticides, bacteria that resist antibiotics, epidemics originating in intensive farms, and cruelty to farm animals. Detergents and plastic bags become pervasive nondegradable wastes. It is said that a pair of baskets, discarded in a landfill, will take a thousand years to decompose completely. The notorious *bisphenol A*, widely used in plastics manufacture since the 1960s, turns out to be a cause of hormonal perturbation and probably cancer, too.

We might do better to think more carefully before we innovate. But unrestrained competition does not allow this. It dictates that we innovate as fast as we can and face the resulting problems later. *Stop for lunch and you are lunch*, as someone in Silicon Valley put it.[3]

The Hyperthyroid Economy

We can compare the role of competition in the economy with the role of the thyroid hormones (thyroxine and related substances) in the human body.[4] These hormones stimulate growth. They also promote metabolism, the transformation of food and drink into energy and body tissues. Likewise, competition stimulates economic growth and enhances efficiency; thus it accelerates the transformation of raw materials into saleable products.

The thyroid hormones are essential to life; without them, you die. Thyroid deficiency in children can leave them physically stunted or mentally retarded. In adults, it leads to obesity, lethargy, hypothermia, and constipation. But that does not mean that the more thyroxine you have in your system, the better. On the contrary, excess of the thyroid hormones (hyperthyroidism) provokes other troublesome symptoms: weight loss, hyperactivity, emotional instability, tachycardia, fever, and diarrhea. It can even be fatal.

The body needs hormones in moderation. Like Goldilocks, it needs *not too little, not too much* of each. But economists, by and large, are unwilling to recognize that the economy, too, is like that. A healthy economy needs competition; yet, with too much of it, things can go badly wrong.

Too Much of a Good Thing

Orthodox economic thought holds that we can and should live in a state of permanent, unrestrained competition. That notion perhaps made sense, up to a point, in the eighteenth century, when Adam Smith grumbled about the anticompetitive price-fixing practices of trade guilds. He clearly preferred "the natural price, or the price of free competition"[5] as he described it. This phrase seems to suggest that any deliberate interference with free competition is an unnatural, reprehensible vice. And that has indeed been the prevailing view of free-market economists from Smith himself down to our own times.

But in Smith's day (the mid-eighteenth century) there were plenty of unavoidable, natural restraints on competition. The basic restraints were that transport, in the age of horse-drawn vehicles on rough roads and sailing ships at the mercy of the weather, was slow, difficult, risky, and costly, while communications (transmission of information) were equally slow.

A shoemaker in Edinburgh could hardly come under serious pressure from competitors in Glasgow (forty-five miles away), let alone in Italy or China. Shoes were made to measure in those days, and it took a full day to travel from Edinburgh to Glasgow, on horseback or in a jolting carriage. And a customer in Edinburgh could not discuss business with a Glasgow shoemaker by telephone or e-mail. So even if, as Smith wished, there had been no anticompetitive practices by shoemakers' guilds, competition would still have been quite severely restricted by natural, physical constraints. Most people had, at best, access to a few neighboring shoemakers in the town where, or near where, they lived. So competition was limited.

Thus, at the time when classical economics was born, competition—even when free from "unnatural" constraints—was essentially far more restrained than the competition we know today. We have made life hard for ourselves by allowing our present-day economic thought to be dominated by theories first propounded in a very different age. With today's cheap and rapid transport and instantaneous worldwide communications, it has become possible for everyone to be in competition with everyone, throughout the world. But do we want to live like that? Or, indeed, can we continue to live like that?

Orthodox economists seldom ask that question. They simply assume that, because raw competition, unhampered by "unnatural" man-made rules, seemed right for Adam Smith, so it must be right for us too. Many economists believe that the "laws of economics" are like the "laws of nature": the same at all times and in all places. Franklin Roosevelt, who studied economics at Harvard at the beginning of the last century,[6] held a more realistic view. In his address accepting the presidential nomination in 1932, he remarked that "economic laws are not made by nature. They are made by human beings."[7]

Roosevelt was right; for economics is about human behavior, and human beings, unlike the forces of nature, have free wills of their own. They can and do make their own decisions, which may not conform with the rationality of the physical laws that govern the motion of the planets or the influence of magnetic fields.

Competition Enhances Performance—But Also Brings Problems

I have said that competition is good in moderation. In what ways is it good? We can start by looking at how competition stimulates performance. It encourages us to do better than we thought we could do. This competitive striving to surpass ourselves (and each other) can be a manifestation of true freedom. It can yield results that are useful, valuable, or beautiful. Yet it can be damaging when it is pushed too hard.

In the nineteenth and twentieth centuries, competition at sea between passenger liners, between tea clippers (fast three-masted square riggers), and between freight steamers all helped us develop quicker transport. The *Blue Riband*, an unofficial accolade for the fastest east-west crossing of the Atlantic, has been accorded to some thirty-five ships. The first was the *Sirius*, a paddle-steamer which completed the voyage in 1838 at an average speed of 8.03 knots; the last was the *United States*, which achieved the all-time record of 34.51 knots in 1952. But today's cruise ships go at a gentler pace, generally between 20 and 25 knots. The high speeds achieved in the last years of the great passenger liners demanded voracious consumption of fuel.

Aviation has a comparable history. The quest for higher speeds culminated in the *Concorde*, which achieved supersonic performance averaging around 1,330 mph. But she flies no more; and her Russian competitor, the *Tupolev Tu-144*, made only 102 commercial flights, the last in 1978. The costs of supersonic civil aviation proved exorbitant, and its extravagant use of fuel is no longer acceptable.

So shipping and aviation have demonstrated not only the ability of competition to enhance performance but also the limitations of this process. In any field, the cult of performance can ultimately exceed practicality, becoming futile, wasteful, and damaging.

Competition between musicians has stimulated remarkable development in the techniques of composing, instrument making, and performance. The piano music of Franz Liszt (1811–1886) reflected his own spectacular performing skill, and it was so difficult that many expert pianists of his day found it unplayable. Today, professional pianists can generally cope with it; but they face even greater difficulties in the works of twentieth-century composers such as Stockhausen, Boulez, or Cage. This competition-driven technical progress has indeed allowed music to conquer new horizons, but it has also produced plenty of meretricious showpieces, fearsomely hard to play, but of little real musical value.[8]

And this "progress" has had a sad result: much of our contemporary "serious" music is unplayable by all but the most advanced, specially trained professionals. We have left far behind the world of Mozart or of Schubert, where amateur musicians could enjoy performing the works of their top-flight contemporaries.

Winner Take All

Yet another problem with severe competition in music—and likewise in sports and many other activities—is the *winner take all* effect, ably diagnosed by Robert H. Frank and Philip J. Cook in *The Winner Take All Society*. They point out that solo singers work in a fiercely competitive environment where, thanks to the internet and the CD, the performances of (for example) all the world's operatic sopranos are accessible throughout the world. Thus, everyone is in competition with everyone; "the world's best soprano can literally be everywhere at once."[9] And so can all the other recorded sopranos. But the human "herd instinct" encourages most of us to follow the one regarded as the current leader. When this happens on a global scale, the singer who is considered the best in her class can achieve far greater rewards than anyone else in her class, even though many of the others may be almost as good as the star. Here we have an example of the *winner take all* principle, which generates some of today's most glaring inequalities.

Frank and Cook highlight an even more striking situation in sports. They tell the story of Mary Lou Retton, gold medalist in gymnastics at the 1984 Olympic Games in Los Angeles: "Her endorsement contracts have earned her several million dollars in the years since her medal. But although Retton's victory over the 1984 silver medalist came by only a slim margin, today [1995] almost no one can even remember the runner-up's name."[10]

Winner take all, indeed! Because for number 1, the rewards are vastly greater than for number 2, the competitive pressure to reach the top is huge. Frank and Cook describe how hyperintensive training programs often cause severe medical and psychological problems and how drastic treatments for these can induce further pathologies.

Then we have the vexatious problem of athletes who take steroids to enhance their performance. These too have unhealthy consequences. In less fiercely competitive times, it was simply "not done" for Olympic athletes to take drugs. But the pressure of excessive competition, combined with the legalistic attitude that lets one do whatever is not expressly prohibited, has demolished that informal convention. And so economist John Kay mourns the loss of "that tricky balance between competition and cooperation, which worked so well for many Olympiads, but which seems no longer to exist."[11]

We have an Anglican bishop to thank for the famous slogan of the early modern Olympics, a memorable phrase that warned against hypercompetitive behavior. Baron Pierre de Coubertin, founder of the modern Olympic movement, quoted this remark at an official dinner in London, following the fourth (1908) Olympiad:

> Last Sunday, during a ceremony in St. Paul's Cathedral in honor of the athletes, the Bishop of Pennsylvania reminded us in a happy phrase: "*what matters in these Olympiads is not so much*

the winning as the taking part." Gentlemen, let us keep in mind these striking words. They extend across all aspects of life and form the basis of a serene and healthy philosophy. What is important in life is not the triumph, but the struggle; the essential thing is not to have conquered, but to have fought well. To spread these precepts is to prepare a humanity that will be stronger, more valiant, but also more scrupulous, more generous.[12]

Finding the right balance is indeed "tricky," as Kay observed. We have somehow to relearn how to play to win, without trying so hard to win that we destroy the decency and civilization of true sportsmanship—or, for that matter, of healthy trade and commerce. Economists want us to believe that trade is conducive to peace and harmony; yet they call for a world of unrestrained competition in which business becomes vicious, greedy, unscrupulous, and exploitative.

Competing to Boost Consumption

We favor competition in sports or in the arts because it motivates us to enhance performance. In business, another argument is prevalent and has been ever since Adam Smith. We shall see (chap. 6) how Smith wanted to get rid of the craftsmen's guilds so that consumers could enjoy lower prices at the expense of the master craftsmen and their employees.

A century later, this theme was taken up by the Viennese professor Carl Menger, founder of the "Austrian school" of free-market economists. In his *Principles of Economics* (1871) he explains how an association of producers, acting as a "monopoly," can agree to regulate output and prices like the old-time guilds that so vexed Smith. Such an association may well find it advantageous to crimp production so as to keep prices high. Menger damns this practice as "socially injurious": a group of producers selfishly seeking to increase their profits by gouging the consumers. By contrast, "true competition always puts this malpractice to an end immediately."[13] In a freely competitive market, each producer can only maximize his profits by producing and selling as much as he can. He cannot restrict his output and push up his prices; if he tries that, his customers will desert him and buy from cheaper competitors.

So, says Menger, one of the "socially most injurious outgrowths of monopoly . . . is removed by competition."[14] The word *injurious* translates *verderblich* in the original text, and this word is among the nastiest adjectives in the German language; its meanings include vicious, corrupt, shameful, perverse, and depraved.

We can hardly dispute Menger's claim that "monopolistic" selling by a cooperative association of producers is likely to mean higher prices and lower sales. But we can indeed dispute Menger's insistence that this practice is *verderblich*. There are many good reasons why it may be far from perverse.

Eight Arguments for Restraint on Competition

(1) Avoiding Overconsumption

Competition, as we have seen, leads to growth in consumption. Eighteenth-century classical economists like Smith saw this as a good thing; after all, with world population around one-tenth of its present level, they had little need to worry about depletion of resources. Even nineteenth-century Austrian economists like Menger could get away with calling for further growth, with lambasting those *verderblichen* colluding traders whose behavior kept production and consumption lower than it might have been. In their day, world population was still only one-fifth of what it is today. But we, with our *full world* (full of us), cannot afford to persist with this kind of thinking. We need a new framework of economic thought.

The big problem today is that two centuries of competitive economics have so far enhanced labor productivity, that now, in the more advanced economies, we can produce everything we need and a whole lot more—indeed, far too much for the good of our environment—even with millions of us unemployed. We don't have shortages of output; we have shortages of jobs. Yet we still need to work for our living.

In the past, we had to work to make what we needed to consume. Now we have to make what we have no need to consume simply to keep ourselves working and earning. We swamp ourselves in superfluous paper and plastics, in flimsy objects quickly discarded, in cheap trash of all kinds, overstretching our natural resources and polluting our planet with rubbish. Yet still we feel the need to promote further growth; for how otherwise can we get our unemployed back to work? Is this not absurd? Might we not be happier with a few of our old-time, work-making, restrictive practices?

(2) A Better Life for Us Workers

Restraint of competition may well mean a better deal for ourselves as workers. Smith himself admitted this. Remarking that guilds existed only in towns, he affirmed that "the industry which is carried on in towns is, everywhere in Europe, more advantageous than that which is carried on in the country."[15] Guilds were good for the craftsmen and their assistants. Likewise today, if workers were not compelled to run on the treadmill of all-out global competition, they could be better paid, more secure in their jobs, less vexed by excessive stresses. Is it *verderblich* to wish for that? Why are free marketeers so keen to clobber us workers for the benefit of us consumers?

That question is easily answered. Economists want us to submit ourselves, as workers, to the harsh treatment meted out by the market because, they say, it is worthwhile enduring that present pain in order to earn the future reward of being able to consume more. But we have reached a situation where consuming more threatens grave and irreparable damage to our world. Consuming more is no longer acceptable. So why submit to maltreatment by the market? The ultimate "reward," far from being desirable, is catastrophic.

The distinguished Czech economist Tomas Sedlacek has given us an intriguing theologico-economic speculation: original sin might in reality be linked to *misguided consumption*, rather than, as various Christian theologies have traditionally suggested, to sexual misbehavior. Thus he writes:

> The medieval notion frequently prevails that the first sin in the Garden of Eden was sexual, that the form of the original sin had sexual character. But this is missing convincing argumentation. I offer another possible angle: It would appear to be much more likely that the original sin had the character of (over) *consumption*. After all, in the story of the Garden of Eden, Eve and Adam *literally* consume (the word "ate" is repeated two times) the fruit. "She took some and ate it. She also gave some to her husband, who was with her, and he ate it."[16]

Sedlacek continues, "In our constant desire to have always more, we have sacrificed the agreeable aspects of work. We want too much, and therefore we work too much. We are by far the richest civilization that has ever existed, but we remain as far, if not further, from the word *enough*, or satisfaction, than at any period in our 'primitive' past." Surely there is a message here for present-day America!

(3) Solidarity

A common argument against producers' associations is that they lead to the injustice of minorities profiting at the expense of the majority. But here the logic is faulty. If, for example, there was a guild of brewers but no other guilds, then one might reasonably object that the many beer drinkers were being unfairly obliged to "featherbed" the few brewers. But if there were guilds or unions for every profession, then everyone would featherbed everyone else, and the charge of unfairness would collapse. That's not unfairness, it's all-around *solidarity*. Is that possible in practice? Yes, it is.

In Switzerland, one of the world's most successful and prosperous economies, there is a long tradition of *cartels*, or agreements between similar businesses to restrain competition among themselves. According to a 1992 report in *The Economist*, "Cartels are part of the warp and woof of Swiss society, helping to give cantons and communes their sense of identity. The habit probably dates back to the solidarity that carried villages and valleys through tough winters."[17] And *The Economist* moans that "the government does so little to get rid" of these cartels. It would moan, wouldn't it? That journal has been assiduously preaching the free-market gospel ever since its foundation in 1843.

Until quite recently, cartels existed in most Swiss industries, as well as in banking and insurance. Despite recent moves to dismantle some of them, economists still complain that more needs to be done. The Competition Commission, set up in 2004 to investigate anticompetitive behavior, has been criticized on the ground that some of its members represent business associations. According to prevailing dogma, such a commission should represent only consumer interests; the producers shouldn't get a look in. The OECD's 2007 survey complains that "Competition law still requires proof of abuse for action to be taken against hard-core cartels."[18] In other words, the OECD thinks that any attempt to restrain competition should be treated as a crime, with no need to prove that the restraint is in fact abusive.

Yet, despite her economic "sins," Switzerland ranks among the world's lowest-unemployment countries, while wages are among the highest and "quality of jobs" is high too. So much for those economists who assure us that, if you want low unemployment, you have to have low pay. Is this an example of St. Thomas's paradox: "Many useful things would be obstructed, if all sins were strictly prohibited"?[19]

The OECD's latest (2013) survey complains that there are still too many restraints on competition and that Swiss productivity growth is below that of neighboring countries, as it has been for decades. Prosperous and stable Switzerland, with its unemployment rate of less than 4 percent, apparently works in practice but not in theory; further free-market reforms are called for. Yet Switzerland seems to have demonstrated that a successful economy with a good deal of solidarity is possible. That does not impress economists who base their beliefs on theory rather than on what has been shown to work in practice.

(4) Competition Can Inflate Costs

Does competition always cut costs? No. In fact, it can seriously inflate them. In less competitive times, investment bankers, financial market traders, and top executives in other businesses were well, but not exorbitantly, paid. Those were the days when it was "not done" for a City or Wall Street bank to "poach" a competitor's staff. Just as it was not done for Olympic athletes to take steroids. Healthier values prevailed.

Today, rather than appointing their top people by internal promotion, companies compete to attract those executives and traders who are considered the best profit earners. They bid up the salaries and bonuses of these "stars" to grotesque levels, thus inflating their management costs. But these same companies are under competitive pressure to get their overall costs down. So they compensate for overspending at the top by understaffing in the middle and at the bottom. Here is one cause of the high levels of unemployment and the gaping inequalities that disfigure our economies and societies.

(5) Mis-selling

When competition squeezes profit margins, firms are driven to compensate by selling larger quantities; according to free-market doctrine, that is a very good thing. But is it? In British personal pensions, competitive pressure to sell more has led to huge mis-selling of unsuitable products. Many people have been persuaded by plausible salesmen to buy pension contracts that cost a lot, yet failed to meet their personal needs. The costs of compensating pensioners were estimated by the British Treasury at "up to £11 billion" ($17 billion).[20]

Still worse has been the case of the notorious subprime mortgages. American banks and mortgage brokers competed with each other to induce low-paid families to buy, with the help of mortgages, houses they could barely afford. This overabundant credit drove up house prices to silly levels. Nevertheless, a house buyer could borrow 100 percent, or even more, of the inflated purchase price at an interest rate that was low in the first few years but rose sharply later. The market collapsed when buyers found they could no longer pay their installments. Excessive competition in the mortgage market has led many people into bankruptcy and homelessness.

(6) Excessive Competition in Investment Markets

Fund managers, who hold portfolios of shares in firms listed on the stock markets, have become more demanding than they once were. They expect the businesses in which they invest to grow faster and to pay higher dividends. That is because they, the fund managers, now compete fiercely with each other. They are engaged in a race for the best returns, a race that has grown more grueling, thanks to the spirit of intense competition that is fostered by current technology and ideology.

With the help of electronic techniques, we can now calculate the performance (return on capital) of investment portfolios quickly and often. With the publication of frequent performance comparisons, which look rather like race cards, fund managers are under constant pressure to enhance and accelerate the returns on their investments. Moreover, very large bonuses can be earned by individuals who notch up fat capital gains for the funds they manage.

Fund managers therefore push the managements of companies in which they invest to strive for maximum, rather than adequate, profits, and to give priority to immediate profitability rather than to long-term development. If a company fails to oblige, its shares may be ditched by the fund managers. Its share price will tumble and so may attract a cheap takeover bid. Company managements live in fear of that.

So businesses of all kinds find themselves under continual pressure from the financial markets to enhance their profits. But they are also under relentless competitive pressure to keep their prices down, or preferably cut them. Conventional economic theory insists on maximum competition between businesses in the interests of consumers; it cares very little about the interests of those who work on the shop floor or in the office. Therefore, companies are encouraged to compete against each other as fiercely as possible. Any agreement between competitors to stabilize prices is treated as a serious crime.

Under the two-edged sword of demand for higher profits and lower prices, companies respond with aggressive cost cutting. This leads to "downsizing," to worsening conditions of employment, to severe work-place stresses, to deterioration in quality of production, research, and customer service, to neglect of safety and environmental protection. It frequently leads to closure of American factories and substitution of cheaper imports.

By slashing costs such as payroll, research and development, or provision for pensions, a business can often boost immediate profits, leading to a rise in its share price. The wider and longer-term consequences of this cost cutting do not concern financial investors, who realize quick capital gains. The old Anglican prayer book describes memorably an ancient equivalent of this situation:

> I do also see the ungodly in such prosperity . . .
> therefore fall the people unto them:
> and thereout suck they no small advantage.[21]

(7) Concentration of Firms

Free competition on price has a nasty consequence: it gives bigger competitors an opportunity to eliminate smaller ones. Big firms enjoy the famous "economies of scale"; this technical jargon simply means that if you do anything on a big scale, you can generally do it cheaper. Thus, by trimming prices, they can drive out smaller competitors. The result is that we find ourselves with an economy dominated by a few giants. They acquire too much power; and those who have excessive power tend to abuse it. The downside of economy of scale is that the few big firms will most likely employ fewer people than the many smaller ones they have replaced; that is one of the reasons for their lower costs. Moreover, the giant that becomes "too big to fail" may have to be rescued at taxpayers' expense if it gets into trouble. Remember the hedge fund LTCM, the insurance giant AIG, the Detroit auto manufacturers, the behemoths of the banking world?

Too much competition leads to too few competitors: not a healthy situation. On the London Stock Exchange, before the "big bang" of 1986, stockbroking firms could not compete on price; the Stock Exchange rule book required them all to stick to a fixed scale of commission rates. In those days, there were more than a hundred independent stockbroking firms, owned by the partners who ran them. Today there are only a dozen or so significant broking houses, almost all owned by banks.

(8) Quality and Durability

Competition on price can mean a "race to the bottom" in terms of product quality or product longevity. We have lost the old habit of making "consumer durables" that really were durable; like those elegant, highly decorated Singer sewing machines of which many, fifty or even a hundred years old, are still in good working order. Durability has been sacrificed in the competitive struggle to get prices down. Moreover, products are changing so rapidly in response to our competitive obsession with innovation that durability has ceased to seem worthwhile.

My wife once, in a photographic shop in London, asked to have a camera repaired. The puzzled salesman responded with a memorable question: "*repair*, madam, what does that mean?" Sadly, the belief that we need not repair anything since it is cheaper to buy new, and new is anyway better, is now so widespread that we no longer know how to repair things—or even, in some cases, what the word *repair* means! This frequent replacement of almost everything is a major cause of our current overconsumption of resources and overproduction of rubbish.

And what about quality in the sense of respect for the environment? It would be highly desirable for European governments and industrialists to agree on a cooperative plan to develop wind, solar, and tidal power on a grand scale, thus eliminating emissions from coal, oil, or gas-fired power stations, ceasing to depend on oil from unreliable sources, and creating a large volume of employment, thus pulling Europe out of its present recession. If you think this is technically impracticable, reflect that Spain already has enough wind turbines to supply about a quarter of her electricity needs. There are some 20,000 of these huge "windmills"; and sunny Spain's solar power potential is, as yet, little developed.

But will governments do this? They are trying, but they are inhibited by the fear that energy may become more expensive in Europe than elsewhere, making European businesses "uncompetitive" with the rest of the world. Economists can still be heard denouncing plans for renewable energy development on the ground that "this will ruin our nation's competitiveness."

We shrink from doing what urgently needs to be done for fear of being capsized by competition. Pius XI said it all in 1931, in *Quadragesimo Anno* (par. 88): "The right ordering of economic life cannot be left to a free competition of forces. For from this source, as from a poisoned spring, have originated and spread all the errors of individualist economic teaching."

And now Christine Lagarde, managing director of the IMF, who comes from a strongly Catholic background, has echoed his thoughts. Perhaps, in part, because she is not an economist; not therefore educated in the theories of orthodox economics, which, sadly, seem often to block our progress toward a more civilized economy. We need more emphasis on cooperation and solidarity—less on competition.

Is Competition Good or Bad?

How can we distinguish between good and bad competition? There is, I regret to say, no foolproof criterion. But here is one good way to evaluate any particular competitive practice: does it raise standards, or does it lower them?

Confucius, who was no great enthusiast for competitive behavior, gave us a valuable clue: "Exemplary persons are not competitive, except when they have to be, in the archery ceremony. Greeting and making way for each other, the archers ascend the hall, and returning they drink a salute. Even in contesting, they are exemplary persons [*junzi*, a word often translated as *gentlemen*]."[22]

Here Confucius evokes a form of gentlemanly competition, reminiscent of the kind commended by Baron de Coubertin. The aim of an archery contest is, of course, to promote high standards of archery; these competitors strive to outdo each other in quality of performance. But they do not strive so hyperintensively that abusive or fraudulent practices creep in, as with certain Olympic contestants and *Tour de France* cyclists who resort to illicit use of drugs to achieve unnaturally and unhealthily high performance.

Confucius's archery contest is an example of virtuous competition that aims to enhance standards. Too often, however, commercial competition degrades standards because its primary aim is lower prices rather than higher quality. Thus we have retailers who cut their prices to the bone by selling in spartan warehouses rather than in attractive shops, by providing little or no customer service, by paying their minimal staff at minimal rates, and by selling merchandise of flimsy quality, manufactured under wretched conditions. This is *standards-lowering competition*. It rhymes with unemployment, low-quality jobs, and overconsumption of materials; flimsy products have to be replaced frequently.

Again, there is *fiscal competition* between countries, a practice warmly commended by certain libertarians. This means that countries vie with each other to push tax rates down. A low-tax country attracts businesses to establish themselves on its territory, where they will pay little tax. It may also encourage foreign businesses to pretend that they are operating on its territory; by devious accounting practices they make it appear that their profits are earned in the low-tax country, so that these profits are lightly taxed. This is clearly unfair to the countries where the profits are, in reality, earned.

Once one country has embarked on a policy of tax-cutting fiscal competition, neighboring countries may well feel obliged to respond by cutting their own tax rates. Consequently, the countries involved either run chronic budget deficits and so build up excessive debts, or they cut back their public services. Again, we have lower standards.

So, there is our criterion. Competition to achieve excellence is admirable, so long as it is not pushed to perverse excesses. Competition to reduce standards, to provide everything on the cheap, too often yields results that are cheap and nasty for everybody concerned: producers, sellers, and consumers. This is deplorable. It is stupid to seek to cut the cost of living without considering the wider consequences. The countries with the highest costs of living are often those with the best quality of life, the least unemployment, and the least poverty. That fact contradicts what mainstream economists persist in trying to teach us. But in economics, practical experience is often a better guide than theory.

Biblical Teaching on Competition

Many Christians seem inclined to tolerate highly competitive behavior, perhaps because it is not explicitly forbidden in the Bible. As the sarcastic English poet Arthur Hugh Clough wrote:

> *Thou shalt not covet; but tradition*
> *Approves all forms of competition.*[23]

It is quite difficult to find the word *competition* in an English translation of the Bible. The word is absent from many versions. It does appear in the Jerusalem Bible (Phil 2:3): "There must be no competition among you, no conceit, but everybody is to be self-effacing." Here, *competition* translates the Greek *eritheia*, meaning ambition, self-seeking, rivalry. Another translation has, "Never act from motives of rivalry or personal vanity."[24] The context suggests that St. Paul is talking about behavior in society generally, rather than specifically about economic competition.

But we may well be wrong in assuming that the Bible does not prohibit aggressive or predatory competition in business. The Old Testament in several places condemns the sin of *hasagat gevul* or "infringement of boundary." In ancient Israel, the boundaries between adjacent farms were often marked simply by heavy stones, whose position could be surreptitiously modified. So we read (Deut 27:17): "Cursed be he who removes his neighbor's landmark." This offense meant that an unscrupulous farmer damaged his neighbor's livelihood by encroaching on his land. In Jewish tradition, the Biblical rule against *hasagat gevul* has often been interpreted to cover many other malpractices that can damage a neighbor's livelihood. Thus the Talmud suggests that a fisherman should keep his nets well away from his neighbor's nets, even by "the full length of the fish's swim."[25] In the same place we read that "Rabbi Huna said: If a resident of an alley sets up a handmill and another resident of the alley wants to set up one next to him, the first has the right to stop him, because he can say to him, 'You are interfering with my livelihood.'" And the Talmud records a lively, but inconclusive, debate on this question.

Elsewhere, we find interpretations of certain verses in Psalm 15. On verse 3:

> He that hath no slander upon his tongue,
> Nor doeth evil to his fellow,

the third-century sage Rabbi Simlai explains: "'*Nor doeth evil to his fellow,*' that is, he who does not set up in opposition to his fellow craftsman."[26]

There has long been, and still is, disputation among Jews over just how much competition is acceptable and to what extent new businesses should be allowed to undermine existing businesses. Courts of Jewish law, such as the *Beth Din* of New York, have to adjudicate from time to time on accusations of *hasagat gevul*. Judgments in such cases can be quite controversial when they conflict with the prevailing American belief that competition should not be restricted.

Thus, in the opinion of many Jews, the Bible does indeed contain prohibitions of "unfair" competition, concealed within the law against moving boundary stones and the succinct language of the psalter. Of course, for many free-market economists, even Jewish economists, all this talk about unfair competition is nonsense. Milton Friedman argued that "the more unfair the competition, the better."[27] But he, though Jewish born and bred, was not a practicing Jew; he turned atheist.

Competition in Catholic Social Teaching

In *Rerum Novarum* (par. 3) Leo XIII observes that "it has come to pass that working men have been surrendered, isolated and helpless, to the hardheartedness of employers and the greed of unchecked competition." Accordingly, he warmly commends (par. 49) solidarity among workers, provided historically by craftsmen's guilds, and in his own day by the developing workingmen's unions. One of the main objects of guilds and unions has always been to protect members' livelihood by restraining downward competitive pressure on prices and wages. Solidarity is the antidote to isolation.

We have seen how Pius XI, in *Quadragesimo Anno* (1931), rejected the notion, dear to many economists, that we can leave the regulation of the economy to the blind action of untrammeled markets. In the following year, in the encyclical *Caritate Christi Compulsi* (par. 18), the pope evoked "the marvelous order established by God, which knows not the frenzy of earthly successes nor the futile competitions of ever-increasing speed." He unwittingly foresaw today's high-frequency trading!

In *Mater et Magistra* (pars. 80 and 137), John XXIII observes that "the demands of the common good on the international level include: the avoidance of unfair competition between the economies of different countries" and calls for price protection for agricultural products. Ideally, he says, this "should be enforced by the interested parties themselves, though supervision by the public authorities cannot be altogether dispensed with."

Price protection means that producers and traders avoid unrestrained competition, which sets unstable and often penurious commodity prices for small farmers in developing countries. Such protection used to be provided by international agreements, regulating prices for certain commodities; but those agreements have been swept away by the worldwide tide of deregulation. To a limited extent, protection is now being reinstated by way of "fair-trade" agreements.[28]

Paul VI, in *Populorum Progressio* (par. 26), does not mince his words: "Certain concepts have . . . insinuated themselves into the fabric of human society. These concepts present profit as the chief spur to economic progress, free competition as the guiding norm of economics, and private ownership of the means of production as an absolute right, having no limits nor concomitant social obligations. This unbridled liberalism paves the way for a particular type of tyranny . . . the 'international imperialism of money.'"

John Paul II, in an address to the Academy of Social Sciences in 1997, speaks (par. 4) in terms that still seem hot off the press eighteen years later. He complains that "the easy transfer of resources and production systems, effected only in virtue of the criterion of maximum profit and unbridled competition, can aggravate unemployment in countries with a longstanding industrial tradition." And he goes on to castigate (par. 5) "an unbridled market which, under the pretext of competitiveness, prospers by exploiting man and the environment to excess."

Benedict XVI, in *Caritas in Veritate* (par. 25), delivers a precise and incisive analysis of one of today's major economic problems:

> The market has prompted new forms of competition between States as they seek to attract businesses to set up production centers, by means of a variety of instruments, including favorable fiscal regimes and deregulation of the labor market. These processes have led to a *downsizing of social security systems* as the price to be paid for seeking greater competitive advantage in the global market, with consequent grave dangers for the rights of workers, for fundamental human rights and for the solidarity associated with the traditional forms of the social State. Systems of social security can lose the capacity to carry out their task.

So, after all the strivings of the period from Pope Leo to Pope John Paul to create more just and humane societies, now we are having to reinvent the wheel; as Pope Benedict remarks, "*Rerum Novarum* is even more to be cherished today than yesterday."[29]

Pope Francis, in an address to new ambassadors to the Holy See on May 16, 2013, complains that "solidarity, which is the treasure of the poor, is often considered counterproductive, opposed to the logic of finance and the economy." That little sentence sums up precisely the attitude of many free-market economists, who reject any form of solidarity as an impediment to the untrammeled competition of their dreams.

Proponents of *localism*, a philosophy which has affinities with the Catholic concept of subsidiarity, argue that local economies are healthier in places where people have a strong sense of attachment to their particular territory. This need not be a national territory; it can just as well be a region or district within a nation, such as Béarn in southwestern France, just to the west of Lourdes. In such places, people are keen to support their local economy by giving preference to the produce of their own territory wherever possible. There is thus a kind of voluntary restraint of competition that can help to offset the negative effects of globalization.

The Economists' Shaky Defense

Economists argue that if we prohibit aggressive competition that damages existing firms, or even drives them out of business, then we block the normal action of free markets. According to their theory, the whole point of free markets is to promote progress by replacing old products with new, better ones, or by replacing old production methods with new, more efficient techniques. This is known in the trade as "creative destruction" (*schöpferische Zerstörung*), a phrase invented by the Austrian economist Joseph Schumpeter (1883–1950), who claimed that his ambition was to be the greatest lover in Vienna, the greatest horseman in Austria, and the greatest economist in the world. Words are powerful. Schumpeter's neat little phrase has helped countless economists and businessmen to justify the continual, relentless destruction of whole segments of our economies in the belief that this process is somehow "creative."

Surely, economists argue, it is stupid, indeed obscurantist, to stand in the way of progress by interfering with free markets in order to protect existing entrepreneurs and employees and their families. This argument leads us to a very basic question, which we shall explore more fully in chapter 14: to what extent do we want to live, or can we live, with rapid economic change? We know that it causes much distress by throwing people out of work. We know that new products introduced without adequate testing often turn out to be harmful or dangerous. We know that constantly replacing things entails wasteful consumption of resources. Yet we know too that we cannot simply stand still; our world has always been subject to change and always will be. We sometimes think that our Catholic traditions are, or should be, unchanging; but no, "*change* is the tradition," according to Fr. Timothy Radcliffe, a past Master of the Dominicans.[30]

Our problem, then, is to find an acceptable balance between the need for change and the need for stability. Those economists who despise stability, who long for unhampered competition to impose the quickest possible innovation and change, regardless of its human, social, and environmental costs, are not helping us. We must seek more enlightened advisors.

CHAPTER 6

The Libertarian Disrespect for Labor

*Human work proceeds directly from persons created in the image
of God and called to prolong the work of creation . . . hence
work is a duty . . . work honors the Creator's gifts . . . everyone
should be able to draw from work the means of providing for his
life and that of his family, and of serving the human community.*

—Catechism, pars. 2427–28

*Man cannot do nothing but eat and make love; he needs other
things to occupy his time and his soul. . . . All moral strength
has its roots in work.*

—Gustav Schmoller[1]

*Work itself is one of the things that men and women need, and
that the community must help provide whenever they are unable
to provide it for themselves and for one another.*

—Michael Walzer[2]

A Harsh World of Employment

These are hard times for the world's workers. Throughout the Western world, and in many other places too, unemployment has been on an upward trend for decades; and in many places it continues to worsen. Jobs are harder to find, harder to keep, more stressful, and more insecure. More and more people are unhappy with their working conditions. It may be that we work best under a certain degree of pressure or stress; but today, exorbitant workplace stresses lead to burnout, depression, muscular pains, hypertension, insomnia, loss of appetite, loss of memory, even paranoid disorders and suicide.[3]

In the early 1960s, when I was a student in Edinburgh, finding a job was a pretty simple matter. It was a case of employers pursuing us rather than of us searching for them. I remember being part of a group of students who were invited by a leading Scottish life insurance company to spend three days being shown over their offices, having lengthy discussions with senior management, being entertained to lunch in good style . . . much to the amazement of my parents, who remembered the hard times of a generation earlier, in the 1930s, when the struggle to find employment was even tougher than it is today.

Why have we fallen back toward the conditions of a bad old age which seemed for a while to be ancient history, never to be repeated?

Changing Attitudes to Work

One basic reason is that the resurgence of free-market economics in the last quarter of the twentieth century has brought a profound change in our attitudes regarding work. But this change was not an innovation. It was a giant leap backward toward ideas that prevailed in the nineteenth century. Pope John Paul II described those ideas in *Laborem Exercens* (par. 7): "Work was understood and treated as a sort of 'merchandise' that the worker—particularly the industrial worker—sells to the employer. . . . This way of looking at work was widespread especially in the first half of the nineteenth century." This view of work, and indeed of workers too, as "commodities" can be traced back to the father of Scottish classical economics, Adam Smith himself. In his *Wealth of Nations* (1776) we read: "The demand for men, like that for any other commodity, necessarily regulates the production of men"[4] since greater demand for labor leads to higher wages, with the result that workers can afford to raise more children. Conversely, says Smith, lower demand leads to lower wages, more poverty, and higher mortality among workers' children.

Past Progress Undone

Overcoming these attitudes required generations of struggle by trade unionists, reforming politicians, enlightened economists, and not least by the priests, laity, bishops, and theologians who developed modern Catholic Social Teaching. But the happy outcome, as John Paul II continued, with a cautionary warning, was that "since then, expressions of this sort have almost disappeared and have given way to more human ways of thinking about work. . . . Nevertheless the danger of treating work as a special kind of 'merchandise,' or as an impersonal force needed for production . . . always exists."

When the pope wrote that, in 1981, resurgence of the free-market philosophy was in its early stages. Sadly, the warning in his last few words has been abundantly justified. Since he wrote, the old nineteenth-century attitudes that he deplored have returned in full force. Harvard law professor Paul C. Weiler writes, with disapproval, that "from the neoclassical economic point of view, labor is a commodity, a factor of production for which the terms of exchange are ideally determined in competitive markets."[5] As a lawyer, he may well have had in mind the words of Justice George Sutherland who, writing the opinion of the Supreme Court in the famous case *Atkins v. Children's Hospital* (1923), stated that "in principle, there can be no difference between the case of selling labor and the case of selling goods."

The Austrian economist Ludwig von Mises (1881–1979) was absolutely certain that the pure free market was the only acceptable economic system. In it, he tells us that "labor is dealt with like any material factor of production and sold and bought on the market."[6] This remark appears in his best-known book, *Human Action*, published in 1949 when such views were happily unfashionable. But Mises's works have enjoyed a big vogue in the late twentieth century, and he still has a considerable following, as we can see from the gigantic website of the Ludwig von Mises Institute (founded 1982) in Auburn, Alabama.

The theory that regards labor simply as an economic commodity has a logical and pernicious consequence. If labor is a commodity, then unemployment is logically a lesser evil than inefficient use of labor. After all, it is clearly better to use less oil or paper than to use these materials wastefully. Thus the journalist Henry Hazlitt, a famous propagandist for Austrian views, wrote that "it would be far better . . . to have maximum production with part of the population supported in idleness by undisguised relief than to provide 'full employment' by so many forms of disguised make-work that production is disorganized."[7]

Such "commodification" of labor in effect dehumanizes human work, treating the worker as a piece of equipment and his labor as a raw material. From a Catholic standpoint, this is theologically heretical and morally disgraceful. It seems hardly an exaggeration to say that economists who propagate such ideas are guilty of grave sin.

US federal law embodies a better concept; it has long recognized the principle that "the labor of a human being is not a commodity or an article of commerce," as we read in section 17 of the Clayton Antitrust Act of 1914. One of the purposes of this act was to exempt labor unions from the provisions of the Sherman Antitrust Act of 1890, which prohibited business cartels as unlawful "restraint of trade." US courts had interpreted the Sherman Act as outlawing unions; Clayton aimed to correct this error. But the free-market attitude, that treats labor essentially as a commodity traded in the market, dies hard.

Classical Economics: Hard on the Workers

In free-market theory, work is generally regarded as a *disutility*, which in economists' jargon means something we do not like and would always prefer to avoid. Work is thought to have no human value apart from the market value of what it produces. Labor is seen as simply a cost of production; like other costs, it should be cut to the bone so as to provide the lowest possible prices for the consumer. This negative attitude to labor can be found in Adam Smith: "Consumption is the sole end and purpose of all production; and the interest of the producer ought to be attended to only so far as it may be necessary for promoting that of the consumers."[8] That has been the prevalent view of free-market economists ever since. Their prime objective is to boost overall wealth by expanding production and consumption. The interests of the consumer, and of the capitalist, rule; those of the worker are well down the list of priorities. To put it bluntly, the attitude of these economists and their followers in politics and business is: *pander to the consumers, exploit the workers.*

We need to recognize that work is not merely something we do because we need the money it earns; it is also an essential feature of our lives, something we need to do as part of our pursuit of a healthy and satisfying existence. If we regard work simply as a "disutility," to which we submit unwillingly in order to earn our keep, we grossly misunderstand and devalue work. If we treat labor simply as a tradable commodity, we grossly misunderstand and devalue our very selves.

Classical economics involved a step backward for working people. Before its triumph, at the end of the eighteenth century, various arrangements were in place to protect the interests of workers. In many places, wage rates for laborers were prescribed by the magistrates, not left to the vagaries of the market. Craftsmen's guilds endeavored to keep prices high enough to ensure an adequate livelihood for carpenters, masons, tailors, bakers, grocers, etc.—all the various tradesmen who supplied our needs. They also saw to it that apprentices underwent a long period of training before they were permitted to set themselves up as master craftsmen and suppliers to the public.

By insisting on long apprenticeships, the guilds restricted the numbers of men entering their trades, but also aimed to ensure sound quality of work. Guilds did not tolerate unrestricted competition and price wars. It did not seem right to drive down the earnings of master craftsmen and their assistants just so that consumers could enjoy a bonanza of price cuts. It was thought better that guildsmen should compete to offer good quality rather than low price. Today, that sound principle is one of the keys to success in advanced industrial economies like those of Germany and Japan.

But the classical economists of the eighteenth and nineteenth centuries, even the wisest of them, ridiculed all that. Adam Smith objected strongly to guilds or "corporations" that propped up tradesmen's prices and incomes. So he called for the abolition of craft solidarities. Without guilds, he argued, "The master,[9] indeed, would be a loser. . . . [The apprentice's] wages, when he came to be a complete workman, would be much less than at present. . . . The trades, the crafts, the mysteries, would all be losers. But the public would be a gainer, the work of all artificers coming in this way much cheaper to market."[10]

Did it never occur to Smith that we consumers (the public) are also we workers? We see from his words just quoted that, from its very beginnings, the science of economics has perversely sought to benefit us, the consumers, by squeezing us, the workers. Thus, in effect, *orthodox economics favors cheap labor* and has done so ever since its birth in the eighteenth century.

Even Adam Smith Could Write Nonsense

Smith's attitude to trades and professions was in some ways startlingly unrealistic, and this seems odd to any reader who appreciates the clear thinking and sound common sense that pervades the greater part of Smith's elegant texts. In the chapter from which I have just quoted, we can find two more examples of this aberration.

First, Smith objected to the existence of a public register of the tradesmen in a town. This, he complained, "connects individuals who might never otherwise be known to one another, and gives every man of the trade a direction where to find every other man of it."[11] Thus the tradesmen are enabled to get together with a view to fixing their prices. Smith apparently thought it possible that, in the absence of a trades register, there could be, for example, a dozen independent bakers in Edinburgh who were unaware of each other's existence.

But that is clearly absurd. First, because tradesmen in the same trade inevitably meet by going to the same places to buy their supplies. Second, because tradesmen have to make their presence known to the public in order to attract business. Bakers do this by having conspicuous shops in the main streets. How then could they possibly be unaware of each other's existence?

Again, Smith argued that "long apprenticeships are altogether unnecessary. . . . The arts . . . such as those of making clocks and watches, contain no such mystery as to require a long course of instruction."[12] Well, concerning clocks and watches—and I mean the traditional mechanical ones—I have personal experience of dealing, on various occasions, with so-called "craftsmen" who have obviously not served long apprenticeships. It has been almost entirely bad experience.

In London, watch and clockmakers' guilds disappeared in the early nineteenth century, thanks to the influence of Smith and his followers. I once took a century-old watch, inherited from my grandfather, to a fellow there who claimed to be an expert at repairing such things. When I recovered it, the watch was gaining some twenty minutes a day, and my complaints evoked no sympathy. I was told, "You can't expect a watch of that age to be as accurate as quartz!" The only way I could get this Smithian workman to regulate my watch properly was to consult a technical book on watchmaking and then explain to the "expert" how to do the job. Since then, it has kept very good time.

The Consumer Comes First

In free-market theory, the consumer interest is supposed to come first; "the captain is the consumer"[13] as Mises put it. The capitalists are supposed to be merely the consumers' humble servants; they can only make money by providing King Pourchassa and Queen Hapishoppa with what their majesties want. In practice, as well we know, today it is often the interest of the capitalist that dominates. But there can be no doubt about whose interest always come a bad third; it is that of the worker.

To be fair to Smith and his contemporaries, the "classical" economists, they did recognize that workers need to earn enough to live on. Smith wrote that a man's wages "must at least be sufficient to maintain him,"[14] and claimed that even the "meanest laborer" did in fact earn a living wage: "For what purpose is all the toil and bustle of this world . . .? Is it to supply the necessities of nature? The wages of the meanest laborer can supply them. We see that they afford him food and clothing, the comfort of a house, and of a family."[15]

Perhaps he exaggerated a little. There were surely many very poor laborers in his day. Nevertheless, working people generally earned enough to survive, at a basic level, and to raise a family. Smith's friend Anne-Robert-Jacques Turgot, an early French economist who was briefly Louis XVI's finance minister, argued that laborers could not expect to earn more than a subsistence wage: "In every kind of labor it must, and does indeed, happen that the workers' wage is limited to that which is necessary to provide for his subsistence."[16] Likewise, a few decades later, another classical economist, the London stockbroker David Ricardo, wrote: "The natural price of labor is that price which is necessary to enable the laborers, one with another, to subsist and to perpetuate their race, without either increase or diminution."[17]

That harsh doctrine is aptly known as the *iron law of wages*. But at least it recognizes that wages should not fall below a basic subsistence level. There is, or should be, a natural "floor" for wages.

Worse Than the "Iron Law"

More recently, however, economists have smashed their way through the floor. The Viennese professor Carl Menger (1840–1921) was the first of the "Austrian school" economists, prophets of an extreme and highly theoretical form of the free-market religion. In the same group were Ludwig von Mises, already mentioned, and his pupil Friedrich von Hayek, Margaret Thatcher's guru and favorite economist.

Menger discussed prices and wage levels in his *Principles of Economics*, published in 1871. There he argued that the price of commodities traded in a free market normally settles at the level that the cheapest buyer is willing to pay. He went on to argue that the free-market level of wages or "price of labor" is no different from the price of any other commodity. It is the rate that the stingiest employer is willing to pay. The worker's need for a living wage does not enter into the calculation:

"Neither the means of subsistence nor the minimum subsistence of a laborer . . . can be the direct cause or determining principle of the price of labor services."[18]

In fact, says Menger, on the previous page, "In Berlin, a seamstress working fifteen hours a day, cannot earn what she needs for her subsistence." Despite this manifest injustice, Menger was not in sympathy with those who wanted to see seamstresses and other exploited workers better paid. On the contrary, he lambasted their agitation as futile; they were demanding "nothing else than paying labor above its value."[19]

For Menger, as for free-market economists in general, there could be no true value of labor other than its market value, based on the market value of what the labor produced. Why should employers not push up their prices so that they could afford to pay their workers better? Because, to do that, they might have to agree among themselves not to compete too fiercely. According to free-market theory, any such agreement is equivalent to a mortal sin.

In the writings of the Austrian and neoclassical economists and their followers, this callous attitude toward workers crops up time and again. It was embraced with enthusiasm by Ayn Rand, who admired Mises, and who paraded a fervent devotion to the principles of unbridled capitalism: "There are no 'rights' to a 'fair' wage or a 'fair' price if no-one chooses to pay it."[20]

In other words, the consumer, who ultimately pays the prices of goods and the wages of labor, is in the driver's seat. The role of the worker is simply to accept whatever miserable wage the bargain-hunting consumer is willing to pay. Miss Rand died in 1982, but her books are still best sellers in America. Does this fact help to explain why there are so many wretchedly paid, precariously employed workers in the richest country in the world?

The thrust of modern economic policy is to give top priority to the consumer by keeping retail prices as low as possible. If this means squeezing the workers by employing fewer of them, trimming pay and other benefits, enforcing longer working hours with shorter breaks and fewer holidays, then so be it. If this means letting our own manufactures disappear, replacing them with imports from the countries with the worst-paid workers, then so be it. If this means letting the biggest suppliers drive out or take over the smaller ones, because the *Großkapitalisten* can sell more cheaply, then so be it. All this for the sake of "consumer benefit," and fatter profits for the biggest businesses.

The Fetish of Labor Productivity

The concept of *n-1 staffing* has been recommended by some writers on management as a means of minimizing payroll costs. The idea is to work out the minimum number (n) of staff needed for a particular task or project and then subtract one. Thus you have deliberate understaffing. This is said to foster a high level of effort and efficiency. "Fewer than minimum" staff means, of course, that the people on the job have to do "more than maximum" if the job is to be done properly.

Well, we can all make an extra effort on occasion and force ourselves to do more than is normally feasible. In an emergency, people will rise to the occasion and do what it takes to cope with fire or flood, with epidemic or battle. But are we all able and willing to do, regularly and habitually, more than maximum?

Can it really make sense for businesses to be run on the basis of expecting people to do more than is normally feasible, not just in emergencies but every day? I think not. To demand that is to impose the excessive stresses of which more and more workers today are complaining. Moreover, this practice leaves far too many people without employment.

Economists argue that the people who are pushed out of work by the "fewer than minimum" strategy will find other things to do, such as starting up innovative new businesses and thus pampering the reigning monarchs (consumers) with still more novel gadgets wherewith to clutter their lives. Clearly, if we can get people to do "more than maximum" work, we get more production, which makes possible more consumption.

But what sense can this strategy make in a world that is already overconsuming its resources? Perhaps it made some kind of sense in Adam Smith's day, or even when Menger wrote, a century later. Then, in the 1870s, world population was around 1.4 billion, a mere fifth of today's level. Natural resources were under far less pressure than they are now. And most ordinary working people lived in very poor conditions. So there was a reasonable case for adopting an economic strategy that encouraged maximum production and consumption. But not today.

The Problem of Underemployment

Under current employment strategies, many people are overworked, but many others are underworked. In Britain it has become common to employ people on *zero-hours contracts* which do not specify any particular number of hours' work per week.[21] With a contract like that, one is called on to work only when needed. Hours of work are thus unpredictable, work may be called for or cancelled at very short notice, and many people do not get enough work to provide a livable income. Yet some contracts specify that one may not accept work with other employers. An official estimate (January–February 2014) suggested that there were then "around 1.4 million employee contracts in the United Kingdom that do not guarantee a minimum number of hours."[22]

This is labor flexibility taken to extremes. It is justified by employers who claim that they are compelled by keen competition—or by cost-cutting strategies in public-sector organizations—to minimize their payrolls. It is appreciated by politicians, who see it as a way to keep unemployment figures down. But it hardly amounts to treating workers with dignity. Some observers and victims of this system compare it with the old method of operating the docks in London, San Francisco, and other ports, where dockers and sundry unemployed laborers assembled on the quayside every morning in the hope of being offered a day's— or even just a few hours'—work. This is a prime example of how the world of labor has gone backward since *laissez-faire* principles have reasserted themselves.

New Kinds of Productivity

It is time to face up to the fact that the cult of labor productivity (achieving the same output with less work) is obsolete. That does not mean that the cult of productivity is obsolete. It simply means that we need new kinds of productivity. We need *resource productivity* instead of *labor productivity*. Instead of trying to achieve whatever output we need with fewer people, we should be striving to achieve it with less energy and lower consumption of materials. Even (or especially) if that means employing more people.

A good way to economize materials would be to make longer-lasting consumer goods, rather than ephemeral things that are frequently discarded and replaced. We should go for truly durable goods that lend themselves to repair and upgrading, both of which are labor-intensive processes that cannot easily be outsourced to faraway places. Oak casks used for storage and maturation of wine, whisky, and some traditional beers, can—with careful maintenance—last for many decades, and the wood can be recycled to make smaller casks, so the overall useful life of the timber may be well over a century. The transport system in Milan, Italy, still has in daily use about a hundred trams (streetcars) that were built in or soon after 1928; they are known as *i ventotti* (the twenty-eights).[23]

Yet still we are bent on economizing labor. For example, we encourage low-cost airlines to undermine the older full-service carriers, which not so long ago had large, well-paid, securely employed staffs. So much better, is it not, to have lean and mean cost cutters with the fewest possible overworked, poorly paid workers. Perhaps even (as Michael O'Leary, head of the Irish airline Ryanair, half-jokingly suggested) firing the copilot and employing a stewardess with a pilot's license, ready at any moment to abandon the drinks trolley and take over in the cockpit, should the overstretched real pilot be struck down by a coronary.

Although domestic air passenger traffic in the United States has grown by 55 percent, from 417 million passengers in 1990 to 645 million in 2012, yet total employment in the airline industry, after an increase in the 1990s, fell back by 2012 to very close to the 1990 levels, with a higher proportion of part-timers.[24] This minimum-employment strategy makes it possible to pamper the consumers (passengers) with extraordinarily cheap fares, while "flogging the horses" by running airlines with underpaid, overworked, minimal staffs. This does indeed mean that people can afford to fly more often, though with worse services and in nastier conditions.

But should we really want to encourage more flying? It means more oil consumption and atmospheric pollution, contributing to the dreaded climate change that could eventually make our planet uninhabitable. We would do better to use fast but energy-efficient electric trains for medium-length journeys. And to make the passengers pay what it costs to have good services on the trains and at the stations. With that kind of strategy all around, we could do something that libertarians long for: we could *cut government spending on unemployment benefits*, since there would be fewer unemployed.

What sense can it make to squeeze ourselves as workers in order to indulge ourselves as consumers? Clearly, we are all consumers. But normally we all have to spend much of our lives working for our living. Even those who are not at work—the children, the retired, the sick, the unemployed—depend largely on the support of working relatives, or on state benefits paid for by working taxpayers. We are all in the camp of the workers, as well as in that of the consumers. So why favor us consumers at the expense of us workers? This game is *we versus us*. There is no point in victory for either side. We need a draw.

The Age of Full Employment

In the immediate postwar decades, memories of the terrible 1930s depression were still raw. Therefore, avoiding unemployment was a top priority. Full employment was everyone's aim. There was little support for economic policies that threatened to lead to job losses. Accordingly, today's obsession with efficiency and competitiveness was not much in evidence. There were few witch hunts in pursuit of businesses that were parties to anticompetitive agreements; on the contrary, such agreements were generally tolerated.

In Britain, the government maintained a "register of restrictive trading practices." Businesses that engaged in such practices were required to make them public by registering the details. It was believed that restraints on competition should be permitted, provided they were open and aboveboard and not obviously abusive.

Some major industries were state-controlled monopolies: railways, airlines, coal mining, bulk steelmaking, and telephones. In these industries, there was little or no competition. In private-sector industries, there was competition, but it was often restrained. Therefore, there was no need to be obsessed with labor productivity, with cutting back on staff and staff costs wherever possible.

How did a business, or indeed a country, survive if it was so uncompetitive? Simply because other businesses, and other countries, were also uncompetitive. The struggle to get costs and prices down, at all costs— including the cost of high unemployment and bad working conditions— was far from a top priority. Competition was not seen as a "holy grail."

More recently, we have essentially given up treating full employment as a high priority. We have turned our attention to other objectives: keener competition, lower prices, freer trade, rising consumption, higher returns on capital. This change of direction reflects the excessive political influence of business corporations, the declining influence of labor unions, and excessive competition among investors to achieve maximum returns on capital. And all this is part of the global shift toward free-market ideologies and strategies.

The Hunter in the Steel Mill

In countless work situations, the input of human labor has been cut back in the interests of efficiency, productivity, and competitiveness. Go into any bank branch or post office; you will probably find more automats than employees. Supermarkets are beginning to replace cashiers with automatic checkout systems. Airports and train stations prefer (or oblige) you to buy your tickets from machines. All this is good for labor productivity, but often annoying for the customers, and rotten for the unemployment figures.

Sir Ian MacGregor, chairman of British Steel in the 1980s, once remarked that, in a modern steel mill, "you should be able to fire a shotgun down the shop floor without hitting anyone." Of him it was said, "MacGregor will never go to hell; Satan will not let him in, lest he shut down half the furnaces!" To be sure, the automated production line is not necessarily a bad idea; traditional production line work was an appallingly boring grind, and automatic equipment often does the job better. But should we apply this principle to so many other activities?

Automated Banking

The automation of banking procedures has not only eliminated a lot of good steady jobs; it has also been one of the causes of the current crisis. Traditionally, the arrangement of large personal loans such as mortgages was a laborious process, with good reason. When bank customers asked for mortgages, it was thought necessary to examine their history and circumstances very carefully, to make sure, so far as possible, that they would be able and willing to keep up their repayments and would not become bad debtors. The customer would have to answer many questions and present detailed evidence of his financial situation: pay stubs, tax returns, investment statements, and so on, enabling the bank to complete the task of *underwriting*.

More recently, however, this task has been largely automated. In a recent IMF working paper, John Kiff and Paul Mills note that automated underwriting (using computer models rather than lending officer judgment) has made loan origination more efficient.[25] They cite studies showing cost savings, on average, of more than $900 on each loan; a sweet little bonus for the bankers and (just possibly also) for the borrowers. But it means fewer jobs in the banks. And that is by no means the only problem.

In the United States, a common excuse for this questionable practice is that impersonal computerized decision making avoids racial discrimination. Unfortunately, it can also avoid discrimination between good and bad borrowers. Lax regulation, combined with the use of technological shortcuts in the interests of "efficiency," led to the approval of loans to borrowers who would have been turned down using traditional underwriting methods. Thus, allegedly "efficient" procedures have gotten us into terrible trouble. Careless automated underwriting facilitated the huge buildup of subprime mortgage lending that exploded in the great banking crisis of 2008, whose aftereffects still vex us.

We need urgently to abandon the free-market heresy that treats human labor simply as a commodity. The contrasting Catholic view is clearly that work has a human value quite apart from what it produces. John Paul II wrote (*Laborem Exercens*, par. 9) that "in spite of all this toil—perhaps, in a sense, because of it—work is a good thing for man." Recently, Professor Robert G. Kennedy has expressed the same idea neatly: "Work on the [Catholic] view contributes to what a person becomes, not merely to what he has."[26]

CHAPTER 7

Labor Unions, Full Employment, and Industrial Democracy

Full employment remains a mandatory objective for every economic system oriented towards justice and the common good.

—*Compendium*, par. 93

The Camel's hump is an ugly lump
Which well you may see at the Zoo;
But uglier still is the Hump we get
From having too little to do.

—Rudyard Kipling[1]

Consumption and Employment

Catholic teaching is highly critical of the extravagant consumerism of our modern "affluent societies." Thus Pope John Paul II wrote (*Centesimus Annus*, pars. 36, 37): "It is not wrong to want to live better; what is wrong is a style of life which is presumed to be better when it is directed toward 'having' rather than 'being.' . . . Man consumes the resources of the earth and his own life in an excessive and disordered way." We in the richer countries face a pressing need to consume resources less wastefully.

There is, however, a problem: as matters stand, if we consume less, more of us will be unemployed. We have seen this very clearly demonstrated by recent events. Downturns in consumption (spending), brought on by the need to reduce private and public debts, have led to rising unemployment, which is currently (2015) much too high in many countries. Yet high unemployment is not merely a lingering symptom of the exceptionally severe financial crisis of the late 2000s. It has been troubling us for several decades.

If we restrain our spending, we put ourselves out of work. Our spending pays other people's wages, and vice versa. When businesses cannot sell us as much as before, they suffer a downturn in revenue. So, to keep their own budgets in balance, they are obliged to cut their costs; and this generally means employing fewer people.

The Catholic Church would like us to consume more moderately, but she clearly does not want us to be unemployed. John Paul II, himself a notably hard worker, was most emphatic about this. He wrote of the need "to act against unemployment, which in all cases is an evil, and which can become, when it reaches a certain level, a real social disaster" (*Laborem Exercens*, par. 18). The *Catechism* (par. 2436) observes that "Unemployment almost always wounds its victim's dignity and threatens the equilibrium of his life. Besides the harm done to him personally, it entails many risks for his family."

These comments reflect more than our own distressing experiences in present and recent times. They spring from an age-old tradition of thinking about work; a tradition that sees work not only as being valuable for what it produces but also as an activity and discipline that is valuable in itself, as we have described elsewhere.[2]

So, how can we resolve this dilemma? Are we condemned to consume ever more and more, simply to keep ourselves working? Such a notion would seem to defy common sense. Historically, human beings have always had to work in order to consume; today, it seems, they have to consume in order to work.

Wasteful Use of Materials

In the more developed countries, almost all of us consume more in physical resources than we need to, or even want to—and not always through our own fault. Try a simple example from everyday life. Buy a packet of tea; examine the label to find the "net weight," that is the weight of the tea itself, without the packaging; then weigh the unopened packet. You may very well find that the total weight is double the net weight. The packaging weighs as much as the tea. You are buying twice as much material as you actually want to use! And, whether you like it or not, that is how tea is commonly sold today.

Years ago, you bought tea by asking the shop assistant for a quarter of a pound of Earl Grey or Darjeeling or whatever. He put a quarter-pound weight on the scales and ladled out the tea from a big bin into a plain packet until the scales balanced. The simple packet, of course, weighed very much less than a quarter of a pound. *Voilà, madame!* In certain traditional shops in Paris,[3] it is still possible to buy tea that way. But it costs more than our wasteful modern way, so most of us don't; and, in most shops, we can't. The market dictates that we spend wastefully.

Wastefully, that is, in terms of materials; but economically in terms of labor. Today, tea is elaborately packaged by highly automated machinery and sold in supermarkets that require very few staff. The old-time encounter with the shop assistant with her ladle and scales—a touch of human contact, an opportunity for a friendly chat—is gone; and this saves us money but means less work for shop staff, and thus less employment, not to mention a less agreeable shopping day.

The modern economy consumes materials too greedily and employs labor too sparingly. In countless ways, we consume more and more materials and energy in order to do less and less work. And then we wonder why we are plagued with unemployment and worried about depletion of natural resources. We blame the government for failing to stimulate growth or for spending too much of our taxes on unemployment benefits. Governments do indeed spend far too much on unemployment benefits; but that is because there are far too many unemployed. The real problem lies deeply embedded in the basic philosophy of economics as we think and practice it today.

You may think that I am being ridiculously naïve and nostalgic in suggesting that we would do better to arrange our economies so that we could do our shopping the old-fashioned way. So inefficient! But if you think that such "helpful inefficiency" is obsolete, consider the case of Japanese retailing. Department stores in Japan have long been famous for their unusually lavish customer service, made possible by employing considerably more shop staff than most Western retailers would think necessary. Thus Kazuto Taniguchi, director of the flagship store of the Takashimaya group, in a press interview a few years ago: "We have to make our service more efficient, not by cutting back on our employees, but by training them to meet customers' expectations."[4] Sadly, standards today seem to be slipping; many Japanese retailers are catching the Western disease of lean staffing.

"Err on the Side of Overstaffing"

Yet a change in Western attitudes may be on the horizon. In a fascinating recent study of retail trading, Sloan School of Management professor Zeynep Ton shows that some of the most successful retailers deliberately overstaff rather than understaff. She sharply criticizes firms that minimize payroll costs by employing as few people as possible, with minimal wages and benefits and inadequate training. These employees have little commitment to their work, provide poor service to customers—largely because they are too busy to do any better—and work inefficiently. Ton argues that stores, including low-price stores, that avoid these bad practices perform better, so long as they are well organized and "cut waste everywhere they can find it *except when it comes to labor.*"[5] She praises US retailer Costco and leading Spanish chain Mercadona for "explicitly [putting] customers and employees ahead of their stockholders."[6] Yet Costco shares, traded on NASDAQ, have a long record of strong performance, while Mercadona, which is a family-owned company, has a dynamic growth record based on reinvestment of profits, not on heavy borrowing.

All that is clearly consistent with Catholic teaching: labor should have priority over capital, and labor must not be treated like a commodity, of which any overuse or "waste" is to be avoided. Unlike coffee or corn, which perish in use, we human beings benefit—and not merely financially—by being well employed. And we suffer from not being employed. This does not mean that we should be forced to "fill the unforgiving minute"[7] with unremitting toil. Work is good; overwork is not. Professor Ton is right: employers should "err on the side of overstaffing."[8] And if they all did so, none would suffer in consequence from competitive disadvantage.

Orthodox economists will retort that the "laws of economics" demand maximum efficiency and minimum costs. But Catholics should know better. Jesus' parable of the laborers in the vineyard (Matt 20:1-15) endorses a certain amount of "overstaffing," or payment for more labor time than is strictly necessary.

Toward Full Employment

We need to recognize that the pursuit of full employment, which dominated economic policymaking in the 1940s, 50s and 60s, was not a misguided notion, as many libertarians would have us believe. It was a practical recognition of the fact that everyone needs to earn a living and should have opportunities to do so without facing inordinate difficulties in finding employment. John Paul II made this point very strongly in *Centesimus Annus* (par. 43): "The obligation to earn one's bread by the sweat of one's brow also presumes the right to do so. A society in which this right is systematically denied, in which economic policies do not allow workers to reach satisfactory levels of employment, cannot be justified from an ethical point of view, nor can that society attain social peace."

It is fashionable in America today to dismiss statements like that as irrelevant, idealistic pipe dreams, thought up by cloistered ecclesiastics who do not understand market realities. Yet history shows that we did in fact succeed in achieving near-full employment during periods when we did not allow our economies to be overwhelmingly dominated by market forces.

Full employment policy is a logical consequence of the basic Catholic principle of respect for work. The economy need not and should not be run solely for the benefit of greedy consumers, who want minimum prices at all costs, and of rapacious capitalists, who want maximum profits at all costs. It should also be run for the benefit of workers of all kinds, who need—and are entitled in justice—to be able to earn a decent living.

In *Mater et Magistra* (par. 79), John XXIII discusses the "demands of the common good"; these, he says, "on the national level . . . include employment of the greatest possible number of workers." Forty-eight years later, in *Caritas in Veritate* (par. 32), Benedict XVI demands that we "continue to *prioritize the goal of steady employment* for everyone." This goal hardly accords with the aim of most business managers today, which is to employ as few workers as possible, hoping thus to maximize efficiency, productivity, and profit.

On this topic, today's prevalent business practice clashes head-on with the Vatican. Yet, as we have noted above, it may be possible for an enterprise to enhance its performance by employing more workers, even by a modicum of overstaffing. Could it be that today's prevalent business theory and practice need a major overhaul?

Are Unions to Blame for Unemployment?

The experience of recent decades suggests that capitalism, as it is currently practiced, is generally incapable of providing full employment.

But the more extreme free marketeers still insist that unemployment is all down to the unions. "They are the prime source of unemployment"[9] thundered Friedrich von Hayek, a favorite guru of Reagan and Thatcher; and though Hayek died in 1999, he still has plenty of followers.

On this argument, union members, those selfish bastards, insist on excessive wages, thus reducing the demand for labor and keeping other people out of work. Let's get rid of unions and their collective bargaining and the rigidities it causes; let wage levels float freely! Then everyone will find a job. Whether or not everyone will have a living wage is quite another matter. If we got rid of all the rigidities that "keep wages too high," as some economists allege, then pay levels might well sink rather than float.

In France, only about 8 percent of the working population belong to unions; yet we are stuck with an unemployment rate of around 10 percent. Blame the 8 percent for a problem that afflicts the entire economy? I ask you!

In America, the proportion of workers in unions is a little higher, at around 11 percent, but the unemployment rate is clearly lower, at less than 6 percent. In Europe, the countries with by far the highest levels of union membership (Sweden, 68 percent; Denmark, 67 percent; Finland, 69 percent)[10] show unemployment rates that are habitually below the European average.

It makes little sense, then, to blame unions for unemployment. Yet free-market economists, relying on theory rather than on observation of the real world, still try to tell us that we suffer unemployment because workers insist on being overpaid. But the countries with the best levels of pay are often those with the least unemployment. In Switzerland, it was recently proposed to institute a national minimum wage of four thousand Swiss francs monthly. That is equivalent to about $4,000, or about $24 hourly! That would hardly be out of line with current Swiss conditions. The average hourly rate of pay in Switzerland is reckoned to be CHF53 ($53) while even in "cleaning and housekeeping," the average is CHF20 ($20). Yet the Swiss unemployment rate is among the lowest in Europe, at less than 4 percent.

Although free marketeers habitually insist that high wages mean high unemployment, there is, on the contrary, a clear link between unemployment and low wages: When job opportunities are insufficient, employers have the upper hand in pay bargaining. So they are able to keep wage rates down; sometimes very far down, as we see in America today, where underpaid workers are thick on the ground.

When I studied economics at the University of Edinburgh, around 1960, in those far-off days of widespread full employment, I learned that full employment meant in practice an unemployment rate of a little below 2 percent.[11] This was indeed more or less normal in Britain between the late 1940s and the mid-1960s.[12] Today, when unions have far less clout, we think we are doing well if we get the rate down to 5 or 6 percent. The US bishops' pastoral letter *Economic Justice for All* (1986, par. 15) remarked that "the 6% to 7% rate deemed acceptable today would have been intolerable twenty years ago."

Unions in Catholic Teaching

The importance of unions has been recognized in Catholic teaching at least since *Rerum Novarum*, in which Pope Leo XIII observed that "the most important [workers' associations] of all are workingmen's unions . . . to enter into a 'society' of this kind is a natural right of man; and the State has for its office to protect natural rights" (pars. 49, 51). More than twenty years earlier, in 1869, we find Wilhelm von Ketteler, bishop of Mainz, proclaiming the need for worker solidarity: "The suppression of all the former workers' corporations [guilds] has completely isolated the worker and left him to shift for himself. . . . Human association has been destroyed and we have seen in its place the formidable extension of financial association."[13] That comment, though nearly 150 years old, seems right up to date today.

In *Singulari Quadam*, an encyclical addressed to German bishops in 1912, Pope Pius X emphasized the Church's vocation to assert the moral rights and duties of workers and employers: "controversies, such as the nature and duration of labor, the wages to be paid, and workingmen's strikes, are not simply economic in character. Therefore they cannot be numbered among those which can be settled apart from ecclesiastical authority" (par. 4), and he goes on to "lavish praise upon each and every one of the strictly Catholic workingmen's associations existing in Germany. . . . We wish them success in all their endeavors on behalf of the laboring people" (par. 5).

In *Laborem Exercens* (par. 8), John Paul II described "the impetuous emergence of a great burst of solidarity between workers" in the late nineteenth century and remarked that the need for solidarity now extends beyond the laboring classes to professionals and intellectuals who "are undergoing what is in effect '*proletarianization*.'" A familiar problem in America today! Concerning unions, he wrote (par. 20), "The experience of history teaches that organizations of this type are an indispensable element of social life. . . . Representatives of every profession can use them to secure their own rights."

In *Caritas in Veritate* (par. 64), Pope Benedict XVI reminded us "how important it is that labor unions . . . should be open to the new perspectives that are emerging in the world of work. . . . [They] should turn their attention to those outside their membership, and in particular to workers in developing countries, where social rights are often violated."

The Rise and Fall of American Unions

In the aftermath of the Great Depression, union membership grew strongly in America. Workers were painfully aware of their weak position vis-à-vis employers and thus of the advantages of being organized in unions. The National Labor Relations Act (NLRA) of 1935, also known as the Wagner Act, clarified and extended union rights. "From a low of 3 million members in 1933, membership grew to 5.8 million in 1938, 12 million in 1945, and 16.9 million in 1953."[14] At the 1953 peak, almost a third of the nonagricultural workforce was in unions.

Since then, the proportion of workers in unions, in the private sector, has persistently declined and is now less than 7 percent; but unions remain strong in the public sector, where they have some 35 percent of workers.[15] Observers of the American labor scene have put forward various explanations for union decline.

Changes in Labor Law

The right to strike has been gravely weakened by the employer's "right" to permanently replace striking workers. This was asserted by the Supreme Court in *NLRB v. Mackay Radio and Television Co.* (1938), but little use was made of the precedent until the 1980s. "By the mid-1980s, the *Mackay* rule was fully operational on the ground, and striking was no longer a viable option for most workers."[16] But the right to strike is clearly endorsed by the *Catechism* (par. 2435): "Recourse to a *strike* is morally legitimate where it cannot be avoided, or at least where it is necessary to obtain a proportionate benefit."

Strike action, of course, must be used with care and moderation, since it can easily become counterproductive; it can cause serious damage to the employing firm and thus to its workers' prospects. It may be harmful to the wider community and may anger the public, thus encouraging political opposition to unions. But with a credible threat of strike action in the background, a union's negotiating strength is enhanced, even if it seldom or never actually calls a strike.

In *Textile Workers Union v. Darlington Manufacturing Co.* (1965), the Supreme Court held that "it is not an unfair labor practice for an employer to close his entire business, even if the closing is due to anti-union animus." Management had threatened to close the mill at Darlington, South Carolina, if its workers voted to be represented by the union; and when they did so vote, management carried out its threat. The court's decision has contributed to a situation where "threats designed to deter workers from supporting a labor organization are common in the US, even though they are violations of NLRA sect. 8 (a) (1)."[17]

The NLRA asserts the rights of employees to "form, join or assist labor organizations," to bargain collectively, and (within certain limitations) to strike. It defines as "unfair labor practice" any attempt by an employer to "interfere with, coerce or restrain" employees in their exercise of these rights.[18] The act is therefore broadly in accord with Catholic teaching. The decision of the Supreme Court in *Textile* appears to contradict federal legislation of thirty years earlier and thus may be an anomaly. It is a good example of how, in America, traditional antiunion attitudes die hard.

In many American states, agreements still exist between companies and unions, under which a worker who takes a job with a company may be obliged to join a recognized union, or to pay fees to the union even without joining it. The idea is to prevent "free-riding," whereby workers enjoy benefits negotiated by the union without contributing to the union's funds. But twenty-five states now have so-called "right to work" legislation, which prohibits such agreements. Recently, such legislation has been passed in Michigan and Indiana in 2012 and in Wisconsin in 2015. Here is another factor in the long-running decline of American unionism.

Changes in Business Structure

It is widely recognized that the decline, in America and in other developed economies, of traditional heavy industries with large workforces concentrated on specific sites has made it harder for unions to recruit new members. Another major problem is the internationalization of business structures; employers have become transnational, while unions are still nationally based. American unions are trying to form effective links with comparable unions in other countries, but this process is complex and slow.

According to labor lawyer and academic Julius Getman, "Unions bear significant responsibility for their own demise," because for many years they have given too little priority to organizing, which in the language of unionism means recruiting new members and establishing new locals. "They routinely assigned their ablest staff members to collective bargaining and those least able to articulate and inspire to organizing."[19] They have been like churches that concentrate on looking after their existing faithful but make little effort to spread the Gospel among outsiders.

And it is true that unions, designed to promote collective bargaining by large groups of employees, are not always well adapted to the needs of people who work on a more independent, free-wheeling basis: writers, designers, musicians, consultants, and self-employed contractors of all kinds, to name a few. Yet these people too face the basic problem of a weak bargaining position against the large organizations that provide much of their work.

Some unions have, by necessity, developed strategies that accommodate independent workers. In Britain, around 27 percent of the National Union of Journalists' members are *freelance* (independent) journalists, press photographers, broadcasters, etc. These members have, at best, only limited opportunities for collective bargaining, since they are self-employed, and many work for several different firms. But they can form a network that advises on what rates of pay to demand, organizes protests against misbehaving media firms, provides legal support for members in dispute with publishers, and promotes training. In America, however, the journalists' union The Newspaper Guild finds it very difficult to attract freelance members, of which it has only about 200 out of a total membership of some 24,000. One problem is that American legislation treats self-employed workers (independent contractors) as separate "businesses" which cannot combine in collective bargaining procedures without falling foul of anti-trust law.

It may well be argued that unions today need to become more like the old-time European guilds, which were associations of self-employed tradesmen and craftsmen. Guilds concerned themselves with the training of young apprentices, as well as with upholding quality standards and adequate prices. In many countries, guilds were deliberately suppressed in the early nineteenth century because they offended against the *laissez-faire* principles that then, as now, were in fashion. But they fulfilled a need in their time—the need for self-employed workers to cooperate to protect their interests. And that is a need that clearly exists today.

Changes in Management Attitudes

In recent decades, management—especially in the private sector—has become generally more hostile to unions. This trend does not necessarily mean that managers are increasingly greedy or malevolent. It reflects growing pressures on business in an increasingly competitive world. American businesses have to compete with lower-cost firms in developing countries; they have to satisfy fund managers who compete with each other to squeeze maximum returns from their investments. And unions have not been helped by the vogue for ideologies like that of Milton Friedman, who notoriously declared that business has no responsibility to society, other than to maximize profits.

All this means that employers are less willing, and indeed less able, than before to meet labor's demands for better pay and other benefits. In fact, many employers today want nothing to do with unions. They put out barrages of antiunion propaganda; they threaten to close their businesses if employees vote for union representation; they fire union activists; and even where a union local has been duly established, they often contrive to avoid concluding collective bargaining agreements.

In practice, this kind of behavior can mean that many workers are unable to organize in unions. It may be argued that they are thus deprived of *freedom of association*, to which US citizens are constitutionally entitled under the First Amendment (the right of the people peacefully to assemble), not to mention their right to bargain collectively, and to strike, under the NLRA.

We need stronger unions, not only to carry out the day-to-day jobs of collective bargaining and helping their members, but also to press for radical reforms in labor law, in business practice, and in economic doctrine. The sometimes deplorable behavior of certain unions does not justify juridical and corporate attacks on unions in general, such as we have seen in recent decades. Unions, like businesses, may misbehave;

that does not mean we should try to get rid of them. Catholic teaching tells us that both are necessary.

The Church Calls for Industrial Democracy

Should workers be able to participate in the management of the firms that employ them? This idea is far from new. It has been repeatedly proclaimed by the Catholic Church. Thus, the *Bishops' Program for Social Reconstruction* of 1919, drafted mainly by Msgr. John A. Ryan and issued by a committee of senior American bishops, proposes far-reaching changes in business organization. It insists on the importance of labor's right to organize, which had already been recognized in the earlier setting up by Congress of the War Labor Board. "It is to be hoped," say the bishops, "that this right will never again be called in question by any considerable number of employers." That was in 1919. A century later, we have retrogressed.

But the Bishops' Program goes far beyond that. It says that employees should not "remain mere wage-earners" but should be able to play a real part in the management of enterprises. They should either establish cooperatives, and thus "own and manage the industries themselves," or they should go for co-partnership arrangements, in which they would "own a substantial part of the corporate stock and exercise a reasonable share in the management." The Program was thus not only far ahead of its time; it remains a fair way ahead of our time. Cooperatives and copartnerships are still exceptions to prevailing practice.

In *Quadragesimo Anno* (par. 65), Pope Pius XI takes up the theme of co-ownership: "We consider it more advisable . . . that, so far as is possible, the work-contract be somewhat modified by a partnership-contract. . . . Workers and other employees thus become sharers in ownership and management or participate in some fashion in the profits received."

Pope Pius XII, addressing the Catholic Association of Small and Medium-Sized Businesses in 1956, poses a searching question: "The head of the undertaking values above all else his power to make his own decisions. . . . His natural gifts . . . find employment in his directing functions and become the main means by which his personality and creative urge are satisfied. Can he [then] deny his subordinates that which he values so much for himself?"[20] So, management should be willing to delegate elements of decision making to competent subordinates, allowing them to share in the process of management in accordance with the Catholic principle of subsidiarity.

John XXIII, in *Mater et Magistra* (pars. 91–92), adds his voice to the demand for industrial democracy: "We, no less than Our predecessors, are convinced that employees are justified in wishing to participate in the activity of the industrial concern for which they work. . . . [They should] make their own contribution to the efficient running and development of the enterprise."

The Vatican II pastoral constitution *Gaudium et Spes* (par. 68) calls for "the active sharing of all in the administration and profits of [economic] enterprises."

John Paul II, in *Laborem Exercens* (par. 12) emphasizes the "principle that has always been taught by the Church: the principle of the *priority of labor over capital*." Labor, he says, is "always *a primary efficient cause*, while capital . . . remains a mere *instrument*." This rather technical language simply means that, since labor creates capital, therefore labor is primary, while capital—the equipment that labor creates—naturally takes second place. To allow inanimate capital to dominate human labor is thus an inversion of the proper order of things. It is an example of the more general problem of people who allow their lives to be dominated by their material possessions.

The pope's words seem indeed to echo those of Abraham Lincoln in his First Annual Message (December 3, 1861): "Labor is prior to and independent of capital. Capital is only the fruit of labor, and could never have existed if labor had not first existed. Labor is the superior of capital, and deserves much the higher consideration."

In *Centesimus Annus* (par. 41), John Paul II describes how one should, through one's labor, grow as a person through "sharing in a genuinely supportive community," an aim that is likely to be frustrated when work is "organized so as to show maximum returns and profits with no concern" for the worker. He goes on to explain (par. 43) that Church teaching "recognizes the legitimacy of workers' efforts to obtain full respect for their dignity and to gain broader areas of participation in the life of industrial enterprises."

Pope Benedict XVI, in a long and memorable sentence in *Caritas in Veritate* (par. 63) eloquently describes work as it should be: "Work that expresses the essential dignity of every man and woman . . . effectively associating workers, both men and women, with the development of their community . . . work that permits the workers to organize themselves freely, and to make their voices heard." Here again we have a vision of a society in which workers are no "mere cogs in the machinery" as John XXIII put it (*Mater et Magistra*, par. 92), but play a positive role in the affairs of the organizations in which they work and the communities in which they live.

The Practicalities of Worker Participation

Worker representation and participation can take many forms. Worldwide, traditional collective bargaining by unions is the most widespread form, but it is by no means the only one. We look here at various others.

Worker Rights Organizations

America now has a wide variety of "alternative labor" movements. These are especially popular in places where unions are weak or nonexistent because of strong employer opposition; they attract workers everywhere who are ineligible[21] for membership of collective-bargaining unions. They have expanded in recent years as conventional unions have declined. These organizations are not unions in the generally accepted sense since they do not engage in collective bargaining; but many of them benefit from union support and collaboration. Their aims include educating workers to understand their legal rights, lobbying for worker-friendly legislation, publicizing workplace malpractices, and organizing protests against them.

An early example, dating from the 1970s, is CAFE (*Carolina Alliance for Fair Employment*), based in South Carolina, a state where hostility to unions is notably strong. More recently, many other such groups have developed, e.g., the *Taxi Workers' Alliance* and the *Restaurant Opportunity Center* in New York, and *OUR Walmart*. Probably the biggest is *Working America*, sponsored by AFL-CIO, which welcomes workers of all kinds. Founded in 2003, this nationwide group now has some three million members. It campaigns not only for a fair deal in the workplace but also for better healthcare, pensions, education, and corporate accountability.

Works Councils

The works council is an institution widely used in Europe but scarcely known in America. In the European Union, firms with at least a thousand employees, and with at least 150 in at least two member countries, are required by European law to have consultative bodies (European Works Councils) for the purpose of dialogue between employee representatives and management. This requirement dates from 1994, but works councils have a much longer history in Europe. They were introduced in Germany by the Factory Councils Law of 1920, promoted by two Catholics, Fr. Franz Hitze and theologian Heinrich Brauns, who served in the Weimar government as minister of labor. In France, the *comité d'entreprise* has been obligatory since 1945 for any firm employing fifty people or more. This is a forum for discussion between management and representatives of the employees and of their trade union. At regular meetings of the *comité d'entreprise*, management is required to provide information on the firm's activities, finances, and commercial circumstances, and to consult the employees on changes that may affect them and on forward planning.

Worker Ownership

In his fine survey *The Future of the American Labor Movement*, Professor Hoyt N. Wheeler suggests that "employee ownership may be the ultimate answer to the conflict between labor and capital—labor becomes capital."[22] In various ways, workers can and do acquire partial or even total ownership of the firms that employ them. In America, employee stock ownership is generally more acceptable to management than trade unionism; it implies partnership rather than confrontation. The *employee stock ownership plan* (ESOP) is favored by private (unquoted) companies; there are now more than seven thousand ESOPs with more than thirteen million employee participants. It is estimated that another fifteen million workers participate in other forms of employee ownership.[23]

The British retail chain John Lewis Partnership, wholly owned by its 90,000 staff (called *members* or *partners*), has a constitution whose opening words are: "the Partnership's ultimate purpose is the happiness of all its members." This makes an interesting contrast with Milton Friedman's ideal corporation, whose sole aim is to maximize shareholders' profits, or with the many businesses that claim that their primary aim is to please their customers. In case you may suspect that the customers of this staff-pampering partnership get a poor deal, I can assure you that its John Lewis department stores and Waitrose supermarkets[24] are among the most highly regarded in Britain, with a loyal clientele and a long history of success. They are among the more agreeable places to do one's shopping; by comparison with many other stores, there is less sense of pressure to sell you things whether you want them or not.

Employee Governance without Ownership

Worker participation in the governance of business does not always require worker shareholding. Another method is for workers to elect directors to the management or supervisory boards of the firms they work for. This practice is widespread in Europe. Among the thirty-one nations in the European Economic Area (the European Union plus Iceland, Liechtenstein, and Norway), nineteen have laws providing for *employee board representation*. It is in Germany that this principle has been most fully developed. There, every large firm has a *supervisory board* which determines overall strategy, implemented by the management board. In firms with five hundred or more employees, they elect one third of the directors on the supervisory board; in those with two thousand or more, they elect half.

In Sweden, there is normally only one board, but around one-third of its members are staff elected, even in firms with as few as twenty-five employees.

Thus, much of Europe is in contrast with America, where board representation for employees is not required by law and is relatively rare. Nevertheless, it does exist in companies where the employees have large shareholdings acquired via ESOPs, pension plans, or other stock purchase arrangements.

A distinctive form of profit sharing has been customary in Japan since the middle of the last century. Salaries in Japanese businesses have typically been around two-thirds of what they would have been on a Western-style fixed-salary basis; the shortfall is made up by bonuses based on profits. Thus in an average year, Japanese employees get around a third of their incomes in the form of bonuses. In good years they can earn more, but in a difficult year a company can reduce or even suspend bonus payments. This practice allows Japanese firms to cut back their payroll costs quite sharply, should the need arise, without laying anyone off. The result is more stable employment, and less unemployment, than is usual in America.

Moreover, a Japanese firm will often have a locally based "enterprise union" whose members are employees of that one firm only and include most employees up to lower-level executives. With a prevalent ethos of partnership rather than confrontation between unions and top management, "labor has a major voice in the policymaking process."[25]

The Catholic Church has long called for more civilized and harmonious governance of business enterprises, with greater participation by employees in the running of businesses and significant sharing by employees in company profits. By a variety of methods, many countries are making gradual progress toward these goals.

CHAPTER 8

Sustainability and Environment

The conservation of natural resources is the fundamental problem. Unless we solve that problem, it will avail us little to solve all others.

—Theodore Roosevelt (1907)[1]

We cannot disregard the welfare of those who will come after us to increase the human family.

—Paul VI, *Populorum Progressio*, par. 17

Future generations . . . risk having to live in a natural environment that has been pillaged by an excessive and disordered consumerism.

—*Compendium*, par. 360

We are living as if we had an extra planet at our disposal. We are using 50% more resources than the Earth can provide, and unless we change course that number will grow very fast—by 2030, even two planets will not be enough.

—Jim Leaps, director general of WWF (2012)[2]

Overconsumption

Today we are rather more aware of environmental issues than were our ancestors a century ago, when Teddy Roosevelt made that far-sighted comment. But the problem of overconsumption of resources has grown a great deal worse. This is partly because world population has risen from about 1.7 billion to 7.2 billion, but also because consumption per head has risen strongly in much of the world. There are far more of us, and many of us are consuming far more.

The *Living Planet Report*, published annually by WWF, provides detailed and alarming estimates of the way in which we, the human race, are devouring our heritage of natural resources. Other researchers have sounded equally stark warnings. In 1986, American biologist Peter Vitousek tried a different approach from that of WWF;[3] he estimated the human-consumed proportion of the products of photosynthesis (transformation of solar energy into living matter). Photosynthesis is the basis of all life on earth; plants transform solar energy into leaves, seeds, wood, etc., which are consumed by us and by animals; marine organisms such as plankton and algae also grow by photosynthesis, and these provide nourishment for some kinds of fish, which in turn are eaten by us and by other fish.

Vitousek and his colleagues reckoned that, in 1986, we humans were already consuming 25 percent of all the products of photosynthesis; eating or drinking them or using them as timber, wool, paper, leather, etc. At that time, world population was around 4.8 billion. In the following twenty-nine years, our numbers have grown at an average rate of around 1.5 percent per annum. That may seem a modest rate of growth; yet that 1.5 percent has brought world population up to its present level of 7.2 billion.

At that rate, population would quadruple from 4.8 billion in 1986 to 19.2 billion by 2078. Since in 1986 our 4.8 billion were already consuming 25 percent of available supplies, by 2078 we would be consuming 100 percent. That would leave nothing for other species (animals and plants). But without them we would have no food! So that scenario is biologically impossible.

Ecological economist Herman Daly has described our predicament in a vivid metaphor: the "ship" of the human race, floating in the "sea" of the habitable world, is approaching the Plimsoll line that indicates a fully loaded state.[4] If we continue to grow much further, our ship will be seriously overloaded. And, as we all know, a seriously overloaded ship is liable to sink.

Obsolete Theory and Practice

The theories that dominate our economic thinking, business practices, and government policies are still based on the "classical" economics of the late eighteenth and early nineteenth centuries, developed by (among others) Adam Smith in Scotland, David Ricardo in England, and Anne-Robert-Jacques Turgot in France. Their writings date from an age when world population was a fraction of its present size. We are 7.2 billion; in 1800 they were about 950 million. And standards of living in those days were, for most people, much lower than they are in the richer countries today.

So classical economics was born in an age when pressure on natural resources was hardly a problem. It is startling to read Adam Smith's remarks on the abundance and cheapness of raw materials in his day. In the Scottish Highlands, he tells us, timber is so plentiful that often only the bark of trees, used for tanning leather, is sellable. "The timber is left to rot upon the ground," or is given away to builders and carpenters. "When the materials of lodging are so superabundant, the part made use of is worth only the labor and expense of fitting it for that use. It affords no rent to the landlord, who generally grants the use of it to whoever takes the trouble of asking it."[5] Likewise, "in some provinces of Spain . . . the sheep is frequently killed merely for the sake of the fleece and the tallow. The carcase is often left to rot upon the ground, or to be devoured by beasts and birds of prey. If this sometimes happens even in Spain, it happens almost constantly in Chili, at Buenos Ayres, and in many other parts of Spanish America, where the horned cattle are almost constantly killed merely for the sake of the hide and the tallow."[6]

Economists in those days had little need to worry about physical limits to growth in production and consumption. So they were enthusiastic about improvements in labor productivity, or output per worker. Witnessing the beginnings of the industrial era, they saw how newly invented machines enabled workers to produce far more food, clothing, furniture, cast iron, paper, or just about anything else, than was possible by traditional methods. Rising productivity opened the way to huge increases in production and consumption; thus, more prosperity for all.

Naturally, there were complaints from traditional craft workers. Already in the sixteenth century we can observe the beginnings of industrial technology in Europe and the reactions to it. The knitting frame, a mechanical device for knitting socks and stockings, was invented by the English clergyman William Lee in 1589; but Queen Elizabeth I refused to grant him a patent for his invention; she feared that the development of machine knitting would throw thousands of hand knitters out of work at a time when there was already much unemployment.[7] She herself wore hand-knitted silk stockings, which were very expensive.

Karl Marx agreed with Her Majesty. He predicted that the mechanization of production would destroy more and more jobs, describing sarcastically the process that continually "sets free" those laborers who are "immediately turned out by the machines." Ultimately, when the proletariat (working classes) could stand this no longer, the destitute jobless workers would rise in revolt and destroy the capitalists.[8]

Yet in practice, the new technologies did not lead to persistently higher unemployment. The demand for cheaper consumer goods was so strong that there was generally enough work to keep rising populations busy, producing more and more of everything, so that most people could consume more and more of everything. That was all very well in an age when natural resources were not under heavy pressure. Today, we cannot (at least in the more developed countries) continue to pursue that kind of growth. Yet orthodox economic theorists and their followers still seem generally to assume that we can, even if they are no longer so keen to say so out loud.

Economists in Denial

In 1955, economist Victor Lebow observed that "our enormously productive economy demands that we make consumption our way of life . . . that we seek our spiritual satisfactions, our ego satisfactions, in consumption. . . . We need things burned up, replaced and discarded at an ever-accelerating pace."[9]

That was some years before the famous "Club of Rome" report, *The Limits of Growth* (1972), was commissioned from a group of scientists at MIT. Their report warned that "if the present growth trends in world population, industrialization, pollution, food production, and resource depletion continue unchanged, the limits to growth on this planet will be reached sometime within the next one hundred years. The most probable result will be a rather sudden and uncontrollable decline in both population and industrial capacity."[10]

But in 1978, the famous Chicago free-market economist Milton Friedman ridiculed the Club of Rome: "They said we have to adjust our sights, we must recognize that there are limits to growth. . . . This approach is completely wrong."[11] And Friedman continued: "From an economic point of view, oil is not an exhaustible resource. . . . We are not going to have a worldwide shortage of energy."

In his last book, *The Fatal Conceit* (1988), the Austrian economist Friedrich von Hayek claimed that "there is no danger whatever that, in any foreseeable future . . . the population of the world as a whole will outgrow its raw material resources."[12] He held that high standards of living, and of civilization, are only possible in large populations living in densely peopled regions. "We can be few and savage, or many and civilized."[13]

Another free-market fundamentalist, Julian Simon, admirer and admired of Hayek, wrote that "our supplies of natural resources are not finite in any economic sense."[14] Simon was convinced that human inventiveness would always find new sources of raw materials, new ways of recycling them, and substitutes for any materials that might run short. In particular, he insisted that "the potential amount of oil . . . is not finite."[15] This assertion rests on a strange argument. Since we do not know the total amount of oil that exists on earth, therefore, according to Simon, we are not in a position to say that it is limited: "The number of wells that will eventually produce oil, and in what quantities, is not known or measurable at present and probably never will be, and hence is not meaningfully finite."[16]

In any case, he continues, if petroleum runs out, we can still make oil (biodiesel and other fuels) from vegetable matter. Indeed we can, but what about the pollution and derangement of climate caused by burning oil? Simon assumes that it will always be possible to find ways of reducing pollution, even while burning more and more oil. But the plants from which we can make oil (maize, sugarcane, rape, soya, oil-palm, etc.) require land, either taken out of food production or obtained by clearing forests.

Thus, till recently, the theory of unlimited growth was widely trumpeted in resounding tones. They are still audible today in certain die-hard centers of *laissez-faire* thought.

Population Growth

Enthusiasts for population growth argue that, since human life is a good thing in itself, therefore the more there is of it the better. Some of them claim that the Bible supports their view, citing God's famous instruction to Adam and Eve (Gen 1:28) and, nine generations later, to Noah (Gen 9:1): "Be fruitful and multiply, fill the earth." But that was in the earliest days of the human race (Adam) and in its early centuries (Noah). Even in the time of Moses, around 1200 BC, it is thought that the entire population of the earth was only around 100 million. The commandment to fill the earth seems by now to have been pretty well respected. God did not command us to overcrowd the earth.

In ancient times, the commandment in Genesis was taken to mean that, as a general rule, everyone had a duty to marry and beget children. Thus we read in the Talmud: "a man shall not abstain from the performance of the duty of the propagation of the race."[17] Nevertheless, some Jews were excused from this duty on the ground that they were excellent scholars and preachers; thus the mystic Simeon ben Azzai (second century AD), criticized for remaining a bachelor, replied that "my soul is in love with the Torah; the world can be carried on by others."[18]

In the thirteenth century, as St. Thomas observes, some people were still arguing that "in ancient times men were obliged to marry, lest the human race cease to multiply . . . seemingly that obligation to marry still exists."[19] But realistic Thomas riposted that "there is no imminent danger of depopulation, since there are always many men who choose to marry." Not to mention (and Thomas does not) those who beget children without marrying.

Yet even today, some still seem to fear lack of population growth as an "imminent danger," and to see even a modest decline in population as a "demographic disaster." They apparently want as many people as possible to be alive at the same time. As Simon puts it, "Even if more people implied a somewhat lower long-run income level—which is not the case—I would be in favor of a somewhat lower standard of living per person if there were more people alive to enjoy it."[20]

It is right to deplore the fact that many people now alive do not enjoy a decent standard of living. But does it make any sense to regret that people *who do not yet exist* are not at present enjoying the good life? A memorable riposte to this argument has been given by economist Herman Daly and theologian John Cobb, "as far as we know, God is not impatient for all lives to be lived soon."[21]

Indeed, the notion of God being "impatient" is absurd in the light of St. Thomas's insight that "eternity knows no succession of events, the whole exists simultaneously."[22] Or, as Plato put it, "Time is a moving image of eternity,"[23] while eternity itself is timeless. From God's standpoint, all the human beings that have lived, are alive today, and will live in the future are "now in existence"; for the "now" of eternity embraces the entirety of earthly time. Thus in the text from *Populorum Progressio*, quoted at the head of this chapter, Paul VI sees the human family being increased by those who will come after us; not necessarily by an increase in numbers living in our time.

The Population "Bull Market"

Nonreligious growth enthusiasts like Hayek and Friedman rely on other arguments. They observe that historically, especially since the rise of the modern industrial economy, human population and human prosperity have often increased in parallel. Why, they ask, should this process not continue indefinitely?

One is reminded of the bullish salesman who assures investors that a stock that has already risen impressively still has the potential to rise much further. In the stock market, however, there is also a more realistic and prudent saying: *trees don't grow to the sky*. The graph of world population from the Middle Ages to the present day[24] looks alarmingly like the chart of a stock that has recently enjoyed a phase of Alan Greenspan's "irrational exuberance."

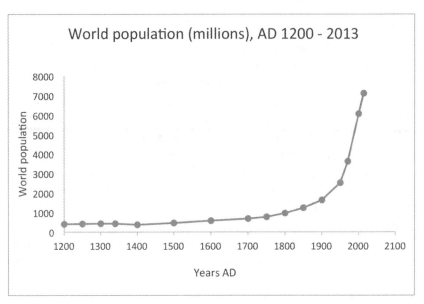

As we well know, stocks that are driven up by the market to stratospheric levels sooner or later come down to earth. History shows that human economies and societies can follow similar patterns, though generally over longer time scales. After a period of exaggerated expansion, with all that that entails in damage to the natural environment, "mother nature" takes her unmotherly revenge. There follows a period of marked decline that is painful for human beings, but which provides a respite for the environment, a chance to recover.

World population, in millions, by Broad Regions at Different Dates, 400 BC to AD 2000

Region	BC 400	BC 200	JC	AD 200	400	500	600	700	800	900	1000	1100	1200
China	19	40	70	**60**	**25**	32	49	44	56	48	56	83	**124**
India, Pakistan & Bangladesh	30	55	46	45	32	33	37	50	43	38	40	48	69
Southwest Asia	42	52	47	46	45	41	32	25	29	33	33	28	27
Japan	0.1	0.2	0.3	0.5	1.5	2	4	5	6	7	7	7	6
Rest of Asia (excl. Soviet Union)	3	4	5	5	7	8	11	12	14	16	19	24	31
Europe (excl. Soviet Union)	19	25	31	**44**	**36**	**30**	**22**	22	25	28	30	35	49
Soviet Union	13	14	12	13	12	11	11	10	10	11	13	15	17
North Africa	10	13	13	16	13	12	11	9	10	10	10	8	8
Rest of Africa	7	9	12	14	18	20	17	15	16	20	30	30	40
North America	1	2	2	2	2	2	2	2	2	2	2	2	3
Central & South America	7	8	10	9	11	13	14	15	15	13	16	19	23
Oceania	1	1	1	1	1	1	1	1	1	1	1	2	2
World Total	152	223	250	255	204	205	211	210	227	227	257	301	399

table continued on next page

World population, in millions, by Broad Regions at Different Dates, 400 BC to AD 2000

Region	1250	1300	1340	1400	1500	1600	1700	1750	1800	1850	1900	1950	1970	2000
China	112	83	70	70	84	110	150	220	330	435	415	558	774	1273
India, Pakistan & Bangladesh	83	100	107	74	95	145	175	165	190	216	290	431	667	1320
Southwest Asia	22	21	22	19	23	30	30	28	28	31	38	75	118	259
Japan	6	7	7	8	8	12	28	30	30	31	44	83	104	126
Rest of Asia (excl. Soviet Union)	31	29	29	29	33	42	53	61	68	78	115	245	386	653
Europe (excl. Soviet Union)	57	70	74	52	67	89	95	111	146	209	295	395	462	492
Soviet Union	14	16	16	13	17	22	30	35	49	79	127	180	243	290
North Africa	8	9	9	8	8	10	9	10	9	13	23	44	70	143
Rest of Africa	49	60	71	60	78	104	97	94	92	90	95	167	266	657
North America	3	3	3	3	3	3	2	3	5	25	90	166	228	307
Central & South America	26	29	29	36	39	10	10	15	19	34	75	164	283	512
Oceania	2	2	2	2	3	3	3	3	2	2	6	13	19	30
World Total	413	429	439	374	458	580	682	775	968	1243	1613	2521	3620	6062

Source: Jean-Noël Biraben, *The History of the Human Population*, chap. 66 in Caselli, Vallin & Wunsch, *Demography, Analysis & Synthesis*, vol. 3, 13. Emphases added.

According to sociologist Sing C. Chew, "Over world history, it seems that when social systems reach a certain level of complexity . . . their relationship with Nature turns degenerative. . . . Ecological degradation and crises emerge when cultural transformations of Nature occur too rapidly, leaving little time for Nature to regenerate itself."[25]

History shows many examples of sharp regional declines in population. Though it is seldom possible to find accurate population figures from ancient times, diligent detective work by demographers has yielded estimates, based on census returns, land registers, tax statistics, and military records, revealing trends which can be confirmed by contemporary observers' comments. The distinguished French demographer Jean-Noël Biraben, drawing on a wide variety of sources, has compiled a population table covering the entire world from 400 BC to the present, which we reproduce on pages 113 and 114.

This table shows a number of startling depopulations. In China, the population appears to have shrunk from around 60 million in AD 200 to 25 million by AD 400, reflecting disordered conditions following the fall of the Han dynasty (206 BC–AD 220), which had been a period of economic growth but also of widening inequalities.

In Western Europe, population appears to have halved from 44 million to 22 million between AD 200 and AD 600, during the decline and fall of the Roman Empire: "From the third century onward, converging testimonies leave no room for doubt: the demographic decline of the Empire is manifest; various explanations are put forward: outbreaks of plague, military anarchy, barbarian invasions, massacres and famines. . . . It is clear that difficult conditions have aggravated mortality in a context of crisis."[26]

More recently, Europe suffered a severe loss of population in the Black Death of the late 1340s, an exceptionally virulent outbreak of bubonic plague, probably aggravated by malnutrition following a period of poor harvests.

Following the arrival of European colonists in the sixteenth century, the native population of Latin America fell calamitously—perhaps by as much as 80 percent—primarily through the spread of European diseases, against which the native peoples had no immunity.

So it is all too clear that population trends, like stock market trends, can go down as well as up. Those who think that, even after the huge population growth of the last century, our planet can still support further massive growth, would do well to think again. In an increasingly crowded world, the risk that something will go disastrously wrong is almost certainly rising.

Catholic Teaching on Population

It has often been said that the Catholic Church encourages, or even demands, large families. Yet authentic Church teaching has traditionally held that it is at least as important to have well-brought-up and well-educated children as it is to have many children. We can trace this tradition back a long way. The *Roman Catechism* (the Catechism of the Council of Trent) of 1566 does not call for large families, and indeed suggests that there is no pressing need for further population growth: "Now that the human race is widely diffused, not only is there no law rendering marriage obligatory but, on the contrary, virginity is highly exalted."[27] That was in the sixteenth century, when world population is thought to have been only around 550 million. Moreover, the old catechism clearly stresses the duty of parents to bring up and educate their children decently: "[T]he Apostle . . . says [1 Tim 2:15]: *The woman shall be saved through childbearing.* These words of the Apostle are not, however, to be understood to refer solely to the procreation of children; they refer also to the discipline and education by which children are reared to piety."[28]

In *Populorum Progressio* (par. 37), Paul VI acknowledges that "the accelerated rate of population growth brings many added difficulties to the problems of development, where the size of the population grows more rapidly than the quantity of available resources to such a degree that things seem to have reached an impasse. . . . It is for parents to take a thorough look at the matter and decide upon the number of their children." And in *Humanae Vitae* (par. 10) he states that "responsible parenthood is exercised . . . by those who, for serious reasons and in respect of the moral law, decide not to have additional children for either a certain or an indefinite period of time."

In more recent Vatican documents we find a strong emphasis on conservation of the environment and avoidance of overconsumption of natural resources. And we find clear endorsement of "family planning," so long as it is done by natural methods. Thus the *Catechism* (pars. 2368, 2372) states that "for just reasons, spouses may wish to space the births of their children." Moreover, "the state has a responsibility for its citizens' well-being. In this capacity it is legitimate for it to intervene to orient the demography of the population . . . by objective and respectful information, but certainly not by authoritative, coercive measures." The *Compendium* (par. 235) adds that "The desire to be a mother or father does not justify any 'right to children.'" Pope Francis, in a recent press conference, observed that "Some people believe that . . . in order to be good Catholics, we should be like rabbits. No. Responsible parenthood."[29] He suggested that the normal birth rate should be three children per couple,[30] *para mantener la población*, to maintain the population; he did not suggest that we should increase it.

Reasons for Denial

Why are some economists, and their followers, determined to deny the evidence that growth in the human economy and population is reaching its limits? The answer, it seems, is not far to seek. If they were to recognize the need to move to a world of stable, rather than ever-growing, economy and population, this would undermine a whole body of orthodox economic ideology. For the project of ever-continuing expansion forms part of the very foundations of conventional economics.

A bicycle collapses if it ceases to move but performs perfectly well when moving at a steady pace. The free-market economy is different. It collapses if it ceases to run at an ever-accelerating pace; stable performance alone will not keep it upright. It is obliged to expand or grow continually. The economist Walter Heller, arguing that a high-growth economy would provide more resources with which to tackle the problems of pollution, stated that "I cannot conceive a successful economy without growth." This provoked the Catholic economist E. F. Schumacher to comment: "If a high-growth economy is needed to fight the battle against pollution, which itself appears to be the result of high growth, what hope is there of ever breaking out of this extraordinary circle?"[31]

The free-market economy fails if it does not continually expand. Why should that be? Why cannot the economy behave like the bicycle? What prevents us from having successful, stable, nonexpanding economies? The short answer is *excessive competition*. This was explained in more detail in chapter 5; here we very briefly summarize the argument.

Competition on price, the drive to win more business by selling cheaper, forces every business continually to search for ways of cutting its costs. This generally means automating its processes and reducing customer services, thus employing fewer people than before for any particular level of activity. Think of robotized production lines, automated telephone switchboards, or low-cost airlines. Economists call this rising productivity or, more correctly, rising *labor productivity*: producing the same output with less input of labor. Orthodox economists generally see this as an indispensable condition for economic health.

But if we persist in enhancing our labor productivity, what if the total volume of output does not grow? Then we have ever-rising unemployment. We have seen this recently in France and other countries; output is generally steady, but unemployment creeps remorselessly upward, month after month, year after year. This is morally, socially, politically, and financially unacceptable. The *Compendium* (pars. 287–88) is emphatic: "Work is a fundamental right and a good for mankind . . . because it is an appropriate way for him to give expression to and enhance his human dignity. . . . 'Full employment' therefore remains a mandatory objective for every economic system oriented towards justice and the common good."

But fully competitive economies cannot maintain full employment unless they continue to expand, in the usual sense of the word, producing and consuming more and more.

The Sustainable State

If we are to develop an economy that can function well at a stable pace, without continual growth, we shall have to discard many of the basic doctrines of the libertarian economists; in particular, the doctrine of free competition. But those economists love their doctrines. They are convinced that, if we restrain free markets, we will lose our freedom. As we have seen, however, the "freedom" of the libertarians is very different from the Catholic understanding of true freedom.

Deeply committed to their ideology, many economists still feel obliged to argue that endless growth is both possible and desirable. Yet science and hard evidence and common sense are against them; and so is the Bible (Ps 62:10):

> if riches increase,
> set not your heart on them.

The human race needs to learn to live with a stable, rather than increasing, level of material riches. But that does not mean no growth in intangible riches. There will remain scope for improvement in the quality of what we produce and consume, though generally not in its quantity. With intangible "goods" such as theatrical and musical performance, literature, sports, and philosophy, there will always be room for innovation and renewal (change rather than expansion), since these activities consume little in material terms.

Historically, some of the leading classical economists envisaged an eventual *stationary state* in which there would be no further economic growth. Adam Smith briefly discusses this concept in pessimistic terms. He describes an economy "which could . . . advance no further, and which was not going backwards." In this situation, he says, "Both the wages of labor and the profits of stock would probably be very low. . . . The competition for employment would necessarily be so great as to reduce the wages of labor to what was barely sufficient to keep up the number of laborers, and, the country being already fully peopled, that number could never be augmented."[32]

Not an attractive prospect! By contrast, the English economist John Stuart Mill (1806–1873) presents a much brighter image of the stationary state. His *Principles of Economics* (1848) is essentially a restatement of the economics of Smith and his followers as it had developed up to the mid-nineteenth century. Here he envisions the stationary state as a mature economy that will have attained a decent level of all-around prosperity, rid itself of exorbitant inequalities, and ceased to pursue growth in output and consumption. This, he says, "implies no stationary state of human improvement. There would be as much scope as ever for all kinds of mental culture, and moral and social progress; as much room for improving the Art of Living, and much more chance of its being improved, when minds ceased to be engrossed by the art of getting on."[33]

We continue to resist such a reorientation. Many people still think it is neither practical nor desirable. But we are reaching a historic turning point as we find ourselves forced to accept that humanity cannot persist in endlessly expanding its population, production, and consumption. Such continuing expansion would, sooner or later, lead to intolerable pressures on available resources; the global economy would "hit the buffers" in some form of cataclysm.

If we are to avoid such a fate, it would seem that we have no realistic choice but to move, gradually but without delay, toward a stationary state—or rather, as we prefer to call it today, to a sustainable state.

CHAPTER 9

The Catholic Concept of Property

Man should regard the external things that he legitimately possesses not merely as his own but also as common in the sense that they should be able to benefit not only himself but also others . . . it is the right of the public authority to prevent anyone from abusing his private property to the detriment of the common good.

—Vatican II, *Gaudium et Spes*, pars. 69, 71

Catholicism Contradicts Libertarians

The Catholic view of property is a stumbling block for many conservatives and libertarians. For they are inclined to the view that property owners should enjoy the widest possible rights to do whatever they please with their own property. They feel that social, legal, and regulatory restraints on their property rights threaten their personal freedom and so must be kept to an absolute minimum. This attitude often reflects reaction against the evils of communism, under which private property rights were habitually violated. It is understandable that people who have suffered from such treatment should be extremely touchy about any interference with their personal property rights.

A notable example was Ayn Rand, whose family's pharmacy in Petrograd was confiscated by the Bolsheviks in 1918. She created the character Dominique Francon, fearsome heroine of *The Fountainhead*, who smashed a valuable statue she had recently bought "so that no-one else would ever see it."[1] She could not bear the thought of sharing her property with anyone else, even to the extent of letting anyone else enjoy the sight of her statue.

That is an extreme example of the hyperindividualist philosophy. But today many libertarians hold hardline views on "absolute" rights to the ownership and use of individual property. Anarcho-capitalist

Murray Rothbard asserted that "there are *no* human rights that are separable from property rights"[2] and regarded all taxation as theft. Yale professor Robert Nozick took a similar stance: "Taxation of earnings from labor is on a par with forced labor."[3] He argued that, if we have to pay (say) 20 percent of our earnings in tax, this means, in effect, that the government is forcing us to spend 20 percent of our time working without pay. Thus, both Rothbard and Nozick argue that a tax-collecting government immorally confiscates part of our property without compensation.

It seems that they were mistaken. First, because in a democracy we elect the government and authorize it to collect taxes for public purposes. And second, because there is, in fact, compensation. By paying taxes, we buy public services from which we all benefit. But *we as a community*, rather than *we as individuals*, buy and benefit. It is not a matter of individual choice. This does not appeal to whole-hog individualists.

Property Rights in the Bible

But the idea that private property rights are *limited, not absolute*, is fundamental in Catholic doctrine. This can be traced back to the beginnings of Christianity, and beyond, into Old Testament times. For it is a basic scriptural teaching that everything in this world belongs primarily to God; we, therefore, are tenants or stewards of God's property, not absolute owners.

Thus Moses tells the Israelites that they must not sell farmland outright, for God says: "the land is mine; for you are strangers and sojourners with me."[4] Only a lease for up to forty-nine years could be sold; in the jubilee year (once in fifty years), the land reverted to the vendor. In Psalm 24:1 we read that

The earth is the Lord's, and all that therein is.[5]

King David offers a beautiful prayer over the gifts that his people have brought for the building of Solomon's temple (1 Chr 29:11, 14): "Thine, O LORD, is the greatness, and the power, and the glory, and the victory, and the majesty; for all that is in the heavens and in the earth is thine. . . . For all things come from thee, and of thy own have we given thee."

The law of Moses hedges property round with many limitations on the use of it. Farmers are not entitled to keep the entire produce of their land for their own and their families' use; there are tithes to be paid on the produce, both for religious purposes (the stipends of the priests and the upkeep of the Temple) and for aid to the poor. Various commandments require other portions of the fruits of the earth to be made available for those in need.[6]

Property in Roman Law and Its Successors

Classical Roman law embraced the principle that one may make whatever use one wishes of one's own property, so long as one stays within the law. "While it would be going too far to say that Roman law gives property owners unlimited rights, it is nonetheless true that it insists on owners' prerogatives, without envisaging their obligations to society."[7]

We find the same basic principle in present-day French law; article 544 of the *Code Civil* states that "property is the right to enjoy the benefits of things and to make use of them in the most absolute manner, provided one does not use them in ways prohibited by law or regulation." This dates back to the *Code Napoléon*, drafted at Napoleon I's command at the beginning of the nineteenth century.

Needless to say, both ancient Roman and modern French law contain restrictions on what one may do with one's property. For example, under French law you cannot totally disinherit your own children; a portion of your estate is by law reserved to them and thus falls outside the scope of your will. Absolute or unlimited property rights are a libertarian dream that never comes true in practice, basically because whatever one does (or does not do) with one's own property generally affects other people.

Aristotle's View

Greek philosophy proposed a more community-oriented view of property ownership. Aristotle (*Politics* 1263a) states that "it is clearly better that property should be private, but the use of it common," and he gives a practical example: "The Lacedaemonians . . . use one another's slaves, and horses, and dogs, as if they were their own; and when they lack provisions on a journey, they appropriate what they find in the fields throughout the country."[8]

In medieval Europe, and indeed up till the eighteenth century, country dwellers often had "rights of common" over certain pieces of land;

even though these lands belonged to local landowners, villagers and peasants were entitled to graze animals on the "common," gather firewood, dig peat, and so on. A century ago, *memsahibs* giving dinner parties in British India benefited from a custom of common usage of tableware: "Unexpected guests were always catered for. . . . Cutlery and utensils passed along the servants' grapevine from bungalow to bungalow as the need arose and guests frequently found their own dishes—'sometimes even your own vegetables'—laid out before them."[9] Today, we go for car sharing, home exchange, garden sharing, swapping of books and clothes, peer-to-peer renting; this kind of activity is expanding with the help of internet communications.

Aristotle considers (*Politics* 1263a) three possible dispositions of property: (a) private in ownership, common in use, as he preferred; (b) vice versa; and (c) common both in ownership and in use. He does not consider the fourth possibility, private both in ownership and in use, presumably because this would rule out any giving or sharing of property; for him, such an economy would have been out of the question.

We may note in passing that, for Ayn Rand, it was not out of the question. In her little Western utopia, "Galt's Gulch," John Galt explains to Dagny Taggart that "there is one word which is forbidden in this valley: the word *give*."[10] Thus Rand's ideology explicitly rules out any kind of giving or gratuitous sharing. Although Rand was Jewish by birth, in this regard she preached a notion that is totally at variance with both Jewish and Christian teaching.

Property in Early Christianity

There is scriptural evidence (Acts 2:44; 4:32) that some of the first Christians abjured private property and held all their assets in common; this practice has been followed by monastic communities since early Christian times.

Some of the Church Fathers argued that, had it not been for Adam's fall, there would have been no private property; its introduction was a consequence of original sin. In St. Ambrose's words, "Nature has poured forth everything for everyone in common";[11] moreover, "nature . . . has created common rights, usurpation has made rights private,"[12] and "the earth belongs to everyone, not to the rich."[13]

St. Augustine offers a rather more positive view of property rights. For him, private property is necessary in view of the fallen condition of humanity, even though ownership in common would be the ideal. In practice, what is wrong with private property is not possession in itself but misuse: "Anything that is wrongly possessed is really another's; moreover, anyone who misuses his property possesses it wrongly."[14] By divine law, says Augustine, everything belongs to God. "By human law, however, one says, *This estate is mine, this house is mine, this slave is mine.* . . . Why? Because God has distributed to mankind, through the emperors and kings of this world, these rights in human law."[15]

So, in Augustine's view, it is for the ruler to decide on who should possess what property; it is not for individuals to appropriate it for themselves. But only a ruler who acts in accordance with the divine order is a just ruler.

The Fathers of the Church insisted that those who owned property had a duty to share its benefits with others. St. Basil the Great (330–379), archbishop of Caesarea, preached a famous homily on the parable of the rich farmer whose motto was "eat, drink, and be merry" (Luke 12:16-20); here he argued that, if everyone kept what was sufficient and gave what was superfluous to the needy, then "nobody would be rich and nobody poor."[16] In fact, even if we could achieve a near-equal distribution of assets, inequalities would very soon reappear because of the different behaviors of individuals. Redistribution therefore needs to be a continuing process.

Basil also reproved "the rich who deem as their own property the common goods they have seized upon . . . like those who by going beforehand to the play prevent others from coming, and appropriate to themselves what is intended for common use."[17] The history of opera shows that it is not unknown for a very rich person to reserve an entire opera house for an evening and thus attend the performance alone—or perhaps with a boxful or two of relatives or friends.

St. Thomas Follows Aristotle's View

St. Thomas discusses property in a well-known passage in the *Summa Theologiae*, citing Aristotle, Ambrose, Basil, and Augustine. The quotation from *Gaudium et Spes* at the head of this chapter is clearly a paraphrase of Thomas's words.

He accepts that communal ownership is "natural" but argues that the division of property among individuals is a matter of human law, which legitimately supplements natural law. Individuals take care over obtaining or producing what they need for themselves; whereas, if they were working for the community, "each one would shirk the labor and leave it to another, as happens where there is a great number of servants." Secondly, each man should be "charged with taking care of some particular thing himself, whereas there would be confusion if everyone had to look after any one thing indeterminately." Thirdly, "a more peaceful state is assured to man if each one is contented with his own. . . . Quarrels arise more frequently where there is no division of the things possessed."[18]

Thomas, like Aristotle and Augustine, distinguishes between *ownership* and *use*. "Man ought to possess external things not as his own, but as common, to wit, he is ready to communicate them to others in their need."[19] Thus, while *ownership* may be individual, *use* should be social and shareable with others.

Thomas's reticence toward communal ownership is based on the same arguments as Aristotle's: private property offers stronger incentives to work, better maintenance of assets, and less risk of disputes.

Pope Leo XIII

Moving on to *Rerum Novarum*, we see that this famous encyclical begins with a vigorous defense of private property and rejection of socialism. Indeed Pope Leo, unlike the early Fathers and St. Thomas, affirms that property ownership is a natural right of man, not merely a right that has been added by human law. "Every man has by nature the right to possess property as his own. . . . Man not only should possess the fruits of the earth, but also the very soil. . . . Those who deny these rights do not perceive that they are defrauding man of what his own labor has produced" (pars. 6, 7, 10). The pope defends inheritance rights and insists that "the main tenet of socialism, community of goods, must be utterly rejected" (par. 15). This rejection applies, of course, to the politics of socialism or communism, which would impose common ownership on everyone; not to the community of goods in monastic life, which is voluntary.

But, he continues (par. 22), "it is one thing to have a right to the possession of money and another to have a right to use money as one wills," and here he quotes the words of Thomas cited above, "Man ought to possess external things not as his own." Thus, the right to *use* money or other property is limited by the need to consider the good of others, of the community, not merely one's own good.

Pope Pius XI

In *Quadragesimo Anno*, Pope Pius calls on Catholics to steer a middle course between "twin rocks of shipwreck," namely, individualism and collectivism (par. 46). Ownership has an "individual and at the same time social character. . . . Men must consider in this matter not only their own advantage but also the common good. To define these duties in detail when necessity requires and the natural law has not done so, is the function of those in charge of the State. Therefore, public authority . . . can determine . . . what is permitted and what is not permitted to owners in the use of their property" (par. 49).

So the state has a clear right to regulate the *use* of property in the public interest. But what about the grossly unequal *ownership* of property? A little later in the same document, the pope laments that "the distribution of created goods . . . is laboring today under the gravest evils due to the huge disparity between the few exceedingly rich and the unnumbered propertyless" (par. 58).

His response is that workers ought to be substantially better paid, so that they have the opportunity to put money aside and accumulate some property of their own. To this end, the revenues of business must be divided more equitably between labor and capital, allowing wages to rise to more adequate levels. Moreover, the pope recommends profit-sharing arrangements for workers (par. 65).

As a matter of historical fact, the lower- and middle-class workers' share of GDP (gross domestic product = total of all incomes) in America today is well below the share that was prevalent in the 1960s, while the shares accruing to highly paid employees and to owners of capital are higher.[20] We need not assume that the present depressed level of the workers' share is inevitable. A better and fairer share has been, and is, possible.

Pope Pius XII

Pope Pius denounced "excessive concentrations of economic goods which, often hidden under anonymous forms, avoid their duties to society and make it almost impossible for the worker to acquire his own capital" and regretted the weakness and decline of smaller businesses, "squeezed and constrained in an ever-harder defensive struggle without hope of a successful outcome."[21] Elsewhere he affirmed that "the dignity of the human person normally demands the right to the use of the goods of the earth, to which corresponds the fundamental obligation of granting an opportunity to possess property to all if possible."[22]

Pope John XXIII

In *Mater et Magistra*, Pope John insists that private ownership of property and productive goods "naturally entails a social obligation. . . . It is a right which must be exercised not only for one's own personal benefit but also for the benefit of others" (par. 19). And ownership needs to be much more widely shared; he extends Pius XI's argument for employee share ownership: "Workers should be allocated shares in the firms for which they work, especially when they are paid no more than a minimum wage" (par. 75); "it is especially desirable today that workers gradually come to share in the ownership of their company" (par. 77).

Pope Paul VI

In *Populorum Progressio*, Pope Paul goes a step further: he argues that, in some circumstances, it may be right for public authorities to expropriate private landowners. "If certain landed estates impede the general prosperity because they are extensive, unused or poorly used, or because they bring hardship to peoples or are detrimental to the interests of the country, the common good sometimes demands their expropriation" (par. 24).

Some American readers may find that shocking. Yet, in the early days of the American republic, it was not always considered wrong for the government to take private land, without compensation, for the benefit of the general public. In fact, state governments often took over undeveloped private lands for road building and other public-utility projects and paid nothing for them. This was tolerated partly because land was so abundant and cheap that what the owner lost could easily be replaced, but also because the republican philosophy of those early Americans included a strong belief in the importance of the common good. Many of them felt it was right and proper that private interests should sometimes give way to those of the community.

Indeed, Thomas Jefferson, when drafting the list of "inalienable rights" in the Declaration of Independence (1776), deliberately avoided the phrase "life, liberty, and property," employed by the First Continental Congress in 1774. He chose instead "life, liberty, and the pursuit of happiness." It appears that he did so because "he did not consider property an inalienable right."[23] Benjamin Franklin even wrote that personal property (over and above a certain basic level) "belonged to the Publick, who, by their Laws, have created it, and who may therefore by other Laws dispose of it, whenever the Welfare of the Publick shall demand such Disposition."[24]

This early republican philosophy seems to have been closer to Catholic teaching than the more individualistic attitudes that have developed later in America and elsewhere.

Pope John Paul II

In *Sollicitudo rei socialis*, Pope John Paul introduces *urbi et orbi*[25] the famous phrase *social mortgage*: "The right to private property is valid and necessary, but . . . private property, in fact, is under a 'social mortgage' . . . based upon and justified precisely by the principle of the universal destination of goods" (par. 42). Since a mortgage is a debt, this phrase recalls the ancient tradition—going back to Moses—that the wealthy "owe a debt" to the poor and so are obliged to set aside for them a part of their property or of the revenue it produces.

In the same encyclical, the pope attacks an abuse of property rights in natural resources, namely, wasteful consumption of materials, calling it "a form of super-development . . . which consists in an excessive availability of every kind of consumer goods for the benefit of certain social groups . . . which involves so much 'throwing away' and 'waste'" (par. 28).

In *Centesimus Annus*, his third encyclical on economics, John Paul II pursues this theme further, observing (par. 40), "It is the task of the State to provide for the defense and preservation of common goods such as the natural and human environment, which cannot be safeguarded simply by market forces." The pope seems here to be calling for public regulation of the exploitation of natural resources. Overexploitation, sometimes encouraged by bullish commodity markets, can lead to serious environmental damage and resource depletion.

Property Should Serve Work

The pope makes a very important comment (par. 43) on industrial and agricultural property. He states: "Ownership of the means of production, whether in industry or in agriculture, is just and legitimate if it serves useful work. It becomes illegitimate, however, when it is not utilized or when it serves to impede the work of others." Here there is a reference back to the pope's earlier encyclical *Laborem Exercens* (par. 14), where he states that "the means of production . . . should serve labor, and thus . . . make possible the achievement of . . . the universal destination of goods and the right to common use of them."

This argument overturns conventional economic thought. Free-market economists generally say, either that capitalist business exists to make maximum profits for shareholders (Milton Friedman's view), or that it exists to provide what consumers want to buy (Ludwig von Mises's opinion). The idea that business exists also to "serve labor," to enable workers to earn a living, is commonly regarded as nonsense by economists, policymakers, and financial commentators. They are more inclined to think that workers are there to serve business. And we elect politicians who, whatever they may say, in practice go along with such attitudes.

That surely helps to explain why we suffer high rates of unemployment and deterioration in working conditions. We give low priority to the interests of ourselves as workers. Consumers and shareholders come first and second (or vice versa), workers always come third; and third place is far below second. Yet we all have to spend much of our lives earning our living by working. So why do we tolerate economic philosophies that care so little for workers' interests?

We would do better to take note of what Pope John Paul said. We should recognize that the economy does not exist only to pamper us with abundant consumer goods or to reward investors with fat dividends, let alone to reward top executives with huge "compensation packages." The economy exists also to enable us all to do useful work— and, so far as possible, enjoyable and satisfying work—and to earn a decent living thereby. If economists cannot or will not accept that, they are in the wrong job. They should take up some other occupation where they may do us less damage.

We noted in chapter 7 that the British retail group John Lewis Partnership has a constitution that explicitly puts the interests of its employees first: "The Partnership's ultimate purpose is the happiness of all its members." This is indeed unusual. But John Lewis has a long and successful history. Property at the service of workers? It can be done!

Thus, modern Catholic teaching on property stands in a long tradition which we can trace back to the Old Testament and to classical Greece. Private property is legitimate, but it must be used in ways that are consistent with the common good. And the community, through its government, is entitled to regulate the use of private property in the general interest.

CHAPTER 10

Freedom of Contract

If you are willing to work for seventy hours a week below the minimum wage under unsafe conditions and allow the employer to dismiss you at will, why should the state prevent you from accepting such terms?

—Dani Rodrik[1]

Experience has too frequently shown that the individual can be as deeply injured through an extortionate contract, as at the hands of the thief, the highwayman or the contract breaker.

—John A. Ryan[2]

Promises must be kept and contracts strictly observed to the extent that the commitments made in them are morally just.

—*Catechism*, par. 2410

The Bedrock of *Laissez-Faire*

Professor Dani Rodrik of Harvard, an eminent opponent of laissez-faire, asks that rhetorical question in order to highlight the need for certain legal restrictions on contracts of employment. And he answers his own question: "Employers must be prohibited from offering odious contracts, even if some workers are willing to accept them. . . . You may be willing to work for seventy hours a week below the minimum wage. But my employer cannot take advantage of your willingness to work under these conditions and offer my job to you."[3]

Rotten jobs are like contagious diseases; they tend to spread. You, my friend, should be vaccinated against flu, not only for your own good, but also lest you catch the bug and pass it on to me.

Freedom of Contract is the bedrock of *laissez-faire* economics. In its pure and absolute form, it means that any person is entitled to enter into any contract whatsoever with any other person, provided that both parties agree freely and willingly to the terms of the contract. For free marketeers, this is a basic principle. It underpins all their classic doctrines: free trade; free individual pay bargaining; absence of controls on rents, prices, wages, or interest rates; absence of regulations on working hours and conditions; nonrestriction of bank lending; freedom to make whatever use one pleases of one's own real estate.

This principle is based on the idea that, since all human beings are (or should be) free and equal before the law, therefore anyone should be free to contract with anyone else. As law professor Vincent Rougeau explains, "Anglo-American contract law strives to promote the freedom and autonomy of individuals to create their own agreements and see them legally enforced."[4]

Freedom of contract does indeed facilitate enterprise. But equally it can leave the way open to serious misbehavior. Overblown speculation, bad lending practices, penurious wages, wretched working conditions, destructive competition, neglect of the environment: all these abuses may be made easier by the current tendency to let people set up whatever contracts suit their own interests without regard to the welfare of others. That is why restraints on freedom of contract are necessary.

What Is a Contract?

The word *contract* covers a very wide range of agreements. In law, a contract is simply a legally enforceable agreement between two or more parties. It need not be a major transaction with formal documentation. Many contracts are small-scale, informal, unwritten agreements.

A contract involves an agreement, or promise, to do or pay something in the future. Thus, if you buy something on credit, promising to pay for it later, you enter into a contract. An agreement, however informal, to work for someone for x hours at y dollars per hour is a contract, provided that y is not less than the legal minimum wage. If it were less, the agreement would not be enforceable by law; it would not be a valid contract.

In fact, most business activities require legally enforceable agreements on delivery of goods or services and payment for them. That is why the law of contract is so important in the modern economy.

Limitations on Freedom of Contract

Many libertarians argue that almost any freely agreed bargain should be legally, morally, and socially valid. The free-market economist Milton Friedman explained that, in the ideal market economy, "individuals are effectively free to enter or not to enter into any particular exchange, so that every transaction is strictly voluntary."[5] In the famous case of *Lochner v. New York* (1905), the Supreme Court struck a big blow for freedom of contract by striking down the Bakeshop Act, enacted by the state of New York in 1895. This act limited the hours of work in bakeries to ten per day and sixty per week; not enough for master baker Joseph Lochner, who demanded more of his workers. Justice Rufus Peckham, writing the majority opinion, stated that the Bakeshop Act was an "unreasonable, unnecessary, and arbitrary interference with the right and liberty of the individual to contract."

In a somewhat similar case, *Adkins v. Children's Hospital* (1923), the Supreme Court overturned the District of Columbia Minimum Wage Law of 1918, which imposed a minimum wage for women. Here Justice George Sutherland argued that, if minimum wage laws were accepted, there would be no logical barrier to legislating maximum wages. Today, given the outrageous inequalities in remuneration in certain businesses, that might not be such a bad idea!

These decisions have been widely seen as reactionary measures authorizing the exploitation of workers. In *West Coast Hotel Co. v. Parrish* (1937), the Supreme Court adopted a very different attitude. It ruled that a minimum wage law passed by the state of Washington was constitutionally valid. Chief Justice Charles Hughes, delivering the opinion of the court, observed, "The Constitution does not speak of freedom of contract. . . . There is no absolute freedom to do as one wills or to contract as one chooses. . . . Liberty implies absence of arbitrary restraint, not immunity from reasonable regulations and prohibitions imposed in the interests of the community." Hughes, nevertheless, was a Republican politician who had run for the presidency against Woodrow Wilson in 1916.

In the real world, the right to freely set up any contracts one fancies is not sacrosanct; it has to be subject to limitations imposed by law or by social convention. Arthur Corbin, one of America's most famous and respected writers on contract law, put it bluntly: "We have never had and never shall have unlimited liberty of contract."[6] But today, certain libertarians are bent on rehabilitating *Lochner*.

Young persons who have not yet reached the age of majority may be unable to enter into legally binding contracts. And clearly the law cannot recognize, as contracts, agreements that involve criminal activity. If you enter into an agreement with a hired assassin or "contract killer" to eliminate someone you would rather not have around, then that agreement is legally void and unenforceable; it cannot properly be called a contract. Indeed, the act of setting up such an agreement, even if the killing is never carried out, may be punishable as attempted murder.

In ancient Egypt, it was possible for a man to contract marriage with his own sister. Queen Cleopatra VII (69–30 BC), last and most famous of a long line of royal Cleopatras, was married successively to her two younger brothers, King Ptolemy XIII and King Ptolemy XIV. Marriages like that were common within the royal family of the Ptolemies; a drastic method of keeping the crown in the family! Indeed, according to some historians, such incestuous marriages were widespread in ancient Egyptian society. But throughout history, most societies have outlawed that kind of contract, even if both parties were to agree to it freely and willingly.

Contracts of "voluntary slavery" were common and legally recognized in ancient Babylon, Greece, and Rome. People could sell themselves into slavery in order to pay off debts or to secure a livelihood. One could agree to a *contract of sale of oneself*—and that was perfectly legal. One could also be bought out of slavery (redeemed). One could even buy oneself out if one could accumulate as much cash as one was worth in the slave market; in classical Greece, for example, certain slaves engaged in business on their own account and earned money. So, in some cases, they could and did buy themselves out.

Few of us, one imagines, would wish to reinstate these practices. Yet some libertarians have, in all seriousness, argued that we should do so. Thus the anarcho-capitalist Robert Nozick considered the question of "whether a free system will allow [an individual] to sell himself into slavery" and replied, "I believe that it would."[7] He admitted, however, that "other writers disagree." It is strange, is it not, that libertarians, apparently so deeply concerned with the importance of individual "freedom," should argue the case for slavery! Yet this paradox is not new. In the eighteenth century, the famous English writer Dr. Samuel Johnson, compiler of the first English dictionary, asked: "How is it that we hear the loudest yelps for liberty from the drivers of negroes?"[8]

In the late twentieth century, a certain London businessman was reported as saying that, if it were lawful to trade in nuclear weapons, he would trade in them. Yet another kind of contract that few of us would wish to see legalized.

The "contract" of prostitution is illegal in some countries, tolerated in others. In America it is governed primarily by state law and is currently illegal in all states except Nevada. Whether legal or not, however, it is generally considered immoral, even when both prostitute and customer are adults who agree freely and willingly to their bargain. It is clearly disapproved by Christian, Jewish, and Muslim teaching, but not by certain libertarians. We have already seen (chap. 3) how the anarchist Murray Rothbard argued for "freedom" to engage in "victimless crimes" such as prostitution and pornography.

In France,[9] in many other countries, and in many American states, gambling debts are legally unenforceable. If you lose a bet and refuse to pay up, the winner cannot sue you for payment. A bet creates a kind of social obligation since nonpayment is considered dishonorable and may lead to social ostracism. But there is no legal obligation. That is because gambling, though not necessarily illegal, is considered contrary to the public interest or the good of society. So the law tries to discourage it by limiting the ability of gamblers to get their debts paid. Wagers are seen as undesirable agreements that, even if they cannot be prevented, should be discouraged.

Thus, on the whole, we agree that unlimited tolerance for the setting up of mutually binding agreements does not make sense. Some agreements, even if they are fully voluntary, are considered to be unjust, criminal, immoral, harmful to the parties involved, or contrary to the public interest. So we prohibit them; or, at least, we do what we can to discourage them.

The Libertarian Approach

Yet economic thought and practice, in recent times, has moved toward the opposite view. The more extreme libertarians argue that whatever you can do, you should be allowed to do, so long as what you do is not clearly criminal. If you are prevented from doing things that are not crimes, though they may be immoral or unfair or antisocial, then, they say, your "freedom" (to do wrong) is infringed. Rougeau comments unfavorably on "the 'amoral' nature of contract law. . . .

In most cases, the courts are not interested in policing the 'fairness' of private agreements."[10] This dovetails with the libertarians' "amoral" conception of freedom itself, the belief that you cannot be free unless you have the power to do wrong as well as right.

So, say the libertarians, you should be free to set up any contract you fancy with anybody else, so long as you can persuade the other party to agree to it, or she can persuade you to agree to it. The law should do as little as possible to forbid particular types of contract or to regulate the terms of permitted contracts.

What, you may ask, is wrong with that? Libertarians hold that freedom of contract is a basic human right. They deny that freely agreed contracts can be unjust. The more learned among them harken back to ancient Greek philosophy and remind us of Aristotle's saying, "No one can suffer injustice voluntarily."[11] They say this means that if you voluntarily agree to the terms of a contract, it follows logically that the contract is not unjust to you. If it were, you would not agree to it.

But Aristotle also pointed out that "lack of self-restraint may make a person voluntarily submit to being harmed by another"[12] because he does what he thinks he ought not to do, rather than what he knows or believes to be in his own best interest. Today that remark might apply to people who let themselves be persuaded to buy more than they can afford, borrowing on credit cards at exorbitant rates of interest. *I shouldn't, but I will.* Or, more seriously, to the many Americans who borrowed on subprime mortgages more than 100 percent of the price of the houses they bought. They were persuaded by plausible salesmen that these contracts were fair, even advantageous, to the borrowers. But in fact, such deals were often riddled with hidden pitfalls.

You might willingly agree to a loan contract without knowing or understanding that it is unfair to you; you are not then knowingly and voluntarily consenting to an injustice. Or you might agree to a contract of employment, knowing that it is a very poor deal for you; you take it because you have no alternative. Work for peanuts or starve! A contract of employment is normally considered to be willingly agreed on both sides; but some employment contracts can hardly, in reality, be called willing consent. Thus, we see that unrestricted freedom of contract presents several major problems:

If one party is in a stronger bargaining position than the other, the contract, even though "freely agreed," may well be unfair to the weaker party.

An unfair contract may be struck where one party has better information than the other about the substance of the contract. This is a familiar problem in sales. You are persuaded to buy something; later, you discover defects that were concealed from you.

The "fine print" in a contract between a business and an individual customer is seldom read or understood by the customer. Yet the fine print may be held at law to form part of the contract. So the customer may not get what she expected.

A contract, even if it is fair to both contracting parties, may be prejudicial to third parties or to the wider public interest.

A contract may involve actions that are immoral, even if they are not illegal.

Contracts of Employment

The problem of unequal bargaining power looms darkly over the field of employment. In the early days of classical economics—the last decades of the eighteenth century—employers (at least in the business world) were mostly individuals. There were not many business corporations. There was the Hudson's Bay Company, trading in beaver pelts and other furs, incorporated by royal charter granted by King Charles II in 1670. There was the even older East India Company, originally the *Governor and Company of Merchants of London Trading into the East Indies*, chartered by Queen Elizabeth I in 1600. There was the Bank of England, incorporated in 1694; the Bank of Scotland, born the following year; and the Bank of the United States, chartered by Congress in 1791. But the immense majority of businesses were unincorporated firms, each owned by a single individual or by a small group of partners.

So most contracts of employment were indeed agreements between individuals. A new employee struck a bargain with the one or few individuals who owned the firm he was joining. Therefore, economists could plausibly argue that the principle of *freedom of contract between individuals* should apply to contracts of employment.

Yet even in those days, there was generally a discrepancy of bargaining power between boss and worker. Employers were usually richer than their employees. As the industrial revolution got under way, rural laborers migrated to the growing towns to seek work in the new factories, just as they do in developing countries today. A contract between a poor laborer fresh from the country and a rich city industrialist was clearly a bargain between parties of very unequal strength. This unbalanced bargaining situation was vividly described by Cardinal Henry Manning, Archbishop of Westminster, in 1891: "It is clear that there can be no real free contract between capitalist and worker. The capitalist wears golden armor; and the worker, if he remains obstinate, knows that hunger awaits him. Thus the 'free contract' has become the employers' gospel; that is why they are so indignant at the idea of intervention by an arbitrator; and why they have protested against all outside interference in their private affairs."[13]

Fr. Henri-Dominique Lacordaire, a Dominican friar who reestablished his order in France, was an eloquent orator and a member of the *Académie Française*. He gave a famous series of lectures at the cathedral of Notre-Dame in Paris; in one of these, in 1848, he summed up memorably much of what is wrong with freedom of contract: "Between the strong and the weak, between rich and poor, between master and servant, it is liberty that is oppressive and the law that sets free."[14]

Then, as now, employers demanded freedom of contract because, in this context, freedom was to their material advantage; for they were the stronger parties. In developed economies today, things are a little better, since the state normally provides unemployment benefits so that jobless workers seldom starve. On the other hand, employers have become bigger and more powerful. The nineteenth and twentieth centuries saw a fundamental change in the status of employers: the spread of incorporation. Businesses that were simply associations of individual partners have largely been superseded by businesses that are corporate bodies, bearing the title "Inc.," meaning *incorporated*. These corporations are *legal persons* with the right to make contracts in their own name.

Corporate status enables a business to raise capital more easily and thus to grow. The principle of free contract *between individuals* has been extended to include free contract *between individuals and corporations*. Given that the corporation is now the normal form of business structure, most workers cannot avoid entering into contracts with corporations. But the growth of very large corporations means that the imbalance in bargaining strength between employers and workers is now, in many cases, enormous.

Yet certain economists persist in claiming that unequal bargaining power in the labor market is not a problem. They argue that the contract of employment between a worker and a corporation is no different from the trade between an individual customer and a supermarket. We don't generally worry that the shop is more powerful than the shopper, because customers (at least in towns) usually do have a real power against the shop: they can go away and do their shopping elsewhere. Likewise, the worker who does not like the way he is treated by the big corporation he works for can (perhaps) go away and take a job with another corporation. But there is a touch of absurdity in the argument that you can change your job as easily as your shopping habits.

Redressing the Imbalance

Between the mid-nineteenth and mid-twentieth centuries, workers strengthened their solidarity in unions, while governments increasingly regulated working conditions. Not surprisingly, many employers strenuously resisted these developments. But there was equally vehement resistance from others who lacked the excuse of pecuniary motives: the libertarian economists, who objected in principle to any interference with freedom of contract. Workers faced two distinct enemies, low greed and high ideology; who shall say which was the more fearsome?

Clearly, a strong union can face a big corporation on more equal terms than can an individual worker. But free marketeers generally disapprove of unions. They are not keen to admit openly their real motive which, all too often, is simply that they want to be able to employ cheap labor. So they use more sophisticated and idealistic pleas. A favorite of theirs is that workers have a sacrosanct right to the "freedom" to make their own individual contracts with employers. Union members do not have this right; they have to accept whatever terms are negotiated by the union on their behalf, in the process we call *collective bargaining*.

Absence of unions may mean, in theory, that individual workers are "freer." But it leaves them more open to exploitation by powerful employers. Can this really be a gain for the workers? The answer to that question depends on the kind of worker to which it is put. The capable, energetic, and diligent striver may prefer a nonunion shop where she may be able to negotiate better than average pay. But we cannot all be better than average workers, demanding and getting better than average pay! The less brilliant character may feel more in need of protection and so may prefer to be in a union.

If one believes that economic efficiency and "performance" are all-important, then it is logical to want economic policy to favor the top performers. A highly competitive society will naturally privilege this approach; every business wants to employ high-voltage performers so as to gain an edge over its competitors. But such a society may pay little heed to the concerns of those whose performance is average or less. They may be paid and treated badly and fired at a moment's notice. We see here one of the causes of our wide and widening inequalities.

Catholic teaching explicitly calls for protection of the weak: "Our faith in Christ, who became poor . . . is the basis of our concern for the integral development of society's most neglected members" (Francis, *Evangelii Gaudium*, par. 186). That is why the Church favors solidarity among workers; most workers need it.

Concerning employment contracts and labor unions, the position of the Catholic Church is very clear. In *Rerum Novarum* (par. 45), Leo XIII evokes "a dictate of natural justice more imperious and ancient than any bargain between man and man, namely, that wages ought not to be insufficient to support a frugal and well-behaved wage earner. If through necessity or fear of a worse evil the workman accept harder conditions because an employer or contractor will afford him no better, he is made the victim of force and injustice."

The *Catechism* (par. 2434) recalls Pope Leo's insistence that natural human rights take precedence over contractual rights: "Agreement between the parties is not sufficient to justify morally the amount to be received in wages."

The free-market dogma that any freely agreed contract must necessarily be fair and just is just another of those theories that too often fail to work out in practice. That is one reason why contracts need to be supervised and regulated.

The Public Interest

Another reason for regulation is that some contracts, even if they are fair to the contracting parties, are contrary to the public interest. If you own a house in a tranquil suburb, zoned for residential use only, you are not entitled to rent your house to a business that operates noisy nightclubs, even if the terms of the lease are perfectly fair to you and your tenant. That would not be a permissible use; it would offend against the public interest in preserving a quiet environment. Yet many libertarians object to the practice of zoning, with its constraints on the uses of real estate. It is true that zoning regulations can be excessively restrictive and may therefore be harmful to the urban community. But we should not abolish zoning because it is sometimes done badly.

Likewise, when a mining company buys or leases land for the purpose of extracting minerals, the contract between company and landowner may be fair and reasonable for both. Yet neighbors and environmentalists may well object. The contract, though fair to the contracting parties, may be detrimental to third parties, or to the wider public interest.

Restraint of Competition

An agreement between traders to sell at fixed prices and not undercut each other is a contract, provided the law permits such an agreement and will enforce it. But today, in many countries, such agreements are illegal and unenforceable, or even criminal, in obedience to the theory expounded by free-market economists ever since Adam Smith. The theory, and often the law, insists that competing traders should not even talk to each other about pricing, let alone have any formal agreements about it. Indeed, they should not even practice *tacit collusion*, which is generally considered illegal in principle, though since it leaves no tangible trail it is "likely to be unactionable as a matter of law."[15]

Tacit collusion is an agreement that is so informal that it is never even mentioned. It is expressed in a kind of "sign language," whereby traders silently signal to each other the price level they wish to maintain. If one of them trims his price, the others momentarily cut their prices rather more sharply to signal that "this won't do, get back in line." Of course, none of us would even dream of behaving like that. Agreements of this kind can be effective and are thought to be widely used. But they are, for obvious reasons, not legally enforceable; they are not true contracts.

Free Trade

The doctrine of freedom of contract clearly tells us that businesses in different countries should not be restrained from entering into trading agreements with each other. For many economists and libertarians, free trade is a sacrosanct principle. Indeed, the English politician Richard Cobden (1804–1865), who was also a Manchester cotton merchant, had a favorite slogan: *Free trade is the international law of God.* You may have trouble finding that in Holy Scripture. Free trade, however, did generally make sense for Britain in the mid-nineteenth century. She was then the *workshop of the world*, with the world's most advanced industrial base. Free trade enabled her to sell freely to other countries against rather limited competition.

This is a deeply controversial topic that we shall discuss in more detail in chapter 12. Here, let us simply note the advice given in the Vatican note *Ethical Guidelines for International Trade* (2003, pars. 1 and 2): "History demonstrates that ensuring some amount of free exchange of goods and services is indispensable for development and peace. Neither free trade nor any set of rules, however, are fair by themselves. Free trade can only be called such when it conforms to the demands of social justice. . . . Even if trade were completely free, there is no guarantee that free trade would be the best trade policy for all poor countries."

Noble but Fallible

Freedom of contract—the right of anyone to freely agree a deal with anyone else—is, on the face of it, a fine and noble principle. Yet it is weak in practice, since it too readily lends itself to abuse and thus to injustice. Therefore, the principle of free contract needs often to be diluted. Regulation may have to forbid certain contracts, impose minimum terms for employment contracts, protect consumers from unfair contracts of sale, and limit the scope of international contracts. The right to set up contracts is a right that needs limitation.

CHAPTER 11

Justice, Charity, and Distribution

The social doctrine of the Church has unceasingly highlighted the importance of distributive justice *and* social justice *for the market economy.*

—Pope Benedict XVI, *Caritas in Veritate*, par. 35

Charity will never be true charity unless it takes justice into constant account.

—Pope Pius XI, *Divini Redemptoris*, par. 49

Justice and Charity in Tandem

Benedict XVI, like his predecessors and his successor, is emphatic on the importance of *social justice*, and likewise of *distributive justice*, "which regulates what the community owes its citizens in proportion to their contributions and needs," as the *Catechism* (par. 2411) explains. In *Caritas in Veritate*, the pope also remarks (par. 6) that "charity transcends justice and completes it."

Yet charity and justice are too often seen as "alternatives" proposed by advocates of competing ideologies. Some conservative writers denounce the whole notion of social justice. In particular, they object to the emphasis on social justice in Catholic teaching, arguing that the Church should confine itself to organizing voluntary charity for those who need help. Some have even accused the Church of attempting to make social justice take the place of charity; as if these two principles were at odds with each other and not, as papal teaching insists, meant to work in tandem.

Poverty and Penury

We may take it that a main aim of both charity and social justice is to tackle the painful problem of poverty. But first we should think a little about what we mean by "poverty." Like "freedom," this is a word that has various meanings. It does not always mean a curse of which we rightly want to rid ourselves. The words of Jesus, "blessed are the poor in spirit," speak of "voluntary humility" and freedom from "immoderate attachment to the goods of this world."[1]

These qualities are quite distinct from the wretched, squalid, disgusting poverty (*miseria* in Latin and Spanish, *misère* in French) of people who are deprived of even a basic minimum of the goods of this world, who exist after a fashion in conditions of filth, hunger, and decrepitude. That kind of poverty, sometimes called *penury*, is certainly not blessed; it is an evil that civilized society should not tolerate. But to eliminate it, or even to mitigate it, can be a difficult matter.

Poverty can also be a relative notion; the American middle classes are "poor" relative to the top dogs on Wall Street, though they may well be "rich" relative to the underclasses. To avoid confusion, I shall generally use the word *penury* to describe the kind of abject poverty that we must aim to eliminate.

Penury may be a result of personal misfortune or "bad luck": accident, illness, handicap, divorce, loss of property; or it may be a result of personal misbehavior: excesses in gambling, drinking, using drugs, or simply careless, improvident spending. The people worst affected by such events are those who are socially isolated, who do not have relatives and friends at hand who can help them get back on their feet.

Sadly, in this age that prizes personal mobility and independence, isolation seems to be increasingly common. That is one reason why there is a need for the safety net of state welfare. Its critics complain that this is "impersonal," but it has the capability to help lonely people for whom more "personal" assistance may be out of reach.

Systemic Penury

Other major causes of penury are *defects or malfunctions in the social or economic system*. An example is famine. We tend to think that this is caused by a breakdown in food supplies, like the notorious Irish famine of the 1840s, when potato crops failed throughout Ireland. Yet famine can occur even in a region where food supplies are near normal, if some people are unable to afford enough food to sustain them. The distinguished Indian economist Amartya Sen, who as a boy witnessed the severe Bengal famine of 1943, argues that famine may occur when prices of craftsmen's products fall sharply; or when food prices rise faster than wages, not because of shortage but because certain classes in society become more affluent and can buy more. He concludes that "a policy of enhancing the incomes of individuals by offering them, for example, a public employment, or by paying an income to very poor people while they are seeking employment, can prove to be one of the best methods of preventing famines. . . . The elimination of famines in India has been largely the result of systematic public intervention."[2]

The Right to Work and to Adequate Wages

Penury is often a consequence of unemployment. Again, this is a systemic rather than a personal problem; a malfunction in the economic system. The real solution is not a matter of handing out cash to the unemployed, either as private charity or as state unemployment benefit. Such payments may well be necessary, but they are palliatives; they do not treat the disease. The real cure is to manage our economies in such a way that there is, so far as possible, always sufficient demand for labor so that everyone has the opportunity to work.

In *Laborem Exercens*, John Paul II wrote at some length about the economic policies needed to avoid unemployment. He emphasized the central role of the state in economic planning but insisted that this "cannot mean one-sided centralization by the public authorities. Instead, what is in question is a just and rational *coordination*, within the framework of which the *initiative* of individuals, free groups and local work centers and complexes must be safeguarded" (par. 18). This reflects the Catholic principle of subsidiarity, meaning that decision making should, so far as is practicable, be local rather than central.

The pope added that "the opposite of a just and right situation . . . is unemployment, that is to say the lack of work for those who are capable of it." Furthermore, concerning international agreements on trade, "the criterion for these . . . must more and more be the criterion of human work considered as a fundamental right of all human beings." Ten years later, in *Centesimus Annus* (par. 43), he reasserted this claim: "The obligation to earn one's bread . . . also presumes the right to do so."

Yet another cause of penury is an inadequate level of wages. We have seen (chap. 6) how free-market economics regards labor as a commodity to be bought as cheaply as possible. We have seen how

Carl Menger, first of the "Austrian School" economists, argued that the "price of labor" (rate of pay) should be determined simply by supply and demand in the labor market, without regard to any calculation of how much laborers actually need to live on.

Penury that reflects flaws in the economic system is not simply a matter of personal misfortune, calling for a personal helping hand from charity. It is a social or economic problem; to put it more bluntly, it is an *injustice*. In *Rerum Novarum*, Leo XIII condemned paltry rates of pay as a form of injustice, even though such rates may have been "freely" agreed between workers and their employers. And the *Compendium* (par. 292) states that "human work is a right upon which the promotion of social justice and civil peace directly depend." The notion that *opportunity to work is a human right* has often been ridiculed by libertarians. But it is well established in Catholic teaching.

Penury, then, is very often a consequence of systemic injustice. This fact brings the theme of *rights* into the picture; people who suffer injustice have, in principle, a right to redress. The avoidance or relief of severe poverty thus becomes an *obligation* rather than purely a matter of voluntary charity. Catholic doctrine on economic rights and obligations is founded on two basic, closely related concepts: *distributive justice* and the *universal destination of goods*.

Distributive Justice in History and Today

We have seen that *distributive justice*, as the *Catechism* defines it, relates to the *contributions and needs* of ourselves as citizens. This clearly differs from the current orthodox view on how personal incomes should be decided. Mainstream economists generally hold that earnings should be based on individual productivity and performance; that is, on each individual employee's contribution to the firm's sales and profits. That may appear reasonable in theory; but in practice it can mean that pay for some people is too little to live on, while for a few others it may be far more than anyone could reasonably need.

It was not always so. The eighteenth-century classical economists (Adam Smith and his followers) accepted that the pay of a laborer should not fall below a basic subsistence level.[3] In the nineteenth century, economists argued that wages and salaries should be determined purely by market forces, without any consideration of how much the workers need for a living wage. Still later, in reaction against that kind of thought and practice, wages came to be set by negotiation between employers and unions, fixing rates of pay for workers in each category of employment, rather than performance-based or market-based individual rates. Today, we have slipped back toward the harsh world of nineteenth-century business.

The concept of distributive justice was discussed long ago by Aristotle and by St. Thomas. Aristotle argued that "all are agreed that justice in distributions must be based on desert [i.e., on what each person is thought to 'deserve'], although they do not all mean the same sort of desert; democrats make the criterion free birth; those of oligarchical sympathies wealth, or in other cases birth; upholders of aristocracy make it virtue."[4] Thus, what each person "deserves" depends largely on his position in society, or on his virtue; it does not, except sometimes in the "oligarchist" view, depend primarily on his wealth.

St. Thomas quoted from this passage in Aristotle and observed that "in distributive justice a person receives all the more of the common goods, according as he holds a more prominent position in the community."[5]

Today, as in Aristotle's day, there are various opinions about what kind of distribution is just. At one extreme we have *egalitarianism*, which calls for a society in which everyone is more or less equally rich (or poor). But, in America at least, this ideal seems to have very little appeal: "Numerous studies of the distributive preferences of people demonstrate almost universal opposition to equality or near equality of income."[6] The philosopher Michael Walzer describes vividly how impractical and disagreeable it would be to try to make everyone equal. Give everyone the same amount of money on Sunday, he says, and it "will have been unequally redistributed before the week is out." Opponents of equality, says Walzer, "describe the repression it would require and the drab and fearful conformity it would produce. A society of equals, they say, would be a world of false appearances where people who were not in fact the same would be forced to look and act as if they were the same. And the falsehoods would have to be enforced by an élite or a vanguard whose members pretended in turn that they were not really there. It is not an inviting prospect."[7]

Glaring contemptuously at the egalitarians from the opposite end of the ideological spectrum sit the hard-line free marketeers and anarcho-capitalists. They hold that one has an absolute right to whatever assets one acquires by lawful means. Therefore, one has no obligation to share these assets with anyone else. One may do so voluntarily if one is charitably inclined. But the notion that there can be an *obligation in justice*, a legal or quasi-legal requirement to share, is anathema to these people. For them, redistributive taxation is totally unacceptable; it amounts to nothing less than theft of private property.

The Universal Destination of Goods

The Catholic concept of distributive justice steers a middle course. It does not call for equality but requires that resources be distributed in accordance with the principle of *universal destination of goods*, which means that God wishes everyone to have at least a basic sufficiency of them: "The right of having a share of earthly goods sufficient for one-self and one's family belongs to everyone" (*Gaudium et Spes*, par. 69).

Conventional economics assumes that this happy state can be achieved through economic growth; we should produce more and more until there is enough to provide at least this basic sufficiency for everyone, without imposing any cutbacks on those who consume far more than they need.

That argument may have been plausible in the past, when world population was much smaller than it is now; it does not make sense today. For it is widely agreed that the human race as a whole is consuming the earth's resources in an unsustainable manner. As long ago as 1987, John Paul II warned in *Sollicitudo Rei Socialis* (par. 34): "Natural resources are limited; some are not, as it is said, renewable. Using them as if they were inexhaustible, with absolute dominion, seriously endangers their availability not only for the present generation but above all for generations to come." Our global consumption of natural resources has swollen to a level that is excessive and unsustainable, even though a great many very poor people still lack the means to consume enough for a decent life.

Therefore, it is vitally important that we who live in more afflu-ent circumstances learn to consume less wastefully. We must learn to consume more in the form of services to each other, less in the form of physical goods. We must abandon the "throwaway" economy in which we produce ephemeral things that are quickly discarded, rather than things that last. Moreover, since we cannot persist in increasing worldwide production and consumption of goods, we have no choice but to distribute our totality of supplies more evenly. That implies a much stronger emphasis on distributive justice than we have at present.

Relieving Poverty Via Distributive Justice

Libertarians and conservatives too often cling to the belief that the relief of poverty should be simply a matter of doling out charitable gifts. But their attitude was forcefully condemned more than eighty years ago by Pius XI in *Quadragesimo Anno* (par. 4). He castigated those "who thought their abundant riches the result of inevitable economic laws and accordingly, as if it were for charity to veil [this] violation of justice . . . wanted the whole care of supporting the poor committed to charity alone."

In his later encyclical *Divini Redemptoris* (1937), Pope Pius takes up the theme again. This document is primarily a formidable tirade against communism, garnished with vivid descriptions of its horrid consequences. Any Catholic who suspects that *social justice* is merely a euphemism for socialism or communism, however, should be aware that this fiercely anticommunist encyclical mentions that phrase several times and always as a Christian obligation.

The pope denounces those employers, including Catholic employers, who treat their workers unjustly but purport to make up for this by supporting charitable efforts to relieve the consequent poverty; a practice that is not unknown in American business today. Thus (par. 49), "a 'charity' which deprives the workingman of the salary to which he has a strict title in justice, is not charity at all, but only its empty name and hollow semblance. The wage-earner is not to receive as alms what is his due in justice."

Pope Pius goes on to criticize Catholic employers and industrialists who neglect and even obstruct the Church's teachings, who (par. 50) "in one place succeeded in preventing the reading of Our Encyclical *Quadragesimo Anno* in their local churches," and who prevent workers from associating in unions. "Is it not deplorable that the right of private property defended by the Church should so often have been used as a weapon to defraud the workingman of his just salary and his social rights?"

Pius continues (pars. 51–52): "It is of the very essence of social justice to demand for each individual all that is necessary for the common good. . . . But social justice cannot be said to be satisfied as long as workingmen are denied a salary that will enable them to secure proper sustenance for themselves and for their families; as long as they are denied the opportunity of acquiring a modest fortune and forestalling the plague of universal pauperism; as long as they cannot make suitable provision through public or private insurance for old age, for periods of illness or unemployment."

The Vatican clearly does not see anything "Bolshevik" in social justice; unlike the libertarian economist Friedrich von Hayek, who wrote that "the greatest service I can still render to my fellow men would be to make the speakers and writers among them thoroughly ashamed ever again to employ the term *social justice.*"[8]

Redistribution in Biblical Tradition

Let us take a closer look at *redistribution* in its two forms: obligatory and voluntary. Both have a long history, reaching back to the Old Testament. The tradition of redistribution has been carried forward from ancient Judaism into modern Catholic teaching.

The law of Moses (Torah) prescribes various provisions for the support of the poor. Among these is a quite complex system of tithes levied on personal resources; in fact, mainly on farmers' crops or livestock, the principal sources of income and wealth in ancient Israel. These tithes serve several purposes: the stipends of the priests of the Temple (the Levites, who had no land of their own), the upkeep and ceremonies of the Temple, and distributions to the poor.

Then there are various benefits in kind for the poor. In Leviticus 19:9-10 we find the "rule of corners": a farmer must not reap the corners of his fields but must leave a part of his crop standing so that poor people may gather it. And we find rules against gleaning one's own fields or vineyards; one must leave any ungathered grain or grapes behind for the same purpose. Another rule (Exod 23:11) stipulates that every seventh year the fields are to lie fallow; in that year, anything that grows there is to be available for the poor.

All those rules form part of the law of Moses. They, and their equivalents in later times, are thus considered as legally binding, not voluntary. Accordingly, "at its foundation Judaism views supporting the needy to be a duty imposed upon each person under the terms of the covenant with God. . . . Supporting the poor is . . . an act of compliance with the covenant that has little to do with free will and everything to do with the fulfilment of one's obligations to God."[9]

This does not mean that Jews are discouraged or excused from making voluntary gifts in addition to those prescribed by law. What it means is that a certain basic level of transfers from richer to poorer is obligatory—just as it is today in virtually all developed countries, which have social security systems financed by taxes. So the principle of paying taxes to support the poor is not a socialist innovation; it goes all the way back to Moses.

In Jewish tradition, there is a clear and helpful distinction between obligatory and voluntary giving. The first is called *tzedakah*,[10] a word closely related to *tzedek*, meaning justice. This is the giving that is required by law, a payment or transfer that is due in justice, on the basis that all the goods of this world belong primarily to God, who wishes that everyone should have at least a basic sufficiency of them. Here we recognize a concept very close to the Catholic doctrine of the *universal destination of goods*.

The second kind of giving is called *gemilut hasadim*, commonly translated as *loving-kindness*; this is what one gives freely, not from legal obligation but out of the kindness of one's heart. It corresponds roughly to what Christians call charity, whereas *tzedakah* is closer to paying one's taxes for social security.

It is said in the rabbinical literature that "an act of loving-kindness is greater than an act of *tzedakah*."[11] Compare this statement with Benedict XVI's remark that "charity transcends justice and completes it." Nevertheless, *tzedakah* takes precedence in the sense that it is obligatory; if you fail to give it, you are acting unjustly and offending against the law; while *gemilut hasadim* is something you give voluntarily, over and above what the law requires.

Obligatory Contributions in Church History

Thus, the Old Testament strongly emphasizes the duty to contribute, in money or in kind, for two main purposes: the practice of religion and the relief of poverty. And these contributions take two forms: obligatory tithes and transfers (*tzedakah*) and free-will offerings or gifts (*gemilut hasadim*). The reasons for obligatory transfers are, again, twofold. First, we have the principle that support for the poor, up to a certain level, is due in justice—it settles a kind of debt; therefore it should be required by law. Second, we have the practical reality that reliance on purely voluntary contributions may not yield enough revenue to provide adequately for the poor and for the Temple. These facts are as relevant for us today as they were in biblical times.

Although Jesus told the Pharisees (Matt 23:23; Luke 11:42) that they should not neglect the duty of paying tithes, this practice seems not to have been followed by the earliest Christians: "We are not in a position to cite any canonical or conciliar text before the fourth century which requires the payment" [of tithes].[12] St. Irenaeus (c. 130–200), bishop of Lyons, observed that our Lord "commanded . . . in place of the rule of tithing, that we should share all things with the poor,"[13] and this text is sometimes quoted today by Christians who reject the idea that we should be required to pay tithes, or any other specified amounts, to our churches. If we follow Irenaeus a little further, however, we find him adding that Jesus was "not abrogating the law, but filling it out, extending and broadening it."[14] So Irenaeus appears to have meant not that we should neglect the rule of tithing but that we should voluntarily give something more.

As the young churches grew and their material needs increased, purely voluntary giving proved to be insufficient; it became necessary to stipulate certain amounts that Christians were morally, or indeed legally, obliged to pay. In the fourth century, St. Ambrose (c. 337–397), archbishop of Milan, preached that tithes ought to be paid on all revenues; a little later, St. Augustine did likewise. As Harvard historian Giles Constable remarks, "These tithes were the property of God, not a voluntary offering by man, and the obligations of charity were in no way fulfilled by paying tithes."[15]

According to St. Thomas, "Man's obligation to pay tithes arises partly from natural law, partly from the institution of the Church; which, nevertheless, in consideration of the requirements of time and persons, might ordain the payment of some other proportion."[16] The Council of Trent, on the penultimate day of its final session (December 3, 1563), wound up its proceedings by rapidly enacting a number of decrees, one of which threatened excommunication for those who withheld tithes or hindered their payment.[17]

We see that there is nothing new about what we now call tax evasion! And indeed, the collection of tithes and other obligatory payments has been a difficult and contentious matter throughout most of Church history. But that does not mean that the practice is wrong or unnecessary.

Compare those ancient and medieval traditions with Pope Benedict's words (*Caritas in Veritate*, par. 6): "I cannot 'give' what is mine to the other without first giving him what pertains to him in justice." It all fits together rather seamlessly, does it not? And does it really make any sense to imagine that, where redistribution of resources is needed, charity should take the place of justice, or vice versa?

Institutional Reform

The idea that we need to adapt our institutions (the functioning of our businesses, the operation of markets, etc.) so as to mitigate inequality and poverty is relatively recent. As we have seen, in ancient and premodern times it was generally understood that inequalities are a fact of life and that where they are excessive, correction is needed via transfers from rich to poor. But another approach, more fundamental, is to try to prevent undue inequalities from developing in the first place.

In modern economies, many injustices are due to the fact that workers, unless they act in a firmly united fashion, are normally in a weak bargaining position relative to their employers. The growth of labor unions, strongly recommended by the Catholic Church ever since *Rerum Novarum* (1891) and indeed before, enables workers to obtain a better deal on wages and working conditions. Regulation of wages, with minimum rates enforced by law, is another method. Worker participation in management, frequently endorsed by recent popes, is a third approach. And perhaps the most important strategy of all is to adopt economic policies that promote full employment. All these precepts can be found in modern Catholic social doctrine.

Can Charity Replace Justice?

What if charity attempts to replace obligatory redistribution or institutional reform, as a good many Americans—some of them Catholics—seem to wish? Reliance on charity alone leads to the humiliating situation deplored by Pius XI, where the worker receives alms to round out an inadequate pay packet or to enable him to survive while unemployed. Most of us, surely, would rather earn a fair and adequate wage for our work than have to ask for it to be topped up out of somebody else's charitable donations. "The laborer deserves his wages" (Matt 10:7), and he should earn a wage worthy of a fair day's work. If he does not, or if he suffers chronic unemployment, then the economic system is somehow faulty. We should endeavor to correct the faults, rather than content ourselves with patching up the problems they cause by acts of charity.

Charity treats the symptoms of the social and economic disease of penury but does not attack its causes. Charity can yield immediate benefits, while correction of underlying causes of penury is generally a long haul. There have always been, and are still, Christians who are unwilling to attempt this, on the ground that they believe that "the end of the world is nigh." They therefore see no point in embarking on any long-term project such as developing more equitable business structures or nonpolluting industrial technologies. But it is surely wrong to *assume* that the present world has no future. After all, Jesus himself assured his followers (Mark 13:32) that they could not know, even that he himself does not know, the date or the hour of its end. Catholic teaching makes it clear that we have a duty to consider the needs of our descendants, that we have no right to act as if there were not going to be any. We must not pillage our environment; we must preserve it in good shape for generations to come. Likewise, we must work toward a fairer society for our successors.

Apart from the millenarians, there are Christians, and many others, who do not want redistribution because they fear that it will hurt them financially; or because they think that redistribution is an unjustifiable interference with their personal "freedom." But, as we explain in chapter 3, they may well have an un-Catholic view of the meaning of freedom.

Can Justice Replace Charity?

Some conservatives accuse proponents of social justice of believing that it can, and should, take the place of charity. And it is true that left-wing writers have sometimes disparaged traditional charity, claiming that in a modern socialist welfare state we would no longer need it. Leo XIII remarked in *Graves de Communi* (1901, par. 16) that "against [almsgiving] the socialist cries out and demands its abolition as injurious to the native dignity of man." The Church, however, has always taught that the practice of charity is good for both donor and beneficiary, indeed (Acts 20:35) that "it is more blessed to give than to receive." Charity can earn a divine reward: "[W]hen you give alms . . . your Father who sees in secret will reward you" (Matt 6:3-4). But some have taken a suspicious view of this doctrine, even claiming that those who give alms are "using the poor as the vehicle of their own salvation."

That notion is a distortion of the Christian doctrine of charity. We should not imagine that we can buy our way out of purgatory, or into heaven, simply by handing out enough cash to the poor: *If I give away all I have . . . but have not love, I gain nothing* (1 Cor 13:3; the word "love" translates *agapē* = affection, friendship, brotherliness). The proper motives for giving to the poor are two: a desire to promote justice in human society, recognizing that it is unjust that people should live in wretched conditions; and a sense of genuine affection and pity for people in that plight.

Justice, in the sense of obligatory redistribution or of institutional reform, cannot eliminate the need for charity. There will always be people who genuinely need help but slip through the meshes of the official safety net or simply deserve and appreciate some extra help in difficult times. Moreover, to quote the Talmud once again, "An act of *tzedakah* is done only for the poor, while an act of loving-kindness may be done for the poor or for the rich."[18] After all, "loving-kindness" includes gifts in love and affection to relatives and friends who are not in material need.

Some people deny the need to practice social justice, claiming that if, by so doing, we were to get rid of poverty, then there would no longer be any scope for compassion and benevolence. This argument is feeble. Poverty is one of many causes of human suffering; there are plenty of others: sickness, bereavement, disability, war, terrorism, and other crimes. Even if we pursued social and distributive justice to the point where no serious poverty remained, there would still be ample scope and need for loving-kindness. "No one," says Pope Leo (*Graves de Communi*, par. 16), "is so rich that he does not need another's help; no one is so poor as not to be useful in some way to his fellow man; and the disposition to ask assistance from others with confidence and to grant it with kindness is part of our very nature."

Obligatory Contribution in the Church Today

The practice of tithing, or otherwise calling for specific levels of giving to one's church, remains a controversial issue. In general, obligatory tithes, payable by farmers or landowners to parishes, dioceses, or monasteries, have died out in Europe and likewise in Latin America, where they existed under the Spanish Empire. The Catholic Church does not generally call for specific levels of contribution by the faithful. Some Protestant churches do so; some indeed demand 10 percent of all income; but Protestants seem on the whole to prefer the stance of the early Christians, who held that all giving should be voluntary and spontaneous.

In the Middle Ages, tithes financed certain "social services" provided by religious houses, such as schooling, hospitals, and assistance for the poor, which are now funded largely by secular institutions; so a full tithe of 10 percent to one's church may well be considered excessive today. If a specific level of giving is to be called for, we may do well to keep in mind the practical view of St. Thomas and "ordain the payment of some other proportion."

Church Taxes

Although tithing in its traditional form has generally fallen into disuse, the practice continues in some countries of paying a "church tax" levied by the state along with other taxes and handed over to the churches. For instance, in Germany there is the *Kirchensteuer* (church tax) payable by practicing Catholics, Protestants, and Jews. One can opt out of paying this tax by declaring that one does not practice any of these faiths. The *Kirchensteuer* amounts to 8 or 9 percent of what one pays in normal income tax, of which the top rate is 45 percent; thus Germans with high incomes have to pay up to 4.05 percent of the top slice of their income to their church. This quite hefty requirement has apparently pushed some Germans into "leaving the Church." But the Catholic bishops have reacted strongly; they have declared that any who do so cannot receive the sacraments.

The German church tax was introduced in the nineteenth century as a substitute for the older system, under which princely families were responsible for the maintenance of churches and clergy in their territories. The idea was to "democratize" the churches, having them financed by the people rather than by the territorial rulers. In many other European countries, there are similar, but generally less onerous, church taxes. To quote just two examples: in Italy there is an income tax of 0.8 percent (*otto per mille* = eight per thousand), which the taxpayer can direct to a religious group of his choice or to a state agency; in Austria there is an income tax of 1.1 percent payable by members of the Catholic Church.

Many Christians today are not in sympathy with the idea that we should be expected, let alone formally obliged, to donate a specific proportion of our revenue to our church. They feel that we should simply be urged to give whatever we think fit. Yet there are several arguments for requesting a defined proportion. One is that reliance on haphazard giving can mean that a great deal of time and effort has to be devoted to fund-raising, by exhortation and by organizing events for this purpose. Time and effort that could perhaps be better spent! In the *American Ecclesiastical Review* almost a century ago, Fr. F. J. Jansen of Elkhart, Indiana complained: "The endless financial harangues which are heard in our churches must naturally beget nausea on account of the frequency of the dose administered. . . . If the energy which is now spent on financial sermons could be directed into Gospel channels, I am confident that before long this country would produce splendid examples of forceful preachers of the Gospel."[19]

Fortunately, such "financial harangues" are not so frequent in our churches today; we have learned to collect more money by way of "planned giving" schemes, which were made tax deductible by the War Income Tax Revenue Act of 1917, just before Fr. Jansen wrote.

Another problem is that, if giving of specific and adequate amounts is not called for, some church members will give little or nothing, thus throwing an unfair burden upon the others; they are the likened by Fr. Jansen to the family of "Mr. Cuckoo, Mrs. Cuckoo and Miss Cuckoo, [who] leave the building and maintaining of the church to others."[20]

Yet another problem is that without adequate contributions from the laity in general, some parishes rely unduly on the large donations of a few wealthy parishioners; but these persons may exert pressure on their priests to soft-pedal the Church's social doctrine, as Pius XI noted in *Divini Redemptoris*. It may indeed be that Pope Francis had this problem in mind when he called recently for a "poor church for the poor"; what he wants may be a Church that does not overly depend on the largesse of the rich. It might be a wise parish strategy not only to ask for a minimum level of contribution (percentage of income) from each parishioner, with exceptions for those with very small incomes, but also to impose a maximum that can be accepted from any one source (person or organization).

Generosity in Times of Recession

If poverty is due largely to unemployment, then giving to relieve poverty should, so far as possible, be done out of savings (capital) rather than by cuts in spending. This may sound odd, but it makes good logical and practical sense. As I am writing from Paris, let us try a French example of this theory.

Since France, at the time of writing, suffers much unemployment-related poverty, should the richer French (call them collectively "R") give up drinking champagne and give the money saved to help the unemployed poor ("U")? That may sound virtuous, in keeping with traditional Christian ideas on the merits of frugality and austerity; "Cardinals and all Prelates of the churches shall be content with modest furniture and a frugal table" as the Council of Trent put it.[21]

But what happens if R give up champagne? Let us suppose (to keep the argument simple) that U spend the money thus transferred to them on red *vin ordinaire*. Then U will indeed gain a benefit at the expense of R; but the result will be loss of income for the champagne industry and some loss of jobs therein. That might be compensated by increased employment for those who make red plonk. But there will probably be no reduction in the overall level of unemployment, the main cause of the poverty one is trying to alleviate.

Now suppose that R carry on drinking champagne, while giving out of their savings (cash in the bank) to help U. In this case there will be a gain in employment in the red wine industry and no loss in the champagne industry. Not only will U gain at the expense of R, but the employment situation will improve. For the cash that was not being spent by R will be spent by U, thus generating more jobs.

Too Much Saving, Too Little Spending

In fact, one of the main causes of unemployment is, quite simply, too much saving; or, to put it the other way round, too little spending. Our spending provides your earnings, and vice versa. Therefore, if spending is too low, logically, earnings must also be too low. In other words, wages are too low; or there are too many unemployed; or, as at present, we have both problems. This happens in every recession, for reasons that we can easily understand.

During a recession, people feel pessimistic, nervous about the future, afraid of losing their jobs, and anxious to pay down their debts. So they trim their spending and save more. Unfortunately, this behavior slows down the economy, increases unemployment, and generally aggravates the situation; we are caught in a vicious circle. Recession is, in fact, largely psychological; the result of a widespread downbeat, fearful, and depressive state of mind.

What seems best for each individual (tightening one's belt and spending less) is, in fact, harmful for the economy and society as a whole. It is a striking illustration of how free-market theory can break down in practice. The theory tells us that if we each act in our own best interest, the outcome will be best for all; our self-interested behavior will further the common good. In practice, during a recession, the opposite happens.

At the time of writing (autumn 2014), much of the world is still in a near-recessionary state, with high unemployment; in some places (Europe and Japan in particular) this condition seems to have become chronic rather than transitory. There is too little spending to keep our economies firing on all cylinders. Meanwhile, there is an excess of cash and of various "unproductive" financial assets sitting in our banks and investment funds.

Economists recognize the problem of excessive capital accumulation, but they have mostly concentrated their attention on overinvestment in physical capital (industrial plant, real estate, etc.). We all know how too much housebuilding in America, Spain, and Ireland has left us with whole streets of empty houses that nobody wants to buy, and piles of unrepayable debt racked up by property developers. But overinvestment in financial capital has probably been even more damaging. The economist Sara Hsu at New York State University observes that "there is little written about financial capital overaccumulation." But that excess, she says, has "resulted in falling wages as well as in the most recent global financial crisis."[22] We need, in fact, more spending and less accumulation. Calls for austerity, virtuous as they may sound, are out of place in today's conditions.

Too much accumulation, with consequently not enough spending, is morally and economically unhealthy. It leads to economic stagnation, with too little paid work. The Irish poet Oliver Goldsmith (1730–1774) described this situation succinctly and precisely: "Wealth accumulates, and men decay."[23] The economist Edwin Burmeister evoked a *reductio ad absurdum* of hoarding: "suppose all of output were devoted to capital accumulation. . . . Consumption would be zero."[24] And we would all starve!

What does Catholic teaching have to say about this? The *Compendium* (par. 329) contains a strong warning about the dangers of excessive saving: "Evil is seen in the immoderate attachment to riches and the desire to hoard." It quotes from St. Basil, "Wealth is like water that issues forth from a fountain: the greater the frequency with which it is drawn, the purer it is, while it becomes foul if the fountain remains unused."[25] According to St. Thomas, "it is more praiseworthy that money be spent on acts of liberality and magnificence, rather than hoarded."[26]

Excessive accumulation is a consequence of excessive inequalities. Most of us cannot afford to hoard on a substantial scale; only the very rich can do that. By obliging them to pay more in tax and using the proceeds to reduce taxes (or increase benefits) for the poorer classes, we would most likely get a higher overall level of spending. What the rich could no longer hoard would be spent by the poor. We would have a boost for the economy *without the need for any loosening of the budget.*

Of course, such a plan would not work if the very rich chose to cut their own spending, rather than their savings, in order to pay the extra tax. But that seems, on the whole, rather unlikely. People do not generally like to reduce their accustomed standard of living. Since the very rich usually have surplus income that they do not spend, most of them would be inclined to dip into that saved income rather than spend less on entertaining or going to the opera.

My readers may object that I am encouraging the rich to carry on spending lavishly; that such behavior is contrary to Church teaching and bad for the environment. The Bible, however, does not always condemn lavish spending or conspicuous consumption. The first miracle of Jesus was the conversion of water into wine for the wedding feast at Cana; Jesus provided a bumper quantity, equivalent to something like a thousand of our bottles, of best-quality wine.

Again, Jesus praised the extravagant gesture of Mary of Bethany, who anointed his feet with "a pound of costly ointment of pure nard" (John 12:3-5) said to be worth "three hundred pennies"; these pennies (*denarii* in the Vulgate) are the same small silver coins mentioned in the parable of the laborers in the vineyard, who were paid a penny a day (Matt 20:9). So Mary's nard (spikenard) was worth a laborer's full year's wages. And well it might be. Spikenard is an essential oil, derived from the rhizomes of a plant of the *Valerian* family, that is still used in perfumery and in medicine. It has always been a rare and expensive commodity, highly prized for its aromatic and therapeutic qualities. Yellow flowers of spikenard, traditionally associated with St. Joseph, appear on the coat of arms of Pope Francis. We may note that both these extravagances employed renewable resources (wine and perfume).

The Bible does not mention church buildings, since the fledgling first-century churches were too small to afford or need them. But it does tell us about the great Jewish temples. The first of these, Solomon's Temple, was a magnificent building, whose construction employed tens of thousands of men: "Solomon overlaid the inside of the house with pure gold . . . and he overlaid the whole house with gold. . . . [H]e adorned the house with settings of precious stones" (1 Kgs 6:21-22; 2 Chr 3:6). After this temple was destroyed by the Babylonians in 587, a second, even grander temple was completed in 516; "the latter splendor of this house shall be greater than the former, says the LORD of Hosts" (Hag 2:9).

The Church has continued this tradition of constructing splendid buildings to the glory of God. These do indeed consume nonrenewable resources (stone and other minerals). On the other hand, the best church buildings can last a very long time. Our cathedral in Paris, Notre Dame, has stood since the twelfth century. Certain grand church buildings in France were demolished by the revolutionaries after 1789; a notable example was the huge abbey church of Cluny, in Burgundy. But its stones were not wasted; they were used in the construction of other fine buildings.

There is a tendency today to disapprove of lavish spending on church buildings. Should the Church spend money on embellishing her sanctuaries, constructing and maintaining fine organs, paying musicians to perform beautiful liturgical music, and so on, when out there on the streets people are languishing in poverty? But today, poverty (at least in the richer countries) is due largely to unemployment. Is it not better to pay people to work than to dole out charity, paying them to do nothing? Too many people are not working; and too many of those who are working are doing dismal, unsatisfying work. If the Church can pay people to do good work, should she not do so?

During the Great Depression, Cardinal Verdier, archbishop of Paris, started a major program of church building, with two objectives: to provide new churches for the recently developed outer districts and suburbs of the city, and to put unemployed builders and craftsmen to work. In 1932, Verdier's organization, *Les Chantiers du Cardinal* ("the Cardinal's building sites"), raised a loan of twenty million francs at 5 percent interest to get the project under way. Advertised with the slogan "to fight unemployment, help your archbishop build churches," this loan was fully subscribed in a few days. Further funds were raised by monthly collections in the parishes. A report published by the *Chantiers* in 1932 states that a church seating eight hundred people cost around a million francs, so that loan provided enough cash to build twenty large churches. During the 1930s, around a hundred churches were built, many of them truly impressive.

At the low point of the Depression, in 1933, work began on the church of St. John Bosco, in one of the poorer districts of Paris. It is adorned with splendid mosaics, frescoes, sculptures, and stained glass, making it arguably the finest of the city's more recent churches. Depression? Cardinal Verdier wasn't hearing of it! And the work of the *Chantiers*, constructing new churches and renovating older ones, continues to this day. Since 1932, some 330 churches have been built in Paris and its suburbs.

CHAPTER 12

Free Trade and Fair Trade

We cannot remain passive before certain processes of globalization which not infrequently increase the gap between the rich and the poor worldwide.

—Pope Benedict XVI [1]

One cannot easily find any place so overflowing with the necessaries of life as not to need some commodities from other parts. Also, when there is an overwhelming abundance of some commodities in one place, these goods would serve no purpose if they could not be carried elsewhere by professional traders. Consequently, the perfect city will make a moderate use of merchants.

—St. Thomas Aquinas [2]

Free trade giveth and free trade taketh away.

—Paul A. Samuelson [3]

The Principle of Free Trade

As we saw in chapter 10, the doctrine of free trade follows logically from the libertarian belief that anyone should be free to enter into any voluntary contract with anyone else. There is no reason, in principle, why this freedom should extend only as far as the frontiers of one's country. The essential unity of the human race, one great family all descended from Adam and Eve, rules out the idea that you should be prohibited from trading with me, merely because you are an American citizen living in the United States, while I live in France and have British and French nationalities.

Nevertheless, as we have explained, there are good reasons why not all freely agreed contracts should be permitted. Therefore, we cannot jump to the conclusion that all kinds of international trade, at whatever prices free markets may set, are necessarily acceptable. We remarked in chapter 5 that there are ethical objections to *unfair competition*, whereby a strong and ruthless business can destroy its smaller competitors and deprive people of their livelihood, or where a new business deliberately poaches the customers of established firms. Moreover, Pope John XXIII called for "avoidance of all forms of unfair competition between the economies of different countries" (*Mater et Magistra*, par. 80).

This issue has grown in importance in recent decades for two main reasons. First, in the context of the *General Agreement on Tariffs and Trade* (GATT) and its successor, the *World Trade Organization* (WTO), governments have labored long and hard to reduce barriers to international trade. And they have had considerable success: "Import tariffs and other restrictions that governments impose on international trade have been reduced to the lowest levels the world has ever seen."[4] Second, developments in transport and communications have greatly facilitated trade over long distances.

Why Free Trade?

Any country that aspires to have a well-developed economy must trade with other nations. Even a country as big as the United States, well endowed with a wide variety of natural resources, finds it advantageous to trade because there are many goods that it cannot produce as efficiently as other countries can.

It is possible to obtain natural rubber from *guayule*, a plant that grows in Mexico and parts of the American South, but it is cheaper to use latex from the Pará rubber tree, which needs a humid tropical climate and is cultivated mainly in Malaysia, Thailand, and Indonesia. The *rare earth metals*, used in countless applications including electronic equipment, lasers, LED lighting, rechargeable batteries, and photovoltaic cells, are present in many countries but are now produced almost exclusively in China, where mining costs, generally heavy for these ores, are lower than elsewhere. And clearly, for most countries, there are materials that cannot be produced locally at all.

Certain countries have attempted to dispense with trade and thus be self-sufficient. But this strategy—known as *autarky*[5]—can hardly work well even for the largest countries and is generally disastrous for smaller ones. It was tried by Albania during the Communist era, when the Albanian government broke off relations with the Soviet Union in the 1960s and then with China in the 1970s; but autarkic Albania was generally considered the most backward nation in Europe. North Korea is still largely autarkic. The Spanish economy was in effect isolated from 1939 at least until the Treaty of Madrid (with the United States) in 1953, both because of wartime conditions and because the Franco regime at first favored self-sufficiency. It was only with the easing of trade restrictions in the 1950s that an impoverished Spain was able to enter a phase of modernization and growth.

Theory tells us that trade among nations is conducive to prosperity because production that is difficult and laborious in one country may be much easier in another. So, if countries concentrate on the tasks they can do best (or at least, cheapest), they should all fare better. A little analogy helps explain this: if your trade is shoemaking, you can easily make yourself a pair of shoes, but you will struggle to make yourself a coat. You are better off selling shoes to a tailor and paying him to make your coat. And so it is between countries.

Yet this simple theory does not always work well in practice. One difficulty is that a country that has a strong advantage in one particular product may become overdependent on it. Thus, because Cuba is particularly well suited to growing sugarcane, this was for a long time the country's dominant product and by far its largest export; hence the local saying: *sin azucar no hay pais* (without sugar there is no country). But that meant that Cuba was cruelly exposed to fluctuations in world sugar prices, as well as to the risk of bad harvests in this single all-important crop.

Libertarians today take it for granted that free trade and freedom go together. Yet in antebellum America, the opposite was the case! The South wanted free trade so as to have maximum opportunities to export its staple plantation crops. The North, however, favored protectionism, so that its budding industries could develop without undue competition from Europe. In the Old South, free trade in raw materials rhymed not with freedom and progress but with a primitive economy worked by slaves and relying heavily on the dominant export, cotton.[6]

Just as an exporting country may be in a perilous position when it depends too much on one product, so an importing country may have problems if it depends too much on one exporter. At the present time, this is painfully clear in the case of Ukraine, which depends heavily on Russia for supplies of natural gas. On a wider scale, we have the situation mentioned above of the rare earth metals; for these, countries throughout the world are almost totally dependent on China. In such situations, the dominant exporter has the opportunity to impose its wishes on its clients.

Again, rapid sprouting of an export industry in a low-cost country may wreck the industries of other countries. We shall see later how the explosive development of coffee growing in Vietnam in the 1990s brought misery for coffee farmers in Latin America and elsewhere. Oversupply in the world coffee market pushed prices down to rock-bottom levels; the result was that hundreds of thousands of small growers could no longer make a living. That kind of disaster can easily happen where there is no international regulation of output and prices. But free-market doctrine rules out such regulation.

Catholic Teaching on Trade

The official Catholic attitude toward free trade is by no means entirely negative. References in Vatican documents to *protectionism* (trade barriers that restrict imports to protect local industries) are infrequent, but virtually all of them show disapproval. Thus, for example, John Paul II, addressing a conference of the FAO (the Food and Agriculture Organization of the United Nations) in 1995, criticized "unjust criteria in the distribution of resources and production, policies formulated in order to safeguard special interest groups, or different forms of protectionism." Benedict XVI, in a letter to British prime minister Gordon Brown in 2009, called for avoidance of "solutions marked by any nationalistic selfishness or protectionism."

Papal teaching has, however, often criticized the way free trade works out in practice. In *Populorum Progressio* (par. 22), Pope Paul VI cites the Vatican II text *Gaudium et Spes* (par. 69): "God created the earth with everything in it for the use of all human beings and peoples. Thus, under the leadership of justice and in the company of charity, created goods should flow fairly to all."[7] The pope continues, "All other rights, whatever they may be, including the rights to property and free trade, are to be subordinated to this principle." This clearly implies that the principle of "fair" distribution should take precedence over that of "free" trade. And indeed, in the same encyclical (par. 59), the pope observes that "free trade can be called just only when it conforms to the demands of social justice."

In an intervention by the Holy See at a World Trade Organization conference, Cardinal Silvano Tomasi argued that "free trade is not an end in itself," and observed that "essential services such as health, education, water and food are not normal goods since citizens cannot choose not to use them without harm to themselves. . . . It is the task of the state to provide for the defense and preservation of common goods which cannot simply be addressed by market forces."[8]

Thus, in certain circumstances, the distribution of essential goods should be regulated by the state rather than left to the market. In the case of food, this principle may apply chiefly to crises of severe shortage, when foodstuffs have to be rationed; since otherwise they will trade at exorbitant prices beyond the reach of the poorer citizens.

With other products, there can be a longer-term need for regulation. Thus, if pharmaceutical companies are persuaded to sell patented drugs at sharply reduced prices in poor countries, then it is necessary to prohibit exports of these cheap supplies from the poor countries. Otherwise traders will buy them there and resell them in the rich countries at large profits. Thus they will deprive patients in the poor countries of access to these drugs.

The Vatican's *Ethical Guidelines for International Trade* (2003) explain that "free trade . . . is fair inasmuch as it allows developed and developing countries to benefit in the same way from participation in the global trading system." So free trading is acceptable only when it is beneficial to both parties. We know that, in practice, trade can exploit the poorer countries, if goods are bought from them at unfairly low prices. It can also damage the richer countries, whose industries may be destroyed by cheap imports. Free-market economists usually reject any accusation of damage to the richer countries, arguing that consumers living there benefit from cheap imports. But those economists have a one-sided view in which benefit to consumers is all that really matters; harm done to producers (workers) does not bother them. This attitude may conform with orthodox economic doctrine, but it is certainly not in accord with Catholic doctrine.

Free and Fair Trade in Coffee

Producers of raw materials such as farm crops and minerals are vulnerable to the sharp price fluctuations frequently experienced in commodity markets. For example, unstable prices can make life very hard for small coffee farmers in Latin America. This instability has various causes, some of them natural, some human. The main natural cause is the weather; crops are abundant in some years, meager in others, while demand for coffee is generally stable. Variable supply meeting steady demand: there you have a recipe for violent ups and downs in prices of raw coffee beans. And they can indeed be violent.

Another problem is that it takes several years for newly planted coffee trees to bear fruit. Farmers may respond to shortages and high prices by planting more trees; but once these trees reach maturity, it may be found that there are too many; then, oversupply will push prices down. And sometimes, when prices are low, farmers aggravate the situation by increasing their output in the hope that by selling more bags of beans, they will compensate for the low prices per bag.

Problems like these arise when coffee farmers behave as classical economic theory says they ought to behave; they do not coordinate their activities—each acts independently, ideally without knowing what the others are doing. Adam Smith proposed the odd notion that tradesmen in a Scottish town (and in his day, towns were tiny by our standards) "might never . . . be known to one another,"[9] and might therefore be unable to collude to keep their prices high. And, he thought, a jolly good thing too! But in coffee farming, this situation is quite possible; many growers are isolated from each other in small, remote hill farms. Even farmers in the same district may not know one another, and one farmer may have little or no idea of what the others are doing.

The outcome of this "blind" competition, as Smith frankly admitted, may well be a boon for consumers, but it is not pretty for producers.[10] In the coffee trade, as elsewhere, we see today the result of decades of addiction to economic strategies that indulge consumers but care little for the welfare of producers.

Can We Stabilize Prices?

The problems of free trade in coffee have encouraged attempts to create alternative systems. In the recent past, there was a large-scale plan to stabilize prices: the *International Coffee Agreement* (ICA), a treaty signed in 1962 by the main coffee-producing and coffee-consuming countries. The producers agreed to limit the quantities of coffee put on the market so as to sustain prices within certain specified limits. If they produced more than their agreed quotas, the surplus had to be stored in the hope of selling it later when supplies were scarcer and prices higher. If there was too much surplus to be stored, the excess was destroyed, either by burning it or by dumping it in rivers or in the sea, causing pollution of air or water. In Brazil, during the Great Depression, surplus coffee beans were sometimes burnt as fuel in railroad locomotives, no doubt regaling passengers with pleasing aromas. (With the demise of steam, this fragrant solution is no longer possible!) Despite the practical difficulties of implementing it, the 1962 agreement did have a certain real success in stabilizing prices around levels that gave a reasonable return to coffee farmers.

The ICA still exists, but it no longer attempts to regulate prices by imposing quotas. This practice was abandoned in 1989, ostensibly because the member countries could not agree on quota levels. But at that time, free-market ideology was all the rage; so many governments were disinclined even to try to regulate the coffee market. And the ICA's coffee price stabilization was motivated in part by the desire to avoid popular discontent (and consequent flirtation with communism) in Latin America and elsewhere. With the collapse of communism at the end of the 1980s, this excuse for flouting free-market principles faded away.

Without regulation, prices have been generally lower than under the ICA regime and have fluctuated very sharply. They have zigzagged between a peak of more than two dollars per pound in 1994 and a trough of just over forty cents in 2001.[11] During long periods of low prices, many small producers have suffered extreme hardship, and many have been forced out of business. And it is thought that the quality of coffee has deteriorated in many places through lack of investment.

Another Approach: "Fair Trade"

Following the breakdown of ICA price regulation, the "fair-trade" movement has tried another method of stabilizing prices. Unlike the ICA, a treaty between governments, this is a smaller-scale cluster of private initiatives that concerned only 5 percent of the US coffee market in 2012.[12]

But fair trade is growing fast. *Fairtrade International* is the coordinating and standard-setting body for fair-trade associations, such as *Fairtrade America* and (in Europe) *Max Havelaar*.[13] The annual reports of Fairtrade International show world coffee sales by member associations as 120,300 metric tons in 2011, as against just 15,800 in 2002. In nine years, sales have multiplied by nearly eight.[14]

The fair-trade system guarantees a minimum price (or the market price if it is higher), according to the rules of Fairtrade International. In some cases, premiums over the basic minimum price are payable.

Niche or Norm?

The fair-trade system operates without formal quotas or other arrangements for limiting production or keeping excess production off the market. When prices in the mainstream commercial market are depressed, fair-trade prices are higher than mainstream. These prices are not then "competitive"; *yet consumers pay them*. They do so because they believe that this is a more ethical way to drink coffee, and because fair-trade coffee is generally of better than average quality. To sell coffee beans on a fair-trade basis, farmers have to be small-scale growers who are members of democratically run cooperatives and conform with certain quality standards.

The price of raw coffee beans is a very small part of what you pay for a cup of coffee at the bar or a packet of coffee in the supermarket. This fact "sweetens the flavor" of fair trade for the coffee drinker. Even when the fair-trade price of coffee beans is double or triple the free-market price, the price of a cup or packet of fair-trade coffee should be only slightly higher than the price of free-market coffee of equivalent quality.

Yet fair trade as we know it has serious limitations. Its critics complain that it does little to help the poorest farmers, who usually are not members of well-organized cooperatives growing high-quality coffee. Again, it may be that the practice of paying higher than market prices encourages a certain amount of overproduction and thus depresses prices in the free market, making life even harder for those poor farmers who are not engaged in fair trade. And a system that appeals to rather limited numbers of coffee drinkers who are fussy about quality and willing to pay higher than normal prices for ethical reasons, may seem unlikely to develop into a mainstream system that can benefit the majority of farmers.

Sociologist Keith Brown, in a recent critical study of this topic, admits that "fair trade does have a positive impact on many producers' lives."[15] But he warns that "fair trade does not and probably will not be sufficient to lift producers out of poverty. The entrenched social problems in impoverished (largely agrarian) societies cannot be eliminated through the small economic premiums associated with fair trade."[16]

Another sociologist, April Linton, writing in the same year (2013), takes a more positive view. She admits that "Fair Trade coffee sells mostly within specialty markets," but adds that "it is noteworthy that Fair Trade chocolates and teas are successfully penetrating medium-quality, medium-price markets as well as high-end ones."[17] The range of products sold under fair-trade systems is widening; apart from coffee, chocolate, and tea, it now embraces rice, sugar, fresh fruits, cut flowers, cotton, wine, and other goods.

The Need to Regulate Production

In principle, it could be possible for fair trade in coffee and other crops to become the norm. But this cannot happen unless arrangements are put in place to regulate production on a worldwide basis, so as to avoid price-slashing gluts such as have clobbered coffee farmers in recent years. So long as fair trade remains a niche market, catering to buyers who are not fussy about price, it can maintain "just prices" even in periods of glut, when mainstream prices are temporarily much lower. But this will hardly work if fair trade becomes itself the mainstream. For normally, in any market where demand is stable, the only way to maintain stable prices is to stabilize supply.

We cannot avoid occasional shortages in the coffee market caused by erratic weather; for example, exceptional frosts in Brazil in 1994 drove prices very sharply upward for a time. But with careful international planning, we should be able to avoid massive gluts due to excessive production; these, after all, are caused by human behavior. Rock-bottom coffee prices in 2001 and subsequent years reflected expansion in Vietnamese (and to a lesser extent Brazilian) production: Vietnam's exports increased nearly tenfold, from 96,000 tons in 1992 to 930,000 in 2001.[18] This huge and very rapid growth clearly helped reduce poverty: "Since 1989 . . . the number and proportion of people in absolute poverty declined considerably. . . . Vietnam has a group of farmers in non-rice areas, in cash crops such as coffee and cashew, that . . . have incomes much higher than those of rice farmers."[19]

Sadly, reduction of poverty in Vietnam caused a serious increase in Latin American poverty. This is an example of what can all too easily happen in international trade. It highlights the need for international cooperation in economic development. Under free-market principles, every entrepreneur is supposed to do whatever seems to suit his or her own best interests, without consultation or cooperation (pejoratively called *collusion*) with other entrepreneurs, and without consideration of how his or her actions will affect those others. Likewise, governments may encourage development within their own countries with little regard to how it will affect other countries.

But development in one country can inflict serious damage on other countries—especially if the development is export based. Vietnam, a tea-drinking country which until recently grew little coffee, took only a few years to overtake Colombia as a coffee-producing country; now it is second only to Brazil in sheer volume, growing mainly for export. Could this perhaps be called "unfair competition"?

Coordinated Regulation

In *Centesimus Annus* (par. 58), John Paul II observed that "this increasing internationalization of the economy ought to be accompanied by effective international agencies which will oversee and direct the economy to the common good." The ICA before 1989 was indeed, to a certain degree, an *effective international agency* in which production quotas for each coffee-producing country were agreed on, with a view to maintaining stable prices—and thus an adequate livelihood for coffee growers everywhere.

Output and price regulation by the ICA, whatever its weaknesses, had one vitally important merit: it was done jointly by producing countries (Brazil, Colombia, Indonesia, Ethiopia, etc.) and by consuming countries (the biggest are in Europe and North America). The producers, as well as the consumers, had their seats at the negotiating table.

Today, without this regulation, the coffee market is for the most part managed by a few large American and European corporations which buy coffee beans, process them, and market the finished product. As Benoit Daviron and Stefano Ponte explain in *The Coffee Paradox*, "The bargaining power of operators based in consuming countries now allows them to dominate actors in producing countries, especially farmers and their governments. . . . In the coffee paradox, producers end up on the losing side of things."[20]

The "paradox" described by these writers is that "a coffee crisis in producing countries, with international prices at the lowest levels in decades" coexists with "a coffee renaissance (also known as the *latte* revolution) in consuming countries."[21] Things have gone wrong since bilateral regulation of the market was abandoned.

Here is an example of the "free trade that is not fair" that Paul VI deplored. Just as a "free labor market" can be unfair when employers are in a much stronger bargaining position than workers, so a "free commodity market" can be unfair when the buyers have much more bargaining power than the sellers (or vice versa).

The Reign of the Transnationals

Today, free trade and free international movement of capital are two of the main pillars of globalization and the dominance of transnational corporations. For example, an American motor manufacturer may design cars and plan their production in Michigan while delegating much of the manufacturing to (for example) subsidiary companies in eastern Europe, which in turn may buy many of their components from (for example) suppliers in southeast Asia. This strategy is possible because the American parent company, and its offshoots or trading partners in other countries, are able to move goods easily across national borders; and because the American company can readily provide capital, where necessary, to its overseas suppliers.

Here is the dream come true of the free marketeers and apostles of the religion of globalization. Its advantages are well known. It enables goods to be produced at the lowest possible costs for the benefit of consumers. It provides opportunities for poorer countries to develop new industries and thus, perhaps, to grow more prosperous. And it allows transnational corporations to make large profits by producing at Third World costs and selling at First World prices. Thus, "for a shirt selling at €25 in the boutique, the cost of labor to make it up in Bangladesh is €0.53," i.e., just over 2 percent of the retail price, according to Shahidul Islam Shahid, vice president of the National Garment Workers' Federation in Bangladesh.[22] Another estimate has suggested that the labor cost of a shirt could be a little as 1.2 percent of the retail price.[23]

We see here a major problem. Certain transnationals, having grown very powerful, can often dictate their own terms to their suppliers. As we have seen in the coffee market, the transnationals, as buyers of raw materials, often have vastly more bargaining power than those who actually produce the materials.

Moreover, these corporations are often in a position to impose their will on the governments of producing countries. For this there are three main reasons. First, the biggest corporations are simply bigger, in economic terms, than many countries; for example, the annual turnover of Netherlands-based foods group Unilever is in the region of $68 billion, which we may compare with the GDP of Paraguay ($36 billion) or of Uganda ($17 billion). Second, the larger corporations, because of their wealth, are better able than many other interest groups to lobby politicians effectively. Third, because of the present mobility of capital and freedom of trade, a corporation may often be in a position to blackmail a government: *we'll pull out if you don't oblige.*

A corporation that relentlessly minimizes its costs may be able to concentrate its production in countries that have the lowest wage rates and the worst conditions for workers. If the government of a low-wage country tries to impose better workplace standards, the corporation may frustrate it by shifting its operations (or its orders to subcontractors) elsewhere. The same goes for state regulations to protect the environment, enhance health and safety standards, etc. Thus, corporations may be able keep standards low where this is to their advantage. They may coerce governments and thus undermine democracy. This happens because, while governments are national, big corporations are transnational and footloose. Freedom of trade and capital movements between countries gives such corporations great flexibility.

This problem can be mitigated if a number of governments agree to impose consistent standards, or if there is a supranational authority that can impose such standards. But independent, democratic governments find it difficult to reach such agreements and to enforce them. And if the rules are imposed by a supranational body such as the World Bank or the International Monetary Fund, the objection may be raised that this process is undemocratic; we citizens do not elect the directors of the IMF.

Thus it appears that overpowerful transnationals can be a real threat to effective democracy as well as to decent conditions of employment, especially in the smaller and poorer countries. And the power of the transnationals depends largely on their ability to move goods and capital freely from country to country. We are reminded of Fr. Lacordaire's saying, "It is freedom that is oppressive and the law that sets free."[24] In international trade, it is well-balanced regulation that sets free.

Free Prices or Just Prices?

Free trade is a mechanism for minimizing production costs by concentrating every kind of production into the hands of those who can do it cheapest. Unfortunately, mainstream economists have turned this mundane mechanism into a quasi religion. They regard free trade as a sacrosanct principle, and they have persuaded too many of us to agree with them. This makes it difficult for alternative trading principles to be accepted in the worlds of academic economics, practical business, and politics. Here we have an example of the *misguided experts* principle that I mentioned in the introduction.

The notion that we must strive to minimize the cost of everything is one of the foundations of orthodox economic thought; so it has been ever since Adam Smith. It is based on the underlying assumption that we all want to be able to consume more; therefore, we must make everything cheaper so that we can afford more of everything. But the big problem today, at least in the world's richer economies, is that we are, by and large, consuming too much and thus overstraining the earth's resources. We consume wastefully, which suggests that what we consume is, in reality, too cheap. Yet we persist with our relentless pursuit of higher productivity and efficiency so as to make everything cheaper still so that we can consume still more! We need to heed the warning of John Paul II (*Centesimus Annus*, par. 37): "Man consumes the resources of the earth . . . in an excessive and disordered way."

Maximum "efficiency," as it is generally understood in economics today, is not always the best way. If we moved away from our obsession with efficiency and the *competition on price* that generates it, we would no longer need to be so obsessive about free trade and free markets. We could step back a few paces toward the lost world of agreed restraints on output and trade, with stabilized "fair" prices. This would be a better deal for us producers (workers). It would, of course, be a "worse" deal for us consumers, in the sense that we would not be able buy so many cheap but often low-quality and ephemeral products. But that would surely be better for the conservation of our planet's resources, for the benefit of future generations.

We have looked at two alternatives to conventional free trade: (a) internationally agreed constraints on output and prices, and (b) "fair trade." We have seen that (b) has limited potential without (a). Both approaches represent a partial rejection of conventional economics.

They discard the belief that the right price must always be whatever price is thrown up by the interplay of supply and demand in the marketplace. They appeal instead to the older, and more Catholic, idea that there is, for any article, a *just price* at which buyers and sellers should normally deal.

The "Just Price"

The scholastic theologians of the Middle Ages elaborated this idea, teaching that it is wrong for anything to be bought or sold at other than its "just price" (*justum pretium*): "To sell a thing for more than its worth, or to buy it for less than its worth, is in itself unjust and unlawful,"[25] as St. Thomas famously put it. There has been much dispute, however, over how we should assess the just price, or fair value, of any particular article.

Thomas points out that "the just price of things is not fixed with mathematical precision, but depends on a kind of estimate, so that a slight addition or subtraction would not seem to destroy the equality of justice."[26] Some neoconservative Catholics today try to argue that the scholastic theologians, when speaking of a just price, meant simply the market price. But that is implausible, since market prices are subject not merely to "slight" variations but often to very sharp movements.

In another place, Thomas discusses the comparison between the value of a house and that of a pair of shoes: "As many sandals must be exchanged for one house as the builder . . . exceeds the shoemaker in his labor and costs";[27] this implies that the true value of an artefact reflects the cost of labor and materials needed to make it. In the same text, however, he also states that things are valued in accordance with the demand for them: "They are priced according as man stands in need of them for his own use."[28]

Thus, Thomas endorsed two quite distinct methods of valuation: (a) cost of production, and (b) what buyers are willing to pay. Modern orthodox economics gives overwhelming preference to (b). But this method, if used exclusively, means that value is determined always in the marketplace, never in the workshop. This implies that we should not even attempt to keep prices in line with production costs; we should not be "fair traders" or negotiators of price-fixing agreements.

But we have seen how this approach can lead to producers receiving very inadequate prices—indeed, "unjust" prices—for their products.

It can also lead to highly unstable prices. We cannot, of course, simply ignore market valuations, which give us indications (though they are often erratic and volatile) of what buyers are willing to pay. It is clearly futile to persist in producing things at prices higher than buyers will generally swallow. Yet producers need to have their say too on the matter of pricing. Otherwise, powerful buyers may drive prices down to unjust levels, even to starvation levels. Medieval theologians, surprising as it may seem, knew better on this matter than many present-day economists.

We have to recognize that just price, or fair value, is an elusive concept that is not easily pinned down. Yet to evade this issue is irresponsible. For both practical and ethical reasons, we need to establish values for goods and services, and for the labor that goes into providing them, that are not merely attractive to buyers but tolerably fair to both buyers and sellers.

Free marketeers think they have an infallible short cut to solving this problem: just leave it to the market and accept whatever values the market throws up. Experience shows, however, that market values are erratic and can often be unreasonable and unacceptable. It has been estimated that in 2001, some 300,000 coffee farmers in Mexico were obliged to leave their land and seek work elsewhere because coffee prices were so depressed. Theorists in Chicago may argue that that's how the cookie crumbles. But they are not struggling to make a living by growing coffee in Mexico.

For fair-trade coffee, the guaranteed minimum price is calculated so that it covers the current and capital costs of sustainable production and enables small cooperative growers to earn a modest but decent income. Fair-trade coffee beans may, however, be sold at market price if this is higher than the guaranteed minimum. The essence of fair trading is not to make prices absolutely rigid but to put a floor under price at a level that yields a living wage to the producer.

Thus the fair-trade movement, like the ICA in the era of regulation, expects consumers to pay at least what is deemed to be a "just price" based on production costs, even though the free-market price may sometimes be cheaper. Here we have a clear divergence from normal free-market behavior. We have a system that invites the consumer to consider the "common good" rather than exclusively one's own personal advantage.

The Role of Politics

Capitalism will be a tyranny whenever wealth is not balanced by strong government.

—Michael Walzer[1]

Present-day conservatives . . . wrongly assume that rolling back the power of the national government would liberate individuals to pursue their own ends, instead of leaving them at the mercy of economic forces beyond their control.

—Michael Sandel[2]

Does Economics Need Politics?

The libertarians' dream is the castration of politics. Aristotle's vision of the state, "originating in the bare needs of life, and continuing in existence for the sake of a good life,"[3] is not for them. Neither is that of America's founding fathers, "may God grant that we may be able to gratify them [the American people] by establishing a wise and just Government."[4] They believe that the state is by nature bad; that the private-sector economy, and society as a whole, can run themselves very well without interference by meddling politicians. They have inherited the startlingly naïve view of one of the leading economists of the French Enlightenment, the lawyer and colonial administrator Pierre-Paul Mercier de la Rivière (1728–1794):

> It is of the essence of order that the private interest of an individual can never be separated from the common interest of everyone, and this is what happens under the regime of freedom. *Thus the world runs itself*. The desire for enjoyment imprints upon Society a movement which becomes a perpetual

tendency towards the best possible state . . . the maintenance of property rights and of liberty causes the most perfect order to reign, without the help of any other law.[5]

Here we see *laissez-faire* in its purest form. Leave everyone free to pursue their private, personal interests and all will be well. As Charles Gide remarks in a classic French history of economic doctrine, "The optimism of the French school is thus characterized by an absolute faith in liberty."[6] But this is the liberty of the libertarians—the absence of restraint and constraint—rather than liberty as Catholic teaching understands it, the *power to do good*. Moreover, Gide observes in the philosophy of this school "a certain hardness with regard to the miseries of the people . . . a certain tendency to believe that these miseries are due to their own faults."[7] This is a tendency that proponents of *laissez-faire* have never abandoned.

A Free World without Borders

It is not surprising that libertarians love the idea of worldwide free trade and free capital movements. For not only is this seen to foster maximum economic efficiency; it is also a recipe for minimum political power. International economic freedom can stymie national governments. Any state that tries to impose better than average standards in economic matters, such as fairer treatment of workers, better public services, or stronger protection of the environment, finds that businesses move out of its jurisdiction, escaping to countries that have less demanding standards and therefore lower costs. Free trade makes it easy for companies to have their work done in the countries where wages, taxes, and social security contributions are least; they can import what they need from these countries instead of producing it locally. Free capital movement allows firms to shift their assets to countries with low tax rates and individuals to hide their investments in similar places. Not so long ago, we saw something of a "race to the bottom" in tax rates, as governments cut their rates in the hope of keeping businesses on board. But this contributed to budget deficits, excessive debts, and deterioration in public services.

The City of London objects to stricter regulation of banking and investment, arguing that bankers and fund managers can emigrate to New York or Zurich if they find business in London too difficult. The

French government tried recently to make high-income residents pay 75 percent income tax on the top slice of their incomes; the result was that some of the victims rapidly became nonresidents.

With nasty phenomena like the former Berlin Wall and the present isolation of North Korea in mind, we tend to take it for granted that nonrestrictive borders must be desirable. Many people would like to see a *world without borders*; in principle, the idea is indeed attractive. Unfortunately, it would make life too easy for terrorists, drug traders, tax evaders, and crooks. It would also mean that countries would have little ability to impose any standards higher than the lowest.

If the absence of border controls causes too many problems, there are essentially two solutions. One is the reinstatement of controls; the other is greater cooperation between nations. The British government, habitually uncooperative with its Continental partners, wants tighter supervision of travel between Britain and the Continent. But this would run counter to the spirit and the treaties of the European Union.

Fuller international cooperation seems a better way. Countries that choose to maintain open borders with each other should agree to keep their tax rates, social legislation, and environmental standards broadly in line so that businesses are not tempted to congregate in the "cheapest" jurisdictions. This means that a spirit of international cooperation, rather than competition, should prevail.

The Role of Politics

Behind all this discussion there lurks a very basic question: how far should economic behavior be regulated by the political sphere? This is a controversial topic, and so it has been ever since the birth of *laissez-faire* ideology in the eighteenth century. It is controversial because the economists of the Age of Enlightenment proposed a theory that was then novel and unorthodox. And though later, in various periods (including our own), it has been widely accepted, it has always been problematic and has always provoked objections.

This theory holds that an economy can, and should, function with minimal control or interference by political authorities. The economy should, so far as possible, be separated from politics and left to look after itself. In recent times, libertarians and anarcho-capitalists have revived this theory in even stronger forms than were current in the past. But experience has too often shown that economic and financial systems, left to themselves, can develop serious malfunctions and can even go disastrously wrong.

In earlier times, even until quite recently, economics had another name: it was called *political economy*. For the word *economy* comes from the Greek *oikonomía* = "household management"; so its original meaning was simply domestic. Economy, we may say, meant looking after a household's material resources and needs. To this day, in a French college, hospital, or religious community, the "housekeeping" income and expenditure is managed by a person called the *économe*.

From the seventeenth century onward, the phrase *political economy* came into use, meaning the management of the material resources not merely of a private household or small community but of an entire state or country, a *pólis* or polity. It implied that this was a matter that concerned national politics. Government had a duty to take care of its country's "housekeeping."

The first writer to mention *political economy* seems to have been the colorful character Antoine de Montchrestien (1575–1621). Son of an apothecary in Normandy, in a brief but adventurous life he wrote poetry and drama, fought duels, acquired a dubious baronial title, manufactured steel products, engaged in trade, and met his end supporting a group of Huguenot (Protestant) rebels. He also found time to write a substantial treatise on political economy, published in 1615.

Montchrestien held the traditional view that political economy required extensive involvement by the political authorities. The state was expected to support and develop industries, to regulate trades and professions, to impose tariffs to protect French industry, and to ensure a sufficiency of suitably trained persons to supply the various industries with the skills they needed. He remarked that "the ancients" (the classical Greek philosophers and others) had assumed that a proper distribution of skills and abilities would be provided, as it were, by fate or by the stars: "It is true that, to excuse those great men for their negligence in this matter, one may say . . . that it was due to a received opinion they held, according to which the common necessity, which was the origin of the Arts [skills], would of itself regulate and solve this problem . . . without any provision by the political authority."[8]

Thus Montchrestien recognized, and rejected, the notion that government could afford to leave the economy alone. In this he was in tune with the prevalent thinking of his day. Later, during the lengthy reign (1643–1715) of Louis XIV, the king's finance minister Jean-Baptiste

Colbert (1619–1683) became renowned for his promotion of muscular state-directed economic strategies.

Yet, even in the seventeenth century, the idea that the state should disengage from the economy had begun to emerge. The phrase *laissez-faire* is said to date from around 1680, when Colbert asked a group of merchants what the government could do to help them. One of them, a certain François Legendre, replied: *laissez-nous faire!* (leave us to do our own thing).[9]

The Age of Reason

From the late seventeenth century and into the eighteenth, we enter the *Age of Enlightenment*, or *Age of Reason*. This was an age preoccupied with discovery of the "laws of nature"; in particular, with the laws of physics, so named from the Greek word for nature, *phúsis*. But in those days the science of physics was usually called "natural philosophy," as in the title of Sir Isaac Newton's great treatise on astronomy, *The Mathematical Principles of Natural Philosophy* (1687).

This kind of study enthralled and fascinated intellectual society. Here at last were basic truths that could be discovered by observation of real objects, such as stars and planets, and by the use of reason, logic, and mathematics. This new science pushed traditional religion aside. Rationalism appealed strongly to an age weary of the bitter theological controversies and religious strife of the Reformation and its aftermath. It proposed truths that could be proved beyond reasonable doubt, rather than doctrines that rested largely on faith, giving rise to endless disputes between diverse understandings and opinions on religious texts and traditions.

Rationalist Economics

How did all this affect political economy? In the Middle Ages, economics was discussed in ethical terms by St. Thomas and other theologians, as it had been by the Greeks before them. It was indeed considered as a branch of ethics, dominated by the search for the "just price" that made each transaction fair to both sides. The aim of economic theory and practice was thus to achieve justice or fairness in dealings between buyers and sellers, between employers and employees.

But in the eighteenth century, economics began to be seen as a science that could be studied by methods like those of physics. Adam Smith was by profession a moral philosopher,[10] not a physicist; but he had a tremendous admiration for Newton. In an early essay, *The History of Astronomy*, he wrote that "the system of Sir Isaac Newton . . . [has] gained the general and complete approbation of mankind . . . as the greatest discovery that ever was made by man."[11] This discovery was that the movements of the celestial bodies can be explained and predicted by means of a "one capital fact," namely, Newton's law of gravity.

Accordingly, Smith developed a somewhat "Newtonian" approach to the study of the economy. He saw it, to a certain extent, as a mechanistic system, with the famous *invisible hand* playing a role like that of the law of gravity in astronomy. Smith, however, was on the whole a practical and realistic economist; he knew better than to imagine that the invisible hand could be trusted always to guide us to the best possible outcome.

Since Smith's day, economics has become more like astronomy. It has become a science that depends heavily on intricate mathematics, as you can see by examining almost any modern academic paper or textbook on economics. The comparison with physics has been persistent. In 1900, the distinguished French economist Léon Walras wrote that "It is now quite certain that . . . mathematical economics will take its place beside astronomy and mathematical mechanics."[12] In 2005, at the World Social Forum in Porto Alegre, Olivio Dutra asserted that "the law of the market is like the law of gravity." He is no right-wing anarcho-capitalist; he is a leading Brazilian trade unionist and a founding member of the *Partido dos Trabalhadores* (workers' party).

In its essence, pure classical theory sees the economy as a mechanistic system. It is said to behave, like the solar system, in an orderly, invariable, and predictable manner so long as we do not perversely interfere with it. This theory has grown deep and widespread roots; as we have seen, today even some left-wingers believe in it! But its main supporters have been the classical economists (Adam Smith and others); their successors, the neoclassicals like Milton Friedman and his colleagues of the "Chicago School"; and the theorists of the "Austrian School" like Ludwig von Mises, Friedrich von Hayek, and Murray Rothbard.

But we are digressing; it is time to get back to the eighteenth century. This was the age when classical free-market theory developed simultaneously in Scotland, with Adam Smith and his fellow philosopher David Hume, and in France, with François Quesnay, Anne-Robert-Jacques Turgot, and Jean-Baptiste Say. We have seen that the intellectual climate of the age was unfriendly to revealed religion. But it embraced with enthusiasm the concept of "laws of nature" that are believed to be grounded in the very nature of things and people, and therefore universally valid. These laws belong to no particular time or place. We did not make them and cannot change them; it is for us to do our best to discover what they are and to abide by them. Newton's law of gravity is clearly a law of nature. Economists came to believe that there are similar laws, equally universal, in economics.

Classical Theory Has Radical Consequences

What follows from that notion? If the economy is in fact ruled by fundamental laws of nature, then clearly there should be no interference with the working of those laws. Neither by individuals, nor by governments, nor by civic organizations such as guilds or unions. It is futile to attempt to go against laws of nature. Try getting water to run uphill or electricity to pass through cotton thread.

But if we insist that economics, like physics, is ruled by inescapable natural laws, then we have a big problem. For the result is that *economics is divorced from ethics*. Economic good behavior is not a matter of doing what is morally right; it is simply a matter of acting in accordance with the laws of nature. For example, we have seen (chap. 6 above) how classical economists such as Turgot and Ricardo asserted that the natural and normal rate of wages for laborers was just enough to provide for the survival of a working class of unchanging size. We have seen, too, how the later Austrian School economists such as Carl Menger claimed that the normal free-market wage rate was that which the stingiest employer was willing to pay, even though that might not be enough to live on. If one believes that these statements represent "laws of nature," then it follows that employers can feel justified in paying no more than rock-bottom wages. They have no need to provide "remuneration . . . such that man may be furnished with the means to cultivate worthily his own material, social, cultural and spiritual life and that of his dependents" as Catholic teaching demands (*Gaudium et Spes*, par. 67).

But in *Quadragesimo Anno* (par. 4), Pius XI had harsh words for those in the upper classes who thought that exorbitant inequalities were "the result of inexorable economic laws," and that these laws permitted them to enjoy "abundant riches" while "the workers . . . crushed by their hard lot, were barely enduring it."

The question, therefore, is whether these so-called "economic laws" really are inescapable, unchanging laws of nature. The old "iron law of wages" was based on the observation that workers raised bigger families when they had more money; not because more children were actually born, but because, in more affluent conditions, more of them survived and grew to maturity. In periods of prosperity, the working class expanded until there was an oversupply of labor; then wages fell, and increasing poverty led to more children dying very young. Adam Smith remarked that "poverty, though it does not prevent the generation, is extremely unfavorable to the rearing of children. . . . It is not uncommon . . . in the Highlands of Scotland for a mother who has borne twenty children not to have two alive."[13]

But that was in the days when reliable methods (natural or artificial) of family planning were unknown. Today, at least in the more developed countries, they are in general use; and, as we noted in chapter 8, the Catholic Church approves the practice of family planning, so long as it is done in a responsible manner and by natural methods.

In practice, it is generally observed that, as populations grow more affluent, birth rates decline; whereas, in the days of Smith and Ricardo, rising prosperity left birth rates little changed, while survival rates improved. It follows that the "iron law of labor," far from being an immutable law of nature, has become largely irrelevant. Greater affluence leads not to population growth but to stability or even decline. One may indeed say that the "iron law" has been stood on its head. It turns out to be an aspect of human behavior, not a fixed law of nature. Remember Franklin Roosevelt's remark, "Economic laws are not made by nature, they are made by human beings."

Is it not reasonable that the economy should, to some degree at least, be governed by the consensus of the citizenry, acting through the machinery of politics? If we reject this idea, then we are stuck with the situation where our society is not what most of us would like it to be; it is merely what arises unintentionally from our individual behaviors as we each seek what we think is best for ourselves.

Of course, if you believe in the theory that what best suits each individual person (or firm) is always the best for all of us, then you will be happy to accept that. According to Adam Smith, that theory "frequently" holds good; but he never said that it always holds good. And we know that it does not. It may suit us as individuals to go to downtown Manhattan comfortably in our own cars rather than in crowded subway trains; but we know that if we all tried to do that, traffic would be so jammed that nobody could go anywhere. It may suit each business to pay its workers as little as possible; but we see that the result of many firms doing that (and unrestrained competition sometimes compels them to do so) is a population of miserable, discontented, underpaid workers, who need help from the public subventions that libertarians decry, and who cannot afford to buy what our businesses are trying to sell.

Untidy Mixtures

Fortunately, we do not have to choose between two mutually exclusive systems: on the one hand the total deregulation favored by free-market zealots, on the other hand total regulation and central planning. In practice, virtually every society lives with an untidy mixture of both. We plan and control some things; we leave others to (more or less) free markets. Not even the Soviet Union succeeded in planning everything. It had an extensive undergrowth of markets, with varying degrees of legitimacy. They handled a very wide range of items ranging from everyday consumer goods and services to industrial materials and components.[14] In general, unofficial markets were tolerated because they provided things that everyone, including loyal communist planners, wanted, but that the planned economy could not readily provide.

In capitalist economies, free enterprise in its normal for-profit form coexists with public-sector operations, cooperatives, and not-for-profit organizations. Freely negotiated individual pay rates coexist with legally prescribed minimum rates and with other rates negotiated by labor unions.

Academic economists tend to dislike these untidy mixtures. They feel that there should be a single, intellectually coherent recipe that can be applied to the entire economy. Classical Marxists wanted universal planning and the disappearance of markets. Modern proponents of "democratic Marxism" have envisaged a world in which essentially all major economic activity would be planned, in a democratic fashion, by the workers: "The system we have described would not yet be a 'pure' socialism. . . . It would still be a transition towards socialism. . . . Private and cooperative enterprises would survive in small-scale production."[15] Pure, thoroughbred socialism would presumably have no place even for small-scale capitalist or cooperative enterprise.

Likewise, the more extreme free marketeers argue that everything should be done their way. According to Hayek, "Competition and central direction become poor and inefficient tools if they are incomplete. . . . A mixture of the two means that neither will really work and that the result will be worse than if either system had been consistently relied upon."[16] Since Hayek detested central planning, that socialist bugbear, clearly he wanted the entire economy to run on the basis of free competitive markets.

But it is clear in Catholic teaching that private enterprise and state regulation are both necessary.

Pope Benedict XVI

In *Deus Caritas Est* (par. 26), Pope Benedict vigorously insists on the essential role of the state in building a just society. "The pursuit of justice must be a fundamental norm of the state. . . . The aim of a just social order is to guarantee to each person . . . his share of the community's goods."

But how can we achieve a just social order? Libertarians argue that the only way to have a free society is to leave it to the unhampered market to create a "spontaneous order," as Hayek put it.[17] Yet they themselves do not claim that this market order is "just." Hayek even wrote that, in a free-market system, "the question of whether the resulting distribution of incomes is just or unjust has no meaning."[18] In our quest for a just society, Hayek and his kind offer us no help at all.

Indeed, Milton Friedman and his wife Rose were brutally frank about this: they wrote that "there is a fundamental conflict between the *ideal* of 'fair shares' . . . and the *ideal* of personal liberty."[19] You can, perhaps, have economic justice (fair shares), or you can have freedom; but you cannot have both. And for the Friedmans, "freedom" was clearly what mattered; social or economic justice were of secondary importance; they were indeed little more than vague notions that could in no way be clearly defined.

The Friedmans ridiculed the very notion of fair shares, claiming that this would mean making everyone the same. Fairness, however, does not really mean that everyone has to have the same amounts of income and capital; that would be unnatural and impracticable, if only because human personalities are so different. What fairness means is (among other things) that exorbitant inequalities should be avoided, especially if they mean that the people at the bottom of the pyramid suffer severe deprivation.

Pope Benedict has a clear answer (*Deus Caritas Est*, par. 28): "A just society must be the achievement of politics." Achieving a fair distribution of property is a political task; the Church's duty is "to offer . . . her own specific contribution towards understanding the requirements of justice and achieving them politically."

"To take a stand for the common good," says the pope in *Caritas in Veritate* (par. 7), "is on the one hand to be solicitous for, and on the other hand to avail oneself of, that complex of institutions that give structure to the life of society, juridically, civilly, politically and culturally, making it the *pólis*, or 'city.'" Thus the common good is not achieved simply by individuals doing the right things in their own corners and handing out suitable amounts of cash to the beggars. It requires us to diagnose and correct the faults in the structure of our society, in the way its various institutions function. This, says the pope, "is the institutional path—we may also call it the political path—of charity, no less excellent and effective than the kind of charity which encounters the neighbor directly." Accordingly, "every Christian is called to practice this charity, in a manner corresponding to his vocation and according to the degree of influence he wields in the *pólis*."

Here is an understanding of the common good that challenges the views of many "conservative" thinkers today, who argue that no good can come through political action; for this could interfere with our individualistic negative freedom, and government is anyway incurably incompetent. Instead, they say, we must rely wholly on individual good behavior and private charity.

Pope Francis

In *Evangelii Gaudium* we meet again this crucial topic of structure. Paragraph 202 of this exhortation is brief, but it is so fundamental and challenging that I quote it almost in its entirety:

> The need to resolve the structural causes of poverty cannot be delayed . . . because society needs to be cured of a sickness that is weakening and frustrating it, and which can lead to new crises. Welfare projects, which meet certain urgent needs,

should be considered merely temporary responses. As long as the problems of the poor are not radically resolved by rejecting the absolute autonomy of markets and financial speculation and attacking the structural causes of inequality, no solution will be found for the world's problems, nor for that matter for any problems. Inequality is the root of social ills.

Here the pope develops a theme that he had already touched on a little earlier in the same text (par. 188): "The word *solidarity* . . . refers to something more than a few sporadic acts of generosity. It presumes the creation of a new mindset which thinks in terms of community and the priority of the life of all over the appropriation of goods by a few." In particular, the pope calls for more adequate wages for poor workers (par. 192): "A just wage enables them to have adequate access to all the other goods that are destined for our common use"; and here he refers back to John XXIII's *Mater et Magistra*, which, as we have seen, calls not only for just rates of pay but also for workers to share in the ownership of the firms that employ them.

With Pope Francis, even more clearly than with his predecessors, we have come a long way from the old religious attitude that Christians had to accept the status quo and concentrate on helping those who suffered from it; trying to change society was not part of their duty. Yet sadly, there are many who still think that way. There are many who complain that changing society requires political action, as Pope Benedict explicitly stated; they deploy their contempt for government and state this as a reason for not proposing, or accepting, any such action. Are they, perhaps, using their libertarian philosophy as an excuse to avoid reforms that might cost them something extra in higher taxes, or in better treatment of their employees, or in higher prices for consumer goods?

CHAPTER 14

Stability and Change

The free-market approach can indeed serve as the motor of change, but . . . the costs are immediate and tend to be levied on the weakest members of the population. The benefits arrive with time and tend to go to the most talented people.

—Stefano Zamagni[1]

The Tension between Stability and Change

Human nature is torn between the desire for continuity and the thirst for novelty. There have always been tensions between those who love tradition and those who find it deadening; between those who fear change and those who welcome it; between those who want to preserve the existing order and those who want to abolish it, who even dream of "maintaining the revolution in permanence,"[2] as Karl Marx and his comrades put it.

It seems that most of us, most of the time, are less than enthusiastic about change. I once asked a psychoanalyst friend whether she had many patients who complained of stresses induced by continual change and upheaval in their working lives. Not surprisingly, her answer was a clear *yes*. I then put it to her that, in my opinion, most people dislike too many changes. But my friend did not agree. She maintained that, in her opinion, most people dislike any change whatsoever!

That is probably an overstatement. A more mainstream view would be that most of us appreciate novelty and change up to a point, but do not want too much of it. We tend to be "conservative" in the basic nonpolitical sense of the word; we prefer what is familiar. Especially in religious matters. Many churchgoers will have seen how a new parish priest who makes a few minor changes of detail in the way Mass is celebrated on Sunday morning risks provoking irate complaints, or even departures, from his congregation!

Stability Disfavored

Nevertheless, the prevailing ideology of our times is, in many ways, positively hostile to stability. It encourages, even demands, chronic discontinuity and incessant mutation in every aspect of our lives. A major late twentieth-century tendency in philosophy and the arts, known as *postmodernism*, "doesn't lament the idea of fragmentation, provisionality or incoherence, but rather celebrates that. The world is meaningless? Let's not pretend that art can make meaning then, let's just play with nonsense."[3] The high rates of divorce in most Western societies today suggest that many people set rather a low value on stability in personal relationships. The dearth of religious vocations is another sign of our aversion to long-term, stable commitments. In the business world, unrestrained competition stimulates perpetual upheaval and change.

Free-market economist Friedrich von Hayek, a favorite guru of Ronald Reagan and Margaret Thatcher, was a passionate advocate of market-driven change. Progress, he insisted, is "movement for movement's sake."[4] He lambasted his opponents for their "fear of uncontrolled social change," arguing for "preparedness to let change run its course even if we cannot predict where it will lead," and for "faith in the spontaneous forces of adjustment, which makes the libertarian[5] accept changes without apprehension, even though he does not know how the necessary adjustments will be brought about."

That is an excellent description of an attitude that is widespread among free marketeers. They have a blind faith in the notion that, if we strip away constraints and let the markets rip, then somehow—they do not even pretend to know how—it will all work out for the best.

A good story concerning Hayek is told by Richard Cockett in *Thinking the Unthinkable*, a lively history of the resurgence of libertarian economics in Britain from the 1970s onward. Cockett describes a visit by Margaret Thatcher in 1975 to the Conservative Research Office in London. Finding that some of the researchers showed too little commitment to free-market ideals, she took from her briefcase a copy of Hayek's magnum opus, *The Constitution of Liberty*. Thumping the table with that tome, she declared: "*This* is what we believe."[6] But the final chapter of that tome is a vehement essay titled "Why I Am Not a Conservative"!

I have often recounted this tale to British Conservatives, whose reactions were incredulous. But Hayek, on this point, was right; his philosophy is, in reality, anything but conservative. Unleashing free markets destroys stability, or "conservatism" in the basic sense of the word. It leads to tumultuous and often very troublesome changes. Yet devotees of Hayek's dogma persist in calling themselves Conservatives (in Britain) or conservatives (across of the Atlantic)!

Theology and Change

The adage "change is the only sign of life" is a favorite with enthusiasts for change; it is attributed to the great nineteenth-century English churchman Cardinal Henry Newman. But it seems not to be one of his wiser sayings. Many changes, after all, can hardly be called signs of life. We see changes in inanimate or lifeless things: rusting iron, rotting timber, weathering stone, evaporating water; a decaying corpse changes much faster than a living body.

The present-day discomfort with the notion of stability even extends, with some thinkers, to their conception of God. Scripture and tradition assure us that God himself is changeless. Thus we read, "For I the LORD do not change; therefore you, O sons of Jacob, are not consumed" (Mal 3:6); and "Every good endowment and perfect gift is from above, coming down from the Father of lights, with whom there is no variation or shadow due to change" (Jas 1:17). A famous old hymn, attributed to St. Ambrose (340–397), begins:

> O strength and stay, upholding all creation,
> who ever dost thyself unmoved abide.[7]

St. Thomas explains, "Anything that is moved [or changed] acquires something by its movement, and extends to something to which it did not extend before. But since God is infinite, containing in himself the fullness of perfection of all being, he cannot acquire anything, nor extend to anything to which he did not previously extend. Hence movement does not belong to God."[8]

Yet certain modern theologians reject the idea of an unchanging God. They prefer to believe in a God who is himself subject to change, who undergoes change as a result of interaction with his own creation. This view is a key feature of *process theology*, a school of thought associated with the English mathematician and philosopher Alfred North Whitehead (1861–1947) and his American follower Charles Harteshorne (1897–2000).

This notion is far from new; the first Council of Nicaea, in 325, pronounced an anathema against those who "affirm that the Son of God is subject to change or alteration";[9] the fourth Council of Lateran, in 1215, thought it necessary to reaffirm the belief that God is "unchangeable."[10] The theory that God undergoes change would appear to deny the timelessness of God's eternity. For change occurs along the line of time; therefore, if eternity is timeless, it must be changeless; as St. Thomas tells us, "Eternity knows no succession of events, the whole exists simultaneously."[11] That does not mean that Heaven is a monotonous place with no variety; on the contrary, in timeless eternity, all good things are present together and always.

The Catholic Church, and normally other churches too, hold that divine eternity is outside and beyond earthly time: "At the end of time, the Kingdom of God will come in its fullness" (*Catechism*, par. 1042). It follows logically that God is, indeed, unchanging. The heterodox view that God's eternity is not timeless, and therefore that God changes, seems to reflect the obsession with change and rejection of stability that are characteristic of so much present-day thinking.

At Berne University of the Arts, in Switzerland, the organist and composer Daniel Glaus has designed a curious organ, on which you can vary the loudness of the notes by pressing the keys down more or less far. This is quite different from the normal organ, where you depress the keys as far as they will go, and the volume of sound does not change until you change the stops. This steadiness, or stability, of organ tone has often been thought particularly suitable for religious music, since it seems to reflect the unchanging nature of God.

But Glaus has designed his peculiar instrument because, he says, contemporary composers no longer write music for the conventional church or concert-hall organ. They feel frustrated by the stability, or inflexibility, of its tone. They are like present-day employers, always urging their workers to more and more flexibility! Here is yet another example of today's dislike of stability. And the creators of the Berne organ claim that it is in tune with certain trends in modern theology. We can hazard a guess as to what they mean.

Anti-Institutionalism

Our modern aversion to stability manifests itself in widespread *contempt for institutions*. Leading French sociologist Bruno Latour, writing in 2002, launched a withering tirade against this attitude: "Ah! The institution, the only real scapegoat of the last century! It is described always as tyrannical, archaic, worn-out, dominating, smothering, castrating, hierarchical, obsolete, sterile, legalistic, formalistic. . . . There is hardly a contemporary who has not wanted to break away from it to 'find' at last freedom, fecundity, initiative, progress, spiritual authenticity."[12]

This florid language may seem a little overblown, but Latour has a point. Change lovers do indeed have a chronic tendency to abhor institutions, which by their nature tend to be "conservative." In particular, sarcastic comments on the "institutional church" abound in modern religious publications. Those who think themselves "progressive" seem at times to want a "Church" that has no institutional structure and no agreed or established doctrine; a "Church" that resembles an informal discussion and social work group, rather than a movement that preserves and transmits a revelation, upholding the philosophy and moral standards based thereon.

Without structure, discipline, and continuity, how could the authentic teachings, traditions, and understandings of Christianity have been preserved through the ages? A famous saying is attributed to Jean Monnet, one of the founding fathers of the European Community: "Nothing is possible without individuals, but nothing lasts without institutions." Christianity, based on the teachings of the individual Jesus, also embodies the vision and inspiration of many other individuals: the Hebrew prophets and the New Testament writers, followed by the great theologians and mystics of later centuries. It is the institution of the Church that has preserved, transmitted, and interpreted this great corpus of history and doctrine for succeeding generations, assuring their continuity. And though continuity implies stability, it can, and should, embrace development in our understanding of the original texts.

Religious Fundamentalism

While some people feel that religion, like economics, should welcome continual, unfettered change, many others seek in their religion an escape from this febrility. The current global epidemic of religious fundamentalism and extremism seems to be, in part, a visceral reaction against a world that is changing faster than many people can tolerate. They seek stability in reversion to antique traditions, rules, and customs, and in rigidly literal readings of ancient texts. Do these archaisms make sense today? The question seems to be irrelevant. All that matters is that they provide clear, stable guidelines that are believed to have divine authority.

While this kind of reactionary thinking has become prominent recently in the Muslim world, it is far from being exclusively a Muslim problem. We see counterparts to Islamic fundamentalism among Christians of various kinds, some of them Catholics; in ultraorthodox Judaism; in certain trends in Hinduism and Buddhism. According to academic Niels Nielsen, "The distinguishing feature of all fundamentalisms has been their defensiveness against modernity."[13]

Historian Laurence Kaplan writes that "social theorists have long recognized that the breakdown of rural community life leaves rootless people with problems of identity, nostalgic for past associations, and susceptible to simplistic alternatives to anomie. . . . Fundamentalism, because of its easily comprehended appeal, remains one of the alternatives that people in various cultures seize when encountering the diverse traumas of modernity."[14]

French academic Mokhtar ben Barka has observed that "fundamentalism is in evidence worldwide in societies that are in economic, political or cultural crisis, affected by rapid evolution. . . . It expresses not only religious feeling but also a state of frustration, of resentment, of being thrown off balance by social, political and cultural changes."[15]

Some may argue that this merely shows what happens when people living in backward societies come into contact with the modern world. We, they think, born and brought up in advanced societies, should be able to live with tumultuous changes; we have no excuse for trying to resist them. Such complacency is foolish. Some of the worst examples of religious extremism can be found among Christians in the United States.

Economic Instability and Its Consequences

In the dreamworld of the ultralibertarians and anarcho-capitalists, everything is in a state of continual and ever-accelerating change. The prices of everything vary every few minutes; every new gadget or piece of software is obsolete within a few weeks; nobody's job lasts more than a few months. We are obliged to live in a world of never-ending, ever-faster transformation.

To some extent, this "dream" has already come true. Continuously fluctuating prices have long been normal on British and American stock exchanges; more recently they have been adopted in the markets of Continental Europe.[16] They are now usual for airline fares and widespread for hotel room rates. In Silicon Valley, new products are seldom at the cutting edge for more than a few weeks. Very short-term employment is becoming more and more prevalent.

Stability, libertarians think, is a sign of ossification. If we do not accept constant changes in our way of life, our habits of work, the things we buy, the recreations we enjoy, then we must be culturally and spiritually moribund. It is not hard to see why these people demand maximum competition in our economies. For all-out competition is inherently destabilizing. In a world of pure, untrammeled competition, every business is under constant threat from competitors that want to grab its customers. Theory holds that in this situation, the consumer gets ever-better value for his dollar as firms compete to provide cheaper products and, of course, continual *innovation*.

The best way to gain a competitive edge in the marketplace is to offer products that differ somewhat from those of your competitors, claiming that yours are *innovative, cutting-edge, state-of-the-art* or some such buzzword. Thus, free competition stimulates change. Indeed, it creates a situation in which businesses cannot survive without ceaseless change. Change becomes an end in itself. And all this is promoted by people who call themselves "conservatives"!

The French philosopher Jean-Michel Besnier argues that, up until the mid-twentieth century, technical innovations such as electricity, automobiles, aircraft, and washing machines generally enhanced human well-being; however, more recently, technologists have designed things solely because they are marketable, "not because they satisfy a need, but because they benefit from a favorable balance of forces in economic competition."[17] Not because there is any real need or desire for them; merely because they help firms get ahead of each other in the competition stakes.

Technological Change

Innovations in technology are clearly among the most destabilizing elements in present-day societies. Historically, such novelties have brought major human progress, and they continue to do so; but nasty, or even disastrous, side effects have been far from rare. In our rush to promote technological "progress," we have inflicted on ourselves extreme pollution, occasional catastrophes in nuclear power stations, medicines that have turned out to be pathogenic, environmental destruction, and severe unemployment in trades and industries that technology has made obsolete.

A recent report[18] by business consultants McKinsey, named, with commendable frankness, *Disruptive Technologies*, suggests that "automation of knowledge work" could potentially eliminate up to 140 million full-time jobs (or an equivalent amount of part-time employment) worldwide over the period 2013 to 2025. Here we are talking about "the use of computers to perform tasks that rely on complex analyses, subtle judgments, and creative problem-solving." Moreover, in industry, thanks to advanced robots, up to sixty million jobs may be potentially automatable by 2025. These are jobs in manufacturing processes; adding them to the 140 million in knowledge work, already mentioned, we reach a total of two hundred million. That is nearly 8 percent of total worldwide employment, and only a little less than the numbers already unemployed worldwide. We risk doubling our already excessive rates of unemployment. *Disruptive technologies* indeed!

Can our societies hope to survive such a high level of disruption? Economists predict that such technologies will foster major economic growth; so, they believe, the hordes of unemployed will sooner or later be reemployed. That is what has generally happened in the past. But that historical growth has brought us to the situation where we are apparently overconsuming the earth's renewable resources by around 50 percent. Clearly, we cannot continue to pursue conventional economic growth throughout the world, even though it is still needed in developing countries.

Howsoever we may in due course resolve these problems, it is clear that we will need time; that if the problems develop too quickly, we may find ourselves unable to cope with them. In that case, they will run out of control and be "resolved" by some kind of disaster. We may then see political revolutions setting up highly controlled economies in which employment-destroying technologies would be outlawed. The libertarian economy, if we leave it unrestrained, may well crash into the buffers of populist resistance. We would do better to adopt more realistic economic policies before we reach that stage.

Beyond Our Control?

Our current free-market mindset sees economic change as something that is driven by impersonal market forces, something that takes place outside the control of individuals or of governments. The theory implies that economic change is like the weather or the tides; we cannot control it, we just have to accommodate ourselves to it. But there is a strange paradox here. Economic changes are the result of our own behavior, yet we see them as being beyond our control.

Moreover, there is a curious disparity between our attitude to weather or tide and our attitude to economic change. We are entitled to defend ourselves against the ravages of foul weather or freak tides; but not—so says the theory—against the destructive effects of market-generated change. Dykes, windbreaks, and seawalls are permissible; obstructing the workings of the markets is a grave economic sin, an offense against the so-called "laws" of economics.

The problem is this: according to libertarian theory, we cannot control, regulate, or moderate economic changes without destroying our own "freedom." Each of us is obliged to accept the consequences of the "free" behavior of other people, including those people who invent or utilize job-destroying machines, environment-poisoning chemicals, or high-risk genetic modifications. That is to say, people who act for their own advantage, or that of their businesses, rather than with regard to the common good.

For we, or our government, must not put constraints on those other people; that would deprive them of "freedom." In effect, then, a "free" human society lives under the dictatorship of the "free" individual behaviors of its own members. *The sum of our independent actions becomes our god*; sometimes, indeed, a malevolent and tyrannical god. In chapter 3 we saw how free marketeers believe that freedom means simply *absence of constraints*. That notion of freedom leads, in logic and in practice, to the dictatorship I have just described.

Free-market economists, determined to impose their views on the world, have only one solution to the problems caused by too rapid change. That is, to sweep away every remaining economic rigidity, every restraint on market freedom, thus making our economies more flexible, more competitive, more able to respond to the changes that confront them, more able to create their own changes. Faster innovation and enhanced competitiveness are held up by these ideologues as the only way forward.

All that appears, on the face of it, realistic and practical. We have to keep up with our competitors. Likewise, they have to keep up with us. *The world is changing faster*, and we have none of us any choice but to make haste to keep abreast of it. But this seemingly pragmatic view leads logically to a perverse conclusion. It tells us that the only cure for societies that have trouble coping with rapid change is to adopt policies that will accelerate the pace of change still further.

Technology and Competition

For the breeding of change, the marriage of electronics and competition is formidably prolific. Information technology opens up ever wider competition. If you are simply a private individual buying a book or a bicycle, the internet lets you compare prices from many more sources than you could have encountered in the past. If you are a business purchaser buying materials or components in quantity, you can compare prices from suppliers all over the world.

Meanwhile, the industries that supply the electronic technology, living in a world of untrammeled competition, strive day and night to launch faster and more powerful systems. Technology strengthens competition, while competition boosts technology. Here is a self-feeding spiral that promotes not merely rapid change, but ever-accelerating change.

Ephemeral and Overcomplex Contraptions

Computers and other electronic devices, like so many products today, have short lifetimes. The prevailing belief is that there is no point in making long-lasting computers, telephones, copiers, or printers, because the technology is developing so rapidly that even the most up-to-the-minute device will be as dated as the top hat or the crinoline in a couple of years. To see how habits have changed in this matter, reflect that the early telephones, though they too used what in their day was advanced and developing technology, were indeed made to last. And they did last, not just for years, but for decades.

The German "W48" was a classic desktop telephone with rotary dial and large handset carrying both transmitter (microphone) and receiver (earpiece). This was introduced in 1948, but it was not in fact very different from the W28, dating from 1928. The W48 continued to be manufactured in large quantities till the 1970s.

Even older and longer lasting was the "candlestick" telephone, whose transmitter was attached to a vertical "stick"; the receiver was on a flexible cable, while the bell was in a separate box fixed to the wall. This design dates back to the 1890s and was in production until the 1930s. I recall that in 1953 my parents bought a house in Aberdeen, Scotland, which was still equipped with a candlestick phone—and it still worked!

Today, it is estimated that mobile phones are replaced, on average, every two to three years. They do, of course, have far more capabilities than traditional telephones; but therefore they are far more complicated. A relatively simple Motorola mobile has an instruction book of thirty-six pages. And every time one replaces it, one has a new plethora of instructions to learn. All this is tedious and time wasting. Why cannot our equipment, and our lives, be simpler? Because we are obsessed with innovation, with introducing countless new options; not necessarily because anyone needs or wants them but because manufacturers feel under compulsion to constantly differentiate their products, to offer consumers more and more choices, so as to gain a transitory competitive advantage.

The recent spate of developments in telephone technology has indeed brought prices down and given telephones greatly enhanced capabilities. Yet, in some respects, communication by telephone has become far more awkward, time consuming, and frustrating than it used to be. Today, any attempt to telephone a business, or other organization, is generally something of an ordeal. There is no one at the switchboard to take your call; you are faced with an automated system that orders you to listen to a long list of options, push various buttons, leave a recorded message, "enjoy" repetitive and usually unpleasant music— the system, it seems, can do anything but connect you rapidly to the person you wish to speak to.

And what if the automated switchboard asks the caller to reply to questions verbally? If the caller is a foreigner who speaks the language of the "vocal server" with a strong foreign accent, her replies may not be "understood" by the machine.

Such innovations have contributed to unemployment by eliminating telephone operators. They have very obviously degraded customer service. What is there to be said in their favor? They are thought to enhance productivity and efficiency. By cutting office expenses they have, perhaps, made organizations a little more profitable and competitive.

But in practice, even that is doubtful. If all offices, in their pursuit of competitiveness and profitability, adopt such measures, in the end they are likely to be no better off.

Yet, under our current economic paradigm, we are obliged to pursue innovation. For our overcomplex contraptions are manufactured in robotized factories by small numbers of people. If we made only enough of them to keep us in long-lasting telephones or printers, replaced every thirty years, the electronics industry would provide precious little employment. We are compelled to carry on innovating, just to keep ourselves (or some of us) at work and earning our living.

Precarious Employment

Rapid economic and technological change means that employment, like the things it produces, is more and more ephemeral. In the quite recent past, many people could expect to stay with the same employer for many years, even for life. Not, of course, generally in the same job; with experience and seniority, one could rise in the hierarchy of the firm or move from one department to another. A capable and diligent worker might progress from a lowly starting position even to the top. The staff of a sound, durable business formed a stable community which, in the bigger and more international firms, could be extensive and varied. Thus employment could be a means not only of producing goods or services, not merely of earning a livelihood, but also of satisfying the normal human need for community. A firm was a social network as well as a refinery, a railroad, or a bank.

But we have been seduced by the libertarians' obsession with individualism and contempt for community. The world of business management has largely embraced the idea that a firm should not even attempt to be a stable community. Nor, perhaps, should it attempt to function as a stable working team; in investment banking, the denizens of the trading room have often been encouraged to behave as a crowd of individuals operating independently, in competition with each other, each aiming for a fatter bonus than anyone else's.

The ideal firm, it is said, is a totally flexible network, taking on employees as and when they are needed and letting them go as soon as their sector is hit by a transient downturn in demand or as soon as they can be replaced by advanced robots. It should outsource as much of its work as possible to subcontractors and should have no stable relationships with them either. It should play them off against each other so as to gain all the alleged benefits of competitive tendering; or, to put it more bluntly, so as to squeeze the most profitable deal out of them.

If firms are run on these lines, no one can have a stable career—not even at the top, where chief executives move frequently and are appointed not by old-style promotion from below but by recruitment in the marketplace, where certain bosses, who acquire a reputation for outstanding profit generation, can command gigantic rewards. This process, however, increases the firm's costs and provides a further motive for cutting costs at the lower levels, whether by firing more workers and middle managers or by trimming product quality.

Early Retirement

There is another problem with an economy where there is no career stability, where one is expected to hop from job to job: it tends to lead to earlier retirement. Not because people want to retire earlier, but because it is very hard for those in their fifties or sixties to find employment. That fact in turn reflects the rapid pace of change; older people are thought, rightly or wrongly, to be unable or unwilling to adapt to changes. So, in our ever-mutating organizations, employers do not want them. But by rejecting older employees, they discard experience. They lose people who have seen serious problems before and learned how to cope with them—or, still better, how to avoid them.

All this is the reverse of what we need in a world in which people are living longer. In 1889, when Bismarck's government in Germany set up the first state pension scheme, the age of seventy was chosen as the normal pension age. It was the same in Britain, where the "Lloyd George" state pension of 1909 was payable from age seventy. In those days, average life expectancy for Englishmen was less than sixty years; yet it was customary to stay at work until around seventy, if one lived that long.

Today, life expectancy is about seventy-five, but for many of us it is impossible to find much paid work beyond the age of fifty-five. Our lives have lengthened, but our working lives have shortened; and these trends continue. It is no wonder that the problem of financing decent pensions grows ever more intractable. And this is not merely a financial problem; it is a social problem too. Not everyone wants two or three decades without the satisfaction of being part of a working community, and quite possibly without an adequate income.

If it is true that older people are less adaptable to change, then since the elderly percentage of our population is expanding, logically we ought to slow down our overall pace of change. Not only to make working life more agreeable for older people but also to enable them to stay at work longer, thus avoiding the unaffordability of pensions and the ill effects of idleness. But the opposite is happening. We are imposing on ourselves acceleration in change when, in fact, we have more need of deceleration.

Plato's Leaky Pots

In the age of the classical Greek philosophers, proponents of change and stability argued in terms that "have acquired no wrinkles" (*n'ont pas pris une ride*), as the French put it. Among the most famous of change lovers was Heraclitus (ca. 535–475 BC). Only fragments of his writings have come down to us, cited by Plato, Aristotle, and other philosophers. But he is credited with the saying *pánta rhei*, "everything flows," or is in a state of perpetual flux; thus, it would seem, there can be no stability.

In Plato's dialogue *Cratylus*, the young philosopher of that name is in dispute with the older Socrates, whose remarks here are generally believed to reflect Plato's own views. Cratylus favors the philosophy of Heraclitus, but Socrates disagrees:

> But we cannot even say that there is any knowledge, if all things are changing and nothing remains fixed. . . . By this reasoning there will be neither anyone to know nor anything to be known. . . . Surely no man of sense . . . will condemn himself and all things and say there is no health in them, but that all things are flowing like leaky pots, or believe that all things are just like people afflicted with catarrh, flowing and running all the time.[19]

Plato argued that, though things in this world evidently do change, yet underlying the changeable things we perceive with our senses there are Forms (or Ideas) which do not change. Thus, your cat is different from my cat, and both of them change over the course of their lives from kittens to mature cats to dead cats; but both are representations of the Form of the cat, the Idea of catness, which is unchanging. The Forms are, of course, abstractions that we cannot see, hear, or touch. But we can know the Form of the cat through our perception of actual cats.

Stability Is Slow Change

Change is a fact of life in this world. But that need not mean that there can be no stability. A slightly cracked pot may leak so slowly that it is, in effect, watertight. A tree changes continuously throughout its life; but a cypress, for example, may live for centuries after reaching maturity. Over that long period, it will show little change. Thus the mature tree is, in effect, stable from our point of view, since it changes very little even over an entire human lifespan. So we may say: in human terms, *stability is slow change.*

From our earthly standpoint, what matters is the rate of change relative to our lifespan. Instability, for us, means change that is rapid in relation to the human lifespan. Sometimes so rapid that we can scarcely live with it. And that is a key problem today. We live in a world where many things are changing, not only at a highly uncomfortable pace but also at a continually accelerating pace.

Today's prevailing climate of opinion holds that rapid, accelerating, and increasingly disruptive change is somehow inevitable; that, whether we like it or not, we are all going to have to live with ever-accelerating changes, and it is up to us to adapt ourselves to them. Is the *revolution in permanence*, dreamt of by the Marxists in 1850, being realized by us capitalists 165 years later? It would appear so.

Yet there is something seriously wrong with our current fatalistic attitude to change. It implies that economic and social change, like the weather, or the tides, or volcanic eruptions, is beyond our control, imposed on us by extrahuman forces. That, of course, is nonsense. These changes are created by us. They are instigated, or impelled, by our hypercompetitive markets.

If we want a more tolerable pace of change, we must modify our economic habits and strategies. We must become less competitive and more cooperative. We must stop letting blind, unrestrained competition drive us toward outcomes that we dread rather than desire.

CHAPTER 15

Ways Forward

We have seen how the teachings of the Catholic Church bear on many aspects of our economic life. Is it possible to describe what an economy run on the basis of these teachings would look like? It is tempting to attempt such a description. But imagined utopias have seldom proved to be realistic or helpful. Indeed, attempts to achieve preconceived utopias have often proved to be not only futile but also harmful.

We can hardly predict what the future will look like more than a decade or two ahead. Anyone who tries to do so faces what a distinguished member of my profession, the British actuary Frank Redington, called an *expanding funnel of doubt*. The narrow end of the funnel represents the present; the wide mouth, the fairly distant future. Its large area encompasses a multitude of possible future scenarios, any of which could conceivably emerge. Since there are so many possibilities, there is much doubt concerning what the future will look like; and the doubt expands as one looks further ahead.

Some of these possible scenarios may be excellent, some horrible; the majority will probably be mediocre, somewhere between those extremes. Even among the minority of excellent scenarios, there will doubtless be many variants. Rather than try to pick one of these and imagine it in detail (the method of the utopianist), it seems better to try to imagine courses of action that could guide us toward one or other of the various possible excellent outcomes. Or, indeed, to a world of divergent excellent outcomes in different places.

For it is surely a mistake to think that there must be a single ideal economic formula for the whole world. That is an error to which conventional economists are prone. They are inclined to believe that their beloved system of untrammeled markets is the right one for everyone, always and everywhere, and to recommend economic strategies accordingly. But peoples of different cultures may prefer different economies.

One of the problems with the concept of unlimited worldwide competitive free trade is that it tends to homogenize everything, to force all human societies into the same mold. For competition drives out any way of doing anything that is not the cheapest, or most "efficient," or most profitable.

Individualism

Every society needs to strike a balance between the basic human need for community and the individual's desire to go it alone, to be oneself, to do it one's own way. There have been many periods in history when the balance has been upset, and our present time is one of them. There have been periods of regimentation, when individuality has been suppressed; there have been periods of social confusion when sense of community has largely evaporated.

Pope John Paul II observed in *Centesimus Annus* (par. 41) that "a society is alienated if its forms of social organization, production and consumption make it more difficult to offer this gift of self and to establish this solidarity between people." There we have a good description of today's often "alienated" and disorientated societies. We need not despair; all this has happened before, and societies have recovered to find a new sense of coherence and purpose. But, to help us recover, we need to understand our sickness, to identify and reject the misguided ideas that have led us astray.

Freedom

Conventional free-market economics is based on a faulty and inadequate concept of freedom. It assumes that freedom simply means the individual's right to act in one's own interests, under a bare minimum of constraints, with little or no regard to the effects of one's actions on the surrounding community. We have come to accept this perverse notion because economists and other libertarians have led us astray; they have convinced us that if we each simply pursue our own private interests and wishes, the outcome will be the best possible for us all. This theory works up to a point, but it has very serious limitations.

What is even worse is the libertarian notion that freedom is amoral, that it means equally the power to do good and the power to do wrong. This implies that rules designed to prevent or dissuade us from doing wrong are a threat to our freedom. Hence the libertarian hatred of regulation in the economy.

We need to recall the older idea that freedom is found in abiding by God's laws and acting for the common good. We find our freedom not alone but in fraternity with others. We need to accept that rules and constraints are not necessarily obstacles to be eliminated or evaded. They can be marker buoys that help us by diverting us from the rocks and shoals of misbehavior and guiding us toward the safe voyage of virtuous conduct. The real challenge, then, is not to get rid of constraints; it is to adopt constraints that help us live better; that restrain us from doing wrong, without preventing us from doing good. "There is no true freedom except in the service of what is good and just" (*Catechism*, par. 1733). There we see a higher and nobler understanding of freedom than mere *laissez-faire*.

Competition

We should not try to eliminate competition; it is a natural mode of human behavior that can encourage progress and higher standards of performance. Yet we need to relearn something that we have forgotten in the era of free-market obsessions: too much competition, or the wrong kind of competition, can be harmful. Papal documents from *Rerum Novarum* onward have repeatedly condemned untamed competition. It can destroy or devalue the livelihoods of those who engage in it. It causes excessive stresses, leading to serious illness. It generates too rapid, ill-considered innovations that often turn out to be harmful. Under excessive competition, people in business behave badly. They crimp their employees' pay and benefits; they sell too aggressively and often "mis-sell," to the detriment of their customers; they neglect health and safety and the protection of the environment; they take excessive risks, which can get them into deep trouble and cause widespread damage.

Rather than considering all restraints on competition as intrinsically criminal—with no need to prove abuse—we should recognize that fierce price-cutting competition leads to lower quality standards, more unemployment, and the elimination of smaller competitors. We should encourage *competition on quality* rather than on price. Better-quality goods that last longer would be easier on the environment; businesses striving to outdo each other in quality of production and service would need to employ more people. We should reject the orthodox notion that all forms of price regulation are pernicious.

Today, agreements to stabilize prices need to be international, and they need to be buttressed by agreements on production levels, to avoid overproduction that can make agreed prices unsustainable. Regulation of production should also help to limit damage to the environment.

The Power of Capital

Too much capital (company stock) is in the hands of institutional investors (fund management organizations) whose sole goal is maximum financial gain—these institutional investors compete fiercely with each other to achieve it. This process has perverse consequences; in effect, it forces businesses to be too greedy. They are under severe pressure to satisfy investors by pursuing maximum profitability, rather than adequate profitability, by putting profit above all other objectives.

We should seek to counter the excessive power of stockholders by building up the power of employees. There are various routes toward this goal: stronger labor unions, works councils, bigger employee holdings of company stock, and worker representation on company boards. Employees have had an increasingly raw deal during the recent free-market decades; it is time to redress the balance.

It is likely that giving more power to the workers would slow down the pace of change in the business world. Workers want steady employment rather than hectic innovation and change. But many of the changes currently in progress are widely seen as threats to society. In particular, we fear the trend toward putting our economic activities under the control of autonomous automated systems; this could lead not only to much more unemployment but also to the automats dominating our societies. A slowdown in this kind of innovation would be widely welcomed.

Labor

Respect for labor is a key element in Catholic Social Teaching. It reflects the belief that human work is our participation in God's work of creation. Work is not simply a burden we must bear in order to produce what we need or desire. Too much idleness is harmful; work provides physical or mental exercise and discipline and so is generally good for us. The Church insists that we ought to manage our economies in such a way that everyone has opportunities to work and to earn an adequate living by working.

Moreover, Catholic teaching tells us that workers should not be mere "cogs in the machinery"; they should participate, so far as they are able, in the running of the enterprises that employ them.

The systems and practices that have developed since the resurgence of free-market thinking and practice in the 1970s have cut back the status and influence of employees, other than those at the top. This trend does not harm workers only. For the retreat of worker power has left a gap that has been filled by the excessive growth of the power of capital; this has been damaging to society in general. The former strength of labor unions provided a check and balance to the power of the stockholders; in its weakness or absence, capital has become overdominant and overdemanding. It needs a countervailing force; but that has been deliberately weakened, in America and elsewhere, by legislative changes and judicial decisions that have undermined the power of organized labor.

One of the worst errors of orthodox economic theory and practice is its tendency to treat labor as just another commodity, and workers themselves essentially as tools in the workshop, to be left idle and unpaid except when needed. At the "Jubilee of Workers," May 1, 2000, Pope John Paul II said: "All must work so that the economic system in which we live does not upset the fundamental order of the priority of work over capital, of the common good over private interest."

Unemployment

Here is a paradox. We are all worried about today's pervasive problem of unemployment. Those who are out of work suffer from it; those who are at work dread it; those who are retired and no longer need to work are saddened by the misery it brings to others. We suffer also from *underemployment*, the situation of people who are at work but cannot earn a living wage because their hours of work are too short. Yet we persist in adopting devices and systems that replace human work; thus we destroy existing jobs faster than we can create new ones.

Why do we do this? Because every business lives under competitive pressures to get its costs down; and every public service lives under similar pressures, because another feature of our current misguided mindset is the notion that *public expenditure is bad* and must be cut back. And that notion is itself part of the Great Competition Obsession; each country feels obliged to trim its public expenditure in order to be "competitive" with other countries.

We hate unemployment, but competition forces us to augment it. Why then are we so addicted to competition? I am afraid the answer is that we have allowed ourselves to be brainwashed by orthodox economists, for whom free competition and free trade amount to a kind of pseudoreligion. We think it more important to be competitive than to have an economy in which everyone can earn a decent living. Old fogeys like myself can recall a time when there was less emphasis on competitive "efficiency," but also less misery. One of our problems today is that we have persisted with perverse policies for so long that many of us (the younger and middle-aged generations) have never known such a time. We should heed the Catholic call for cooperation in community, rather than let ourselves be continually harassed by our own relentless competition.

Environment and Stability

More than two centuries of rapid economic development have made possible huge and unprecedented increases in world population, with much improved standards of living for many of the world's people, though many others still lag behind in conditions of penury. All this growth, however, is causing grave damage to our environment and threatens the exhaustion of our natural resources. The "bull market" of conventional growth is not sustainable indefinitely; if we do not restrain it, we risk some kind of catastrophic correction.

Catholic teaching insists on the vital importance of care for our planet Earth; both out of respect for God himself, for it is his world, and because we have a duty to leave the world in good shape for the benefit of our descendants. But some prominent economists have argued that we need not worry about availability of natural resources, that there is no danger of exhaustion in the near, or even remote, future. This theory is not credible. Those who promote it are generally devout believers in free-market principles. It seems likely that they believe in the unlimited availability of resources because, if they did not, they could hardly continue to believe in the possibility of endless market-propelled growth.

It should be our aim to move toward a stable world economy that consumes raw materials in a sustainable manner. This means that usage of physical resources should not continue to grow indefinitely but should settle at levels that can be maintained in the long term without depleting our planet's stock of resources.

Redistribution

Inequalities of income and wealth arise naturally because of the differences between individuals. But they should not be allowed to become excessive. The Catholic doctrine of the *universal destination of goods* tells us that God wishes every person to have at least enough of this world's goods to be able to live decently, and that we cannot rely on personal charity alone to smooth out exorbitant inequalities. We must strive to organize our economies so that gross inequalities do not arise. We need regulation and labor solidarity to ensure that wages are living wages; we need redistributive taxation; most of all we need economic strategies that make full employment a high priority.

Politics

Libertarians have essentially given up on politics. They assume that governments are incapable of looking after the common good because, they say, state officials are concerned only with furthering their own personal interests. According to libertarian theory, this selfish behavior works well in free markets but badly in the public sector. The market sanctifies selfishness, the state diabolizes it. Therefore, it is said, since everyone behaves selfishly, we must have an all-encompassing market system which, so far as possible, takes over the functions of the state.

It seems more realistic to hold that selfish behavior—acting purely for one's own advantage, with little or no regard to the good of others—works badly everywhere and should be avoided; and to recognize that most people have at least some inclination to do good, not merely to strive for their own advantage.

Libertarians believe that the proper alternative to bad government is minimal government, the miniskirt rather than crinoline state. But we need government to mediate between conflicting interests and to correct excessive inequalities. We need well-designed regulations to limit damaging misbehavior. And we need government to carry out public interest projects that cannot well be financed and maintained by individuals and private businesses.

Since we need government, it follows that the proper alternative to bad government is good government. As Pope Benedict XVI wrote in *Deus Caritas Est* (par. 28), "A just society must be the achievement of politics." It is far from easy to achieve it. With God's help, we must persevere in this never-finished endeavor.

Notes

Chapter 1—pages 1–9

1. Michael R. Griffiths and John R. Lucas, *Ethical Economics* (1996), 26. Griffiths is a partner in Towers Perrin Tillinghast, management consultants; Lucas is a philosopher and fellow of Merton College, Oxford.

2. Adair Turner, *Economics, Conventional Wisdom, and Public Policy* (2010), 1. Lord Turner was chairman of the United Kingdom's Financial Services Authority between 2008 and 2013.

3. Adam Smith, *The Wealth of Nations* (1776), bk. 4, chap. 2.

4. Amartya Sen, *On Ethics and Economics* (1987), 1.

5. Friedrich von Hayek, *The Fatal Conceit* (1988), 13. This remark means, for example, that we should always buy from the cheapest sources, giving no preference to local suppliers.

6. Abraham Heschel, *The Insecurity of Freedom* (1966), 15.

7. Milton Friedman, *Capitalism and Freedom* (1962), 8, 12.

8. Friedrich von Hayek, *The Constitution of Liberty* (1960), 79.

9. Friedrich von Hayek, *The Mirage of Social Justice* (1976), 126.

10. Ibid., 97.

11. Ibid., 66.

12. Paul Krugman, lecture given at Massachusetts Institute of Technology, February 5, 2010.

13. Sen, *On Ethics and Economics*, 29, 79.

14. Joseph Stiglitz, *The Roaring Nineties* (2004), xii.

15. Friedrich von Hayek, *The Political Order of a Free People* (1979), 111ff.

16. Ludwig von Mises, lecture given at Princeton, October 1958, sect. 5.

17. Hayek, *The Constitution of Liberty*, 285.

18. Ludwig von Mises, *Socialism* (1981), 400.

19. See Thomas Piketty, *Capital in the Twenty-First Century* (2014), graphs 8.5 and 10.5.

Chapter 2—pages 10–25

1. Charles Taylor, *The Ethics of Authenticity* (1991), 4.

2. Aristotle, *Politics*, 1253a.

3. Thucydides, *History of the Peloponnesian War*, sec. 2.37, reporting Pericles's funeral oration for Athenian soldiers, around 430 BC. Emphasis mine.

4. *Analects of Confucius* (1998), 51.

5. Jewish tradition holds that the Torah (Law of Moses, in the first five books of the Old Testament) contains 613 commandments. The best-known list of these was compiled by Maimonides in the thirteenth century. It can be seen on www.chabad.org.

6. Daniel J. Elazar, *Judaism and Democracy: The Reality* (1986).

7. Walter Ullmann, *The Individual and Society in the Middle Ages* (1966), 5.

8. Ibid., 9.

9. Aristotle, *Politics*, 1332b.

10. Ullmann, *Middle Ages*, 32–33.

11. More recent scholars have argued that the development of individualism can be traced back further; thus Richard Southern writes that "the emergence of the individual from his communal background" began in the eleventh and twelfth centuries. See Southern, *The Making of the Middle Ages* (1953), 221.

12. Jacob Burckhardt, *The Civilization of the Renaissance* (1945), 81.

13. Ibid., 82n27.

14. Ibid., 262, 279.

15. Jonathan Sacks, *The Politics of Hope* (2000), 210. The author is a former British Chief Rabbi.

16. Immanuel Kant, *What is Enlightenment?* (1784).

17. Isaiah Berlin, *The Crooked Timber of Humanity* (1990), 57–58. The title of this book comes from a famous remark by Kant: "Out of the crooked timber of humanity, nothing perfectly straight can be constructed." Kant was a sociable and hospitable character with a wide circle of friends; it may be that this saying was inspired by a lunchtime conversation with a Königsberg shipbuilder.

18. According to tradition, St. Luke was a painter as well as a physician; he is a patron saint of both professions.

19. Robert Burns (1759–1796), *The Gowden Locks of Anna*. In the second line, *maunna* = must not.

20. Joseph de Maistre, *Du Pape* (1821), 271.

21. Félicité de Lamennais, *Des Progrès de la Révolution et de la Guerre contre l'Eglise* (1829), 26.

22. Jean-Baptiste de Montvalon, "La Manif pour tous, acte II," in *Le Monde* (Paris), September 21, 2014.

23. John Paul II, Address to Visiting Scottish Bishops, October 29, 1992, par. 2.

24. Joseph Ratzinger, *Introduction to Christianity* (1990), 239.

25. Baron Georges-Eugène Haussmann was *Préfet de la Seine* (in effect, mayor of Paris, but there was no mayor then) between 1853 and 1870.

26. In the Tridentine missal, and in the old Anglican prayer book (*Book of Common Prayer*), this is the collect for the Fourth Sunday after Easter.

27. Taketoshi Nojiri, *Values as a Precondition of Democracy* (1998), 91.

28. Ibid., 96.

29. Barry Shain, *The Myth of American Individualism* (1994), 194.

30. Quotations from Tocqueville are from *Democracy in America* (2004), 2:585–87.

31. This striking phrase is reminiscent of Thomas's description of heaven: "Eternity knows no succession of events, the whole exists simultaneously." *Summa Theologiae* I, q. 10, a. 1.

32. Robert Cecil, *The Myth of the Master Race* (1972), 12–13.

33. John A. Ryan, "Individualism," in *The Catholic Encyclopedia* (1910).

34. William G. Sumner, *What the Social Classes Owe to Each Other* (1987), 44.

35. Ibid., 21.

36. Francis, "Message for World Day of Peace," January 1, 2014.

37. Sumner, *Social Classes*, 35.

38. Ayn Rand, *Atlas Shrugged*, 238.

39. Ayn Rand, *The Fountainhead*, 580.

Chapter 3—pages 26–37

1. Aristotle, *Politics*, 1255b.

2. George Orwell, *Nineteen Eighty-Four* (1987), 313.

3. Friedrich von Hayek, *The Constitution of Liberty* (1960), 79.

4. Murray N. Rothbard, *Myth and Truth about Libertarianism* (1980), 10.

5. Murray N. Rothbard, *For a New Liberty* (1973), 9.

6. Milton Friedman, *Capitalism and Freedom* (1962), 12.

7. Aristotle, *Politics*, 1310a.

8. John 8:34; Acts 8:23; Rom 6:18–22; 2 Tim 2:26; 2 Pet 2:19.

9. Augustine, *Enchiridion*, par. 105.

10. Thomas Aquinas, *Summa Theologiae* II/II, q. 88, art. 4.

11. Bernard Häring, *The Law of Christ* (1961), vol. 1, chap. 4.

12. Laurent Gagnebin and Raphael Picon, *Le protestantisme, foi insoumise* (2008), 119, 62.

13. Eric Foner, *The Story of American Freedom* (1998), 5.

14. This translation is from the Anglican *Book of Common Prayer* (1662).

15. Mishnah, *Avoth* 6:2.

16. Abraham J. Heschel, *The Insecurity of Freedom* (1966), 15.

17. Ibid.

18. Abraham J. Heschel, *God in Search of Man* (1959), 411.

19. Thomas Aquinas, *Summa Theologiae* I, q. 62, a. 8 (my translation).

20. André Gide, *Nouveaux Prétextes* (1929).

21. Charles Baudelaire, Letter to Armand Fraisse (1860).

22. Thierry de Duve, *Résonances du ready-made* (1989), 48.

23. Jean Clair, *Sur Marcel Duchamp et la fin de l'art* (2000), 52.

24. Although Duchamp's original urinal was a common mass-produced article, the replicas have been laboriously handmade from a photograph of the original by Alfred Stieglitz. See www.cabinetmagazine.org/issues/27/duchamp.php.

25. Hayek, *Constitution*, 79.

26. In certain circumstances, however, inaction may be considered as positive wrongdoing. Thus, French criminal law punishes the offense of failure to help a person in danger (*non-assistance à personne en danger*).

27. Friedrich von Hayek, *The Road to Serfdom* (1944), 107.

28. *Works of T. H. Green* (1895–1911), 3:372.

Chapter 4—pages 38–52

1. President Franklin D. Roosevelt made this comment in his inaugural address as President, March 4, 1933.

2. John Plender is a senior editorial writer and columnist with the *Financial Times*, London. The quotation is from *Prospect* (London), February 1998, 52.

3. Charles P. Kindleberger, *A Financial History of Western Europe* (1993), 43.

4. Edwin S. Hunt & James M. Murray, *A History of Business in Medieval Europe, 1200–1550* (1999), 64–65.

5. Ibid.

6. See graph "private credit by deposit money banks and other financial institutions to GDP for United States" at http://www.research.stlouisfed.org/fred2/series/DDDI12USA156NWDB.

7. Friedrich von Hayek, *The Constitution of Liberty* (1960), 17.

8. Cited by Larry Harris, *Trading and Exchanges* (2003), chap. 29.

9. Thomas Aquinas, *Summa Theologiae* II/II, q. 77, art. 3.

10. Federal Deposit Insurance Corporation, *The First Fifty Years* (1983), 7. This fascinating history is accessible on the FDIC site.

11. Jean-François Gayraud, *Le nouveau capitalisme criminel* (2014), 153.

12. Thomas Piketty, "Il faut taxer fortement les très hauts revenus," *Alternatives Economiques* (January 2009): 52–54.

13. Philip Augar, *The Death of Gentlemanly Capitalism* (2000), 20.

14. J. Delany, "Jealousy," in *The Catholic Encyclopedia* (1910).

Chapter 5—pages 53–74

1. Pascal Salin, "Vive la concurrence fiscale!" *Le Figaro* (September 17, 2004). The author is professor emeritus of economics at Université Paris-Dauphine.

2. Christine Lagarde, "The Future Global Economy," *Project Syndicate* (December 31, 2012). The author is managing director of the International Monetary Fund.

3. Beverly Kaye and Sharon Jordan-Evans, *Love It, Don't Leave It* (2003), 152.

4. Angus Sibley, "The Hyperthyroid Economy" (1995). This article is accessible on www.equilibrium-economicum.net.

5. Adam Smith, *The Wealth of Nations*, bk. 1, chap. 7.

6. At Harvard, Roosevelt studied under economists William Z. Ripley, whose support for corporate reform foreshadowed the New Deal, and O. M. W. Sprague, who "had a strong belief in central banking and credit controls as devices for stability." See Rexford G. Tugwell, *The Democratic Roosevelt* (1957), 53–54.

7. In this address, Roosevelt also denounced the *trickle-down* theory, the belief that, when the rich grow still richer, their affluence trickles down to everyone else; a theory still widely current today, despite ample evidence against it.

8. Dr. Samuel Johnson (1709–1784), compiler of the first English dictionary, is said to have reacted unfavorably to a piece of crazily virtuosic violin music. On being told that it was extremely difficult to play, he retorted: "would that it were impossible!"

9. Robert H. Frank and Philip J. Cook, *The Winner Take All Society* (1995), 2.

10. Ibid., 131.

11. John Kay, "Business lessons from the sporting world," *Financial Times* (August 16, 1996).

12. Pierre de Coubertin, reported in *The Fourth Olympiad* (1909), 793.

13. Carl Menger, *Principles of Economics* (1976), 223.

14. Ibid.

15. Adam Smith, *The Wealth of Nations*, bk. 1, chap. 10, pt. 2.

16. Thomas Sedlacek, *Economics of Good and Evil* (2009), 217.

17. See "Switzerland and Europe," *The Economist* (November 28, 1992): 28.

18. *OECD Economic Surveys: Switzerland 2007*, 98.

19. Thomas Aquinas, *Summa Theologiae* II/II q. 78 a. 1 (my translation).

20. *Treasury Committee Ninth Report* (session 1997–1998), par. 25.

21. *Book of Common Prayer*, Psalm 73, vv. 3 and 10.

22. *Analects of Confucius* (1998), bk. 3, v. 7.

23. Arthur Hugh Clough, *The Latest Decalogue* (1862). This poem is a satire on hypocritical observance of the Ten Commandments in Victorian English society. It contains the famous lines "Thou shalt not kill, but need'st not strive, officiously to keep alive."

24. J. B. Phillips, *The New Testament in Modern English* (1962), 412.

25. Babylonian Talmud, *Baba Bathra*, fol. 21b.

26. Babylonian Talmud, *Makkoth*, fol. 24a. The translation of Psalm 15 is that given in the Talmud.

27. Friedman made this comment in the second episode of his TV series *Free to Choose* (1980). A transcript can be viewed on www.TheDailyHatch.org.

28. See chap. 12 of this work.

29. Benedict XVI, *Caritas in Veritate*, par. 25. This is my translation from the Latin; it differs from the official English version but is close to the French.

30. Timothy Radcliffe, "An Englishman Making Waves in Rome," Interview with Victoria Combe in *Daily Telegraph*, April 27, 2001.

Chapter 6—pages 75–88

1. Gustav Schmoller (1838–1917), *Grundriss der allgemeinen Volkswirtschaftslehre* (1900–1904), vol. 1, 21, 29. The author, professor at the University of Berlin, was for many years the dominant economist in Germany. He belonged to the "Historical School" of economists, who based their ideas on the study of economic history rather than on academic theory. His book has been translated into French but not into English.

2. Michael Walzer, *Spheres of Justice* (1993), 92.

3. *Report of the European Agency for Health and Safety at Work* (2007), 24.

4. Adam Smith, *The Wealth of Nations* (1776), bk. 1, chap. 8.

5. Paul C. Weiler, *Governing the Workplace* (1990), 121.

6. Ludwig von Mises, *Human Action* (1949), 270.

7. Henry Hazlitt, *Economics in One Lesson* (2008), 56.

8. Smith, *The Wealth of Nations*, bk. 4, chap. 8.

9. In Smith's day, the profit-earning "masters" were self-employed master craftsmen who worked at their trades; they were skilled workers. They were hardly capitalists in the modern sense. In the preindustrial world, most trades did not require large amounts of capital.

10. Smith, *The Wealth of Nations*, bk. 1, chap. 10, pt 2.

11. Ibid.

12. Ibid.

13. Ludwig von Mises, *Human Action* (1949), 589.

14. Smith, *The Wealth of Nations*, bk. 1, chap. 8.

15. Adam Smith, *The Theory of Moral Sentiments* (1759), pt. 1, sec. 3, chap. 2.

16. Anne-Robert-Jacques Turgot, *Réflexions sur la Formation et la Distribution des Richesses* (1769), par. 6.

17. David Ricardo, *Principles of Political Economy* (1817), chap. 5. Ricardo's full text contains various observations, too often overlooked, which mitigate this harsh doctrine.

18. Carl Menger, *Principles of Economics* (1976), 171.

19. Ibid., 174.

20. Ayn Rand, *The Virtue of Selfishness* (1964), 96.

21. See Phillip Inman, "Army of Workers Trapped in Insecure, Badly-Paid Jobs," *The Guardian* (London), July 30, 2014. This article is accessible on www.theguardian.com/uk.

22. Source: Office of National Statistics, www.ons.gov.uk/ons/rel/lmac /contract-with-no-guaranteed-hours/zero-hours-contracts/art-zero-hours.html. Licensed under the Open Government License v. 3.0.

23. A number of trams of this series were sold to San Francisco, where they are still running.

24. Figures from US Bureau of Transport Statistics.

25. John Kiff and Paul Mills, "Money for Nothing," IMF Working Paper 07199 (July 2007), 3.

26. Robert G. Kennedy, *Rethinking the Purpose of Business* (2002), 55.

Chapter 7—pages 89–105

1. Rudyard Kipling, "How the Camel Got His Hump," in *Just-So Stories* (1902).

2. See chap. 6 above.

3. Notably at Mariage Frères, a chain of upmarket tea shops in Paris and elsewhere. This is an old-established firm of tea importers that branched out into retailing in the 1980s. Despite its archaic selling methods and high prices, it is a thriving, profitable, expanding business.

4. Kazuto Taniguchi, interview with Philippe Pons, *Le Monde*, April 9, 2009.

5. Zeynep Ton, *The Good Jobs Strategy* (2014), 154.

6. Ibid., 198.

7. Rudyard Kipling, "If—" (1895).

8. Ton, *Good Jobs* (2014), 15.

9. Friedrich von Hayek, *1980s Unemployment and the Unions* (1980), 52.

10. Proportions in unions are OECD figures for 2012.

11. In practice, the unemployment rate never falls to zero, even in a "tight labor market" when demand for labor exceeds supply. There are always some people who are out of work because they are moving from one job to another or because they are not qualified for the jobs on offer.

12. See B. R. Mitchell, *British Economic Statistics* (1988), 126.

13. Wihelm von Ketteler, sermon at Offenbach am Main, July 25, 1869.

14. Daniel Nelson, *Shifting Fortunes* (1997), 104.

15. Figures from the US Bureau of Labor Statistics for 2013.

16. James Gray Pope, "How American Workers Lost the Right to Strike," *Michigan Law Review* (Dec. 2004).

17. Alvin L. Goldman and Robert L. Corrada, *Labor Law in the USA* (2011), 223.

18. National Labor Relations Act, sections 7 and 8.

19. Julius G. Getman, *Restoring the Power of Unions* (2010), 18–19.

20. Pius XII, address given to the Catholic Association of Small and Medium-Sized Businesses on October 8, 1956; quoted by Jean-Yves Calvet and Michael J. Naughton in *Rethinking the Purpose of Business* (2002), 55.

21. The National Labor Relations Act, which authorizes collective bargaining, does not apply to agricultural laborers, domestic servants, independent contractors, supervisors, and certain other workers. See NLRA sect. 2 (3).

22. Hoyt N. Wheeler, *The Future of the American Labor Movement* (2002), 197.

23. See National Center for Employee Ownership articles, "A Detailed Overview of Employee Ownership Plan Alternatives" and "ESOP Facts," www.nceo.org.

24. The John Lewis group also includes the famous Peter Jones department store in Sloane Square, London.

25. Mary Anchordoguy, *Reprogramming Japan* (2005), 40.

Chapter 8—pages 106–19

1. Theodore Roosevelt, address to the Deep Waterway Convention (Memphis, Tennessee), October 4, 1907.

2. Jim Leaps, director general of WWF International, *Living Planet Report* (2012), 6.

3. Peter Vitousek et al., *Bioscience* 36 (1986): 368–73.

4. Herman Daly, *Beyond Growth* (1996), 50.

5. Adam Smith, *The Wealth of Nations* (1776), bk. 1, chap. 11, pt. 2.

6. Ibid., pt. 3.

7. The Worshipful Company of Framework Knitters, a guild of the City of London, incorporated in 1657, still exists; see www.frameworkknitters.co.uk.

8. Karl Marx, *Capital* (1887), vol. 1, chaps. 25 (sect. 3) and 32.

9. Victor Lebow, "Price Competition," in *Journal of Retailing* (Spring 1955).

10. Donella H. Meadows et al., *The Limits to Growth* (1972), 23.

11. Milton Friedman, *Bright Prospects, Dismal Performance* (1983), 143.

12. Friedrich von Hayek, *The Fatal Conceit* (1988), 125.

13. Ibid., 133.

14. Julian Simon, *The Ultimate Resource* (2006), 6.

15. Ibid., 178.

16. Ibid., 179.

17. Babylonian Talmud, *Yebamoth*, fol. 61b.

18. Ibid., fol. 63b.

19. *Summa Theologiae*, supp. to pt. III, q. 41, a. 2 (my translation).

20. Simon, *The Ultimate Resource*, chap. 40.

21. Herman Daly and John Cobb, *For the Common Good* (1989), 239.

22. Thomas Aquinas, *Summa Theologiae* I, q. 10, a. 1.

23. Plato, *Timaeus*, 37d.

24. This chart is based on world population figures in the table on pages 113–14.

25. Sing C. Chew, *World Ecological Degradation* (2001), 3.

26. François Hinard, Nicolas Corvisier, and Pierre Salmon, *Histoire des populations de l'Europe* (1997), 131.

27. *Roman Catechism* (1829), 228.

28. Ibid., 233.

29. Francis, in-flight press conference between the Philippines and Rome, January 19, 2015. The Spanish text has *paternidad responsable*, i.e., *responsible fatherhood*.

30. A fertility rate of 3.0 (three births per woman) is sufficient to maintain a stable population in less-developed countries where mortality rates at younger ages are relatively high. In some of the poorest countries, the "replacement rate" is almost 3.5. In regions such as America and Europe, it is typically close to 2.1. See Thomas Espenshade et al., *Population Research and Policy Review* (2003), 575–83.

31. E. F. Schumacher, *Small is Beautiful* (1974), 98–99.

32. Smith, *The Wealth of Nations*, bk. 1, chap. 9.

33. John Stuart Mill, *Principles of Political Economy* (1848), bk. 4, chap. 6.

Chapter 9—pages 120–30

1. Ayn Rand, *The Fountainhead* (1952), 145.

2. Murray N. Rothbard, *For a New Liberty* (2006), 52.

3. Robert Nozick, *Anarchy, State, and Utopia* (1974), 169.

4. Lev 25:23. The *New International Version* has "you are but aliens and my tenants."

5. This translation is from the Anglican prayer book of 1662.

6. See below, chap. 11.

7. Jean Gaudemet, *L'Eglise dans l'empire romain* (1989), 571.

8. Lacedaemonia, also called Laconia, is a region in the southeast of the Peloponnese. Its people were "celebrated for their brief and pithy locution," hence our word *laconic*.

9. Charles Allen, *Plain Tales from the Raj* (1975), 94.

10. Ayn Rand, *Atlas Shrugged* (1996), 655.

11. Ambrose, *De Officiis Ministrorum* (On the Duties of the Clergy), bk. 1, chap. 28, par. 132.

12. Ibid.

13. Ambrose, *De Nabuthe* (concerning Naboth; see 1 Kgs 21), chap. 12, par. 53.

14. Augustine, *Epistle* 153, par. 26.

15. Augustine, *Tractates on the Gospel of St. John*, tractate 6, par. 25.

16. Basil, *Homily on Luke 12:18*.

17. Ibid.

18. Thomas Aquinas, *Summa Theologiae* II-II, q. 66, a. 2.

19. Ibid.

20. See Thomas Piketty, *Capital in the Twenty-First Century* (2014), graphs 6.5 and 8.5.

21. Pius XII, radio message, September 1, 1944.

22. Pius XII, radio message for Christmas Eve, December 24, 1942.

23. William M. Treanor, "The Origins and Original Significance of the Just Compensation Clause of the Fifth Amendment," *Yale Law Journal* (1985): 700.

24. Ralph L. Ketham, ed., *The Political Thought of Benjamin Franklin* (1965), 358.

25. *urbi et orbi* = to the city [of Rome] and to the world.

Chapter 10—pages 131–42

1. Dani Rodrik, *The Globalization Paradox* (2011), 190.

2. John A. Ryan, "Individualism," in *The Catholic Encyclopedia* (1910).

3. Rodrik, *The Globalization Paradox*, 191.

4. Vincent D. Rougeau, *The True Wealth of Nations* (2010), 126.

5. Milton Friedman, *Capitalism and Freedom* (1962), 14.

6. Arthur Corbin, *Corbin on Contracts* (1952), 1166.

7. Robert Nozick, *Anarchy, State, and Utopia* (1974), 331.

8. Cited by Eric Foner in *The Story of American Freedom* (1998), 32.

9. Articles 1965 and 1966 of the *Code Civil*. There is an exception for bets on events such as horse races, where the outcome is not purely a matter of chance.

10. Rougeau, *The True Wealth of Nations*, 118, 127.

11. Aristotle, *Nicomachean Ethics*, 1136b.

12. Ibid.

13. Henry Manning, *The Labour and Social Question* (1891), chap. 4.

14. Henri-Dominique Lacordaire, *Du Double Travail de l'Homme* (1848), 238.

15. OECD report *Oligopoly* (1999), 202.

Chapter 11—pages 143–62

1. Matt 5:3; *Catechism*, pars. 2546, 2548.

2. Amartya Sen, *L'économie est une science morale* (1999), 52–53.

3. See above, chap. 6, n14.

4. Aristotle, *Nicomachian Ethics*, 1131a.

5. Thomas Aquinas, *Summa Theologiae* II/II, q. 61, a. 2.

6. James Konow, *Distributive Justice* (2008), 3.

7. Michael Walzer, *Spheres of Justice* (1983), xi–xii.

8. Friedrich von Hayek, *The Mirage of Social Justice* (1976), 97.

9. Alan Avery-Peck, *Encyclopedia of Judaism*, vol. 1, 51–52.

10. Somewhat confusingly, from a Catholic standpoint, Jewish writers often translate *tzedakah* as *charity*.

11. Babylonian Talmud, *Sukkah* fol. 49b.

12. Fernand Cabrol and Henri Leclercq, *Dictionnaire d'Archéologie chrétienne*, tome 4, vol. 1, 995.

13. Irenaeus, *Adversus Haereses*, bk. 4, chap. 24, sec. 2.

14. Ibid., sec. 3.

15. Giles Constable, *Monastic Tithes* (1964), 18.

16. Thomas Aquinas, *Summa Theologiae* II/II, q. 87, a. 1.

17. *Council of Trent*, Twenty-Fifth Session, Decree on Reformation, chap. 12.

18. Babylonian Talmud, *Sukkah* fol. 49b.

19. F. J. Jansen, letter "Church Support," *The Ecclesiastical Review* (1919): 442.

20. Ibid.

21. See note 17 above.

22. Sara Hsu, *Financial Capital Overaccumulation* (2012), accessible on http://mpra.ub.uni-muenchen.de/41698/.

23. Oliver Goldsmith, *The Deserted Village* (1770).

24. Edwin Burmeister, *Capital Theory and Dynamics* (1980), 63.

25. Basil, *Homily on Luke 12:18*.

26. Thomas Aquinas, *Summa Contra Gentiles*, bk. 3, chap. 30.

Chapter 12—pages 163–77

1. Benedict XVI, Apostolic Exhortation *Sacramentum Caritatis* (2007), par. 90.

2. Thomas Aquinas, *De Regno*, pt. 2, chap. 3.

3. *The Collected Scientific Papers of Paul A. Samuelson* (1986), 5:486.

4. Dani Rodrik, *The Globalization Paradox* (2011), 252.

5. Not to be confused with *autarchy*, which means autocracy.

6. Robert O. Keohane, "Associative American Development, 1776–1860" (1983).

7. The official English version of *Gaudium et Spes* has "created goods should be in abundance for all," but that is not an accurate translation of the Latin text. The translation in *Populorum Progressio* (par. 22), quoted here, is more correct.

8. Address by Cardinal Silvano Tomasi at the 6th ministerial conference of the World Trade Organization, Hong Kong, December 18, 2005.

9. See chap. 6, n11.

10. See chap. 6, n10.

11. These are "composite indicator prices" published by the International Coffee Organization. At any one time, there are many prices for different varieties and grades of green coffee.

12. Estimate given by Jennifer Gallegas, Director of Coffee at Fair Trade USA; see their press release of April 10, 2013. This organization is quite distinct from Fairtrade America, which is part of Fairtrade International.

13. The Dutch worker-priest Frans van der Hoff, also called Francisco Vanderhoff Boersma (b. 1939) was a founding member of the association Max Havelaar, named after a character in a nineteenth-century Dutch novel.

14. For 2012, Fairtrade International reported sales of 77,400 metric tons, while Fair Trade USA reported 73,900 tons. Thus it appears that worldwide annual fair-trade coffee sales are now more than 150,000 tons. Total worldwide annual coffee sales are in the region of 8 million tons. Thus the fair-trade proportion is around 2 percent.

15. Keith R. Brown, *Buying into Fair Trade* (2013), 137.

16. Ibid., 128.

17. April Linton, *Free Trade from the Ground Up* (2013), 28, 32.

18. Brian van Arkadie and Raymond Mallon, *Vietnam, a Transition Tiger?* (2003), 185, 272.

19. Bui Van Hung, "Rural Diversification" in *Reaching for the Dream* (2004), 184, 191.

20. Benoit Daviron and Stefano Ponte, *The Coffee Paradox* (2005), 246.

21. Ibid., 245.

22. Nicole Vulser, *Shila Begum, survivant du Rana Plaza*, in *Le Monde*, April 22, 2014.

23. Naila Kabeer and Simeen Mahmud, in *Chains of Fortune* (2004), 142.

24. See chap. 10, n14.

25. Thomas Aquinas, *Summa Theologiae* II/II, q. 77, a. 1.

26. Ibid.

27. Thomas Aquinas, *Sententia Libri Ethicorum*, bk. 3, sect. 9.

28. Ibid.

Chapter 13—pages 178–89

1. Michael Walzer, *Spheres of Justice* (1983), 316.

2. Michael Sandel, "America's Search for a New Public Philosophy," *The Atlantic Monthly* (March 1996): 57.

3. Aristotle, *Politics*, 1252b.

4. George Mason, of Virginia, letter to his son at the opening of the Constitutional Convention, 1787.

5. Pierre-Paul Mercier de la Rivière, *L'ordre naturel et essentiel des Sociétés Politiques* (1767). In *Collection des principaux économistes*, vol. 2, 617.

6. Charles Gide, *Histoire des Doctrines Economiques* (1909), 361.

7. Ibid., 362.

8. Antoine de Montchrestien, *Traicté d'Economie Politique* (1999), 150.

9. See *"Laissez-faire,"* in *Palgrave Dictionary of Economics* (2008).

10. Adam Smith was professor of moral philosophy at Glasgow University from 1752 to 1764; in 1759 he published a major philosophical treatise, *The Theory of Moral Sentiments*.

11. Adam Smith, *Essays on Philosophical Subjects* (1980), 105.

12. Léon Walras, *Elements d'économie pure* (1988), 22.

13. Adam Smith, *The Wealth of Nations*, bk. 1, chap. 8.

14. For a detailed description of these markets, see Aron Katsenelinboigen, *Soviet Studies* (1977), 62–85.

15. Ernest Mandel, *New Left Review* (1986). Mandel (1923–1995) was a prominent Belgian Marxist writer and campaigner.

16. Friedrich von Hayek, *The Road to Serfdom* (1991), 31.

17. See, for example, Friedrich von Hayek, *The Fatal Conceit* (1988).

18. Friedrich von Hayek, *The Constitution of Liberty* (1960), 99.

19. Milton and Rose Friedman, *Free to Choose* (1980), 135.

Chapter 14—pages 190–204

1. Stefano Zamagni, *The True Wealth of Nations* (2010), 87.

2. The phrase *maintaining the revolution in permanence* appears in the constitution of the Universal Society of Revolutionary Communists set up by Marx, Engels, and others in London in 1850. See W. O. Henderson, *The Life of Friedrich Engels* (1976), 1:167.

3. Mary Klages, *Postmodernism* (2012), par. 5.

4. Friedrich von Hayek, *The Constitution of Liberty* (1960), 41.

5. Ibid., 400. Hayek, writing in England, used the word *liberal* here. But since in America that word commonly means something close to *socialist*, to avoid misunderstanding I have substituted *libertarian*.

6. Richard Cockett, *Thinking the Unthinkable* (1994), 174.

7. Translation by John Ellerton (1826–1893).

8. *Summa Theologiae* I, q. 9, a. 1 (my translation).

9. *Profession of Faith* of the Council of Nicaea (325), sec. 2.

10. *Profession of Faith* (first Constitution) of the Fourth Council of Lateran (1215).

11. *Summa Theologiae* I, q. 10, a. 1 (my translation).

12. Bruno Latour, *Jubiler, ou les tourmentes de la parole religieuse* (2002), 189.

13. Niels C. Nielsen, *Fundamentalism, Mythos, and World Religions* (1993), 148.

14. Laurence Kaplan, *Fundamentalism in Comparative Perspective* (1992), 7, 13.

15. Mokhtar Ben Barka, *Les Nouveaux Rédempteurs* (1998), 171.

16. The methods of trading used on the London and New York stock exchanges have historically involved prices that fluctuate continuously throughout each day's trading session. By contrast, the *Bourse de Paris* until recently used a system in which prices were set in a "call-over" held once or twice daily; other stock markets in Continental Europe used similar methods.

17. Jean-Michel Besnier, "Le monde numérique simplifie la pensée," *La Recherche,* no. 484 (February 2014): 78.

18. This report, *Disruptive Technologies* (May 2013), is accessible on www .mckinsey.com.

19. Plato, *Cratylus* (1926), 440a–440d.

Bibliography

Allen, Charles. *Plain Tales from the Raj*. London: Century Publishing, 1975.

Anchordoguy, Mary. *Reprogramming Japan*. Ithaca, NY: Cornell University Press, 2005.

Aristotle. *Nicomachean Ethics*. Translated by Harris Rackham. Cambridge, MA: Harvard University Press, 1967.

———. *Politics*. Translated by Benjamin Jowett. Oxford: Clarendon Press, 1885.

Arkadie, Brian van, and Raymond Mallon. *Vietnam, a Transition Tiger?* Canberra, Australia: Asia Pacific Press, 2003.

Augar, Philip. *The Death of Gentlemanly Capitalism*. London: Penguin, 2000.

Avery-Peck, Alan. "Charity in Judaism." In *Encyclopedia of Judaism*. Leiden: Kon. Brill NV, 2000.

Babylonian Talmud (including the *Mishna*). London: Soncino Press, 1935–1948.

Bellamy, Edward. *Looking Backward* (1888). Oxford: Oxford University Press, 2007.

Ben Barka, Mokhtar. *Les nouveaux rédempteurs: le fondamentalisme protestant aux Etats-Unis*. Paris: Les Editions de l'Atelier, 1998.

Benedict XVI. Encyclical *Caritas in Veritate*. Vatican, 2009.

———. Encyclical *Deus Caritas Est*. Vatican, 2006.

Berlin, Isaiah. *The Crooked Timber of Humanity*. Edited by Henry Hardy. London: John Murray, 1990.

Besnier, Jean-Michel. "Le monde numérique simplifie la pensée." *La Recherche*, no. 484, February 2014.

Biraben, Jean-Noël. "The History of the Human Population." In Graziella, Vallin & Wunsch, *Demography: Analysis and Synthesis*, vol. 3, chapter 66. Amsterdam: Elsevier, 2006.

Brown, Keith R. *Buying into Fair Trade*. New York: NYU Press, 2013.

Burckhardt, Jacob. *The Civilization of the Renaissance* (1861). Translated by S. G. C. Middlemore. London: Allen & Unwin, 1945.

Burmeister, Edwin. *Capital Theory and Dynamics*. Cambridge, UK: Cambridge University Press, 1980.

Cabrol, Fernand, and Henri Leclercq. *Dictionnaire d'Archéologie chrétienne et de liturgie*, tome 4, vol. 1. Paris: Letouzey et Ané, 1920–1921.

Calvet, Jean-Yves, and Michael J. Naughton. *Rethinking the Purpose of Business*. Notre Dame, IN: University of Notre Dame Press, 2002.

Catechism of the Catholic Church (Catechism). English translation. Libreria Editrice Vaticana, 1994.

Catholic Encyclopedia. New York: Robert Appleton Company, 1904–1912.

Cecil, Robert. *The Myth of the Master Race: Alfred Rosenberg and Nazi Ideology*. London: Batsford, 1972.

Chew, Sing C. *World Ecological Degradation*. Lanham, MD: Rowman & Littlefield, 2001.

Clair, Jean. *Sur Marcel Duchamp et la fin de l'art*. Paris: Gallimard, 2000.

Cockett, Richard. *Thinking the Unthinkable*. London: HarperCollins, 1994.

Compendium of the Social Doctrine of the Church (Compendium). Compiled by the Pontifical Council for Justice and Peace. English edition, Libreria Editrice Vaticana, 2005.

Confucius. *Analects of Confucius*. Translated by Roger T. Ames and Henry Rosemont, Jr. New York: Ballantine Books, 1998.

Constable, Giles. *Monastic Tithes*. Cambridge, UK: Cambridge University Press, 1964.

Corbin, Arthur. *Corbin on Contracts* (one-volume edition). St. Paul, MN: West Publishing, 1952.

Coubertin, Pierre de. Reported in *The Fourth Olympiad*. London: The British Olympic Association, 1909. See www.olympic-museum.de/o-reports/report1908.htm

Council of Trent. Canons and Decrees. Translated by J. Waterworth. London: Dolman, 1848.

Daly, Herman E. *Beyond Growth*. Boston: Beacon Press, 1996.

Daly, Herman E., and John B. Cobb, Jr. *For the Common Good*. Boston: Beacon Press, 1989.

Daviron, Benoit, and Stefano Ponte. *The Coffee Paradox*. London: Zed Books, 2005.

De Maistre, Joseph. *Du Pape* (1821). Paris: Garnier Frères, undated.

Duve, Thierry de. *Résonances du ready-made*. Nîmes: Jean Chambon, 1989.

Elazar, Daniel J. *Judaism and Democracy: The Reality*. Jerusalem Center for Public Affairs, 1986. See http://www.jcpa.org/dje/articles2/jud-democ.htm.

Espenshade, Thomas J., Juan C. Guzman, and Charles F. Westoff (Princeton University), "The Surprising Variation in Replacement Fertility." *Population and Policy Review*, vol. 22. Dordrecht, Netherlands: Kluwer, 2003.

FDIC: The First Fifty Years. Washington, DC: Federal Deposit Insurance Corporation, 1983.

Foner, Eric. *The Story of American Freedom*. New York: Norton, 1998.

Francis. Apostolic Exhortation *Evangelii Gaudium*. Vatican, 2013.

Frank, Robert H., and Philip J. Cook. *The Winner Take All Society*. New York: Simon & Schuster, 1995.

Friedman, Milton. *Capitalism and Freedom.* Chicago: University of Chicago Press, 1962.

———. "The Energy Crisis" (1978). Reprinted in *Bright Prospects, Dismal Performance.* Sun Lakes, AZ: Horton, 1983.

Friedman, Milton, and Rose Friedman. *Two Lucky People.* Chicago: University of Chicago Press, 1998.

———. *Free to Choose.* Orlando, FL: Harcourt, 1980.

Gagnebin, Laurent, and Raphael Picon. *Le protestantisme, foi insoumise.* Paris: Flammarion, 2008.

Gaudemet, Jean. *L'Eglise dans l'empire romain.* Paris: Sirey, 1989.

Gayraud, Jean-François. *Le nouveau capitalisme criminel.* Paris: Odile Jacob, 2014.

Getman, Julius G. *Restoring the Power of Unions.* New Haven, CT: Yale University Press, 2010.

Gide, Charles, and Charles Rist. *Histoire des Doctrines Economiques.* Paris: Larose et Tenin, 1909.

Goldman, Alvin L., and Robert L. Corrada. *Labour Law in the USA.* 3rd rev. ed. Kluwer Law International, 2011.

Green, Thomas Hill. *Works of T. H. Green.* Edited by R. L. Nettleship. London: Longmans, 1895–1911.

Greenfield, Gerard. "Vietnam and the World Coffee Crisis." Paper for the Asia-Pacific Regional Land and Freedom Conference, 2002.

Griffiths, Michael R., and John R. Lucas. *Ethical Economics.* New York: St. Martin's Press, 1996.

Häring, Bernhard. *The Law of Christ (Das Gesetz Christi,* 1951). Translated by E. G. Kaiser. Cork: Mercier, 1961.

Harris, Larry. *Trading and Exchanges.* Oxford: Oxford University Press, 2003.

Hayek, Friedrich von. *The Constitution of Liberty.* London: Routledge & Kegan Paul, 1960.

———. *The Fatal Conceit.* London: Routledge, 1988.

———. *The Mirage of Social Justice.* Chicago: University of Chicago Press, 1976.

———. *The Political Order of a Free People.* Chicago: University of Chicago Press, 1979.

———. *The Road to Serfdom* (1944). London: Routlege, 1991.

———. *1980s Unemployment and the Unions.* London: Institute of Economic Affairs, 1980.

Hazlitt, Henry. *Economics in One Lesson* (1946). Auburn, AL: The Ludwig von Mises Institute, 2008.

Henderson, W. O. *The Life of Friedrich Engels.* London: Routledge, 1976.

Heschel, Abraham. *God in Search of Man.* Philadelphia: Jewish Publications Society, 1959.

———. *The Insecurity of Freedom.* New York: Farrar, Strauss & Giroux, 1966.

Hinard, François, Nicolas Corvisier, and Pierre Salmon. "L'Europe gréco-romaine." In *Histoire des populations d'Europe*, edited by Jean-Pierre Bardet and Jacques Dupâquier. Paris: Fayard, 1997.

Hsu, Sara. *Financial Capital Overaccumulation* (2012). Accessible at http://mpra.ub.uni-muenchen.de/41698.

Hung, Bui Van. "Rural Diversification." In *Reaching for the Dream*, edited by Margaret Beresford and Tran Ngoe Angie. Copenhagen: Nordic Institute of Asian Studies, 2004.

Hunt, Edwin S., and James M. Murray. *A History of Business in Medieval Europe, 1200–1550*. Cambridge, UK: Cambridge University Press, 1999.

John XXIII. Encyclical *Mater et Magistra*. Vatican, 1961.

John Paul II. Encyclical *Centesimus Annus*. Vatican, 1991.

———. Encyclical *Laborem Exercens*. Vatican, 1981.

———. Encyclical *Sollicitudo Rei Socialis*. Vatican, 1987.

Kabeer, Naila, and Simeen Mahmud. "Rags, Riches and Women Workers." In *Chains of Fortune*, edited by Marilyn Carr. London: Commonwealth Secretariat, 2004. This book is accessible on http://wiego.com.

Kant, Immanuel. *Was ist Aufklärung? (What Is Enlightenment?)*. Berlinischer Monatsschrift, 1784.

Kaplan, Laurence. *Fundamentalism in Comparative Perspective*. Amherst, MA: University of Massachusetts Press, 1992.

Katsenelinboigen, Aron. "Colored Markets in the Soviet Union" *Soviet Studies* vol. 29, no. 1. Abingdon, England: Taylor & Francis, 1977.

Kaye, Beverly, and Sharon Jordan-Evans. *Love It, Don't Leave It*. San Francisco: Berrett-Koehler, 2003.

Kennedy, Robert G. "The Virtue of Solidarity and the Purpose of the Firm." Chap. 3 in *Rethinking the Purpose of Business: Interdisciplinary Essays from the Catholic Social Tradition*, edited by S. A. Cortright and J. Naughton. Notre Dame, IN: University of Notre Dame Press, 2002.

Keohane, Robert. "Associative American Development, 1776–1860." Chap. 2 in *The Antinomies of Interdependence*, edited by John G. Ruggie. New York: Columbia University Press, 1983.

Ketham, Ralph L., ed. *The Political Thought of Benjamin Franklin*. Indianapolis: Bobbs-Merrill, 1965.

Kindleberger, Charles P. *A Financial History of Western Europe*. Oxford: Oxford University Press, 1993.

Klages, Mary. *Postmodernism*. See www.colorado.edu/English/ENGL2012 Klagespomo.html.

Konow, James. "Distributive Justice." In *Encyclopedia of American Government and Civics*, edited by Michael A. Genovese and Lori Cox Han. New York: Facts-on-File, 2008.

Lacordaire, Henri-Dominique. *Du double travail de l'homme* (52nd Conférence de Notre Dame). Paris, 1848.

Lamennais, Félicité de. *Des Progrès de la Révolution et de la Guerre contre l'Eglise*. Paris: Belin-Mandar et Devaux, 1829.

Latour, Bruno. *Jubiler, ou les tourmentes de la parole religieuse*. Paris: Le Seuil, 2002.

Leo XIII. Encyclical *Graves de Communi Re*. Vatican, 1901.

———. Encyclical *Libertas Praestantissimum*. Vatican, 1888.

———. Encyclical *Rerum Novarum*. Vatican, 1891.

Linton, April. *Free Trade from the Ground Up*. Seattle: University of Washington Press, 2013.

Mandel, Ernest. "In Defense of Socialist Planning." *New Left Review*, no. 159 (September–October 1986).

Manning, Henry. *The Labor and Social Question*. London, 1891.

Marx, Karl. *Capital* (*Das Kapital*, 1867). Translated by Samuel Moore and Edward Aveling. London, 1887.

Meadows, Donella H., et al. *The Limits to Growth*. New York: Universe Books, 1972.

Menger, Carl. *Principles of Economics* (*Grundsätze der Volkswirtschaftslehre*, 1871). Translated by James Dingwall & Bert F. Hoselitz. New York: NYU Press, 1976.

Mercier de la Rivière, Pierre-Paul. *L'ordre naturel et essentiel des Sociétés Politiques* (1767). In *Collection des principaux économistes*, edited by Eugène Daire. Osnabrück: Zeller, facsimile 1966.

Milford, Anna. *Coffee, Co-operatives and Competition: The Impact of Fair Trade*. Bergen: Chr. Michelsen Institute, 2004.

Mill, John Stuart. *Principles of Political Economy*. London, 1848.

Mises, Ludwig von. *Human Action*. New York: Yale University Press, 1949.

———. "Liberty and Property." Lecture given at Princeton, 1958, accessible on www.libertadcarajo.files.wordpress.com.

———. *Socialism* (*Die Gemeinwirtschaft*, 1922). Translated by J Kahane. New Haven, CT: Yale University Press, 1981.

Mishna: see *Babylonian Talmud*.

Mitchell, B. R. *British Economic Statistics*. Cambridge, UK: Cambridge University Press, 1988.

Montchrestien, Antoine de. *Traicté de l'économie politique* (1615), critical edition by François Billacor. Geneva: Droz, 1999.

Nelson, Daniel. *Shifting Fortunes*. Chicago: Ivan R. Dee, 1997.

Nielsen, Niels C. *Fundamentalism, Mythos, and World Religions*. New York: State University of New York Press, 1993.

Nojiri, Taketoshi. "Values as a Precondition of Democracy." In *Democracy—Some Acute Questions*. Vatican City: Pontifical Academy of Social Sciences, 1998.

Nozick, Robert. *Anarchy, State, and Utopia*. Oxford: Blackwell, 1974.

OECD. *OECD Economic Surveys: Switzerland 2007*. OECD Publishing, 2007.

Orwell, George. *Nineteen Eighty-Four* (1949). Edited by Peter Davidson. London: Secker & Warburg, 1987.

Palgrave Dictionary of Economics. New York: Palgrave Macmillan, 2008.

Paul VI. Encyclical *Humanae Vitae*. Vatican, 1968.

———. Encyclical *Populorum Progressio*. Vatican, 1967.

Phillips, J. B. *The New Testament in Modern English*. London: Geoffrey Bles, 1962.

Piketty, Thomas. *Capital in the Twenty-First Century (Le Capital au XXI siècle*, 2013). Translated by Arthur Goldhammer. Cambridge, MA: Harvard University Press, 2014.

Pius X. Encyclical *Singulari Quadam*. Vatican, 1912.

Pius XI. Encyclical *Caritate Christi Compulsi*. Vatican, 1932.

———. Encyclical *Quadragesimo Anno*. Vatican, 1931.

———. Encyclical *Divini Redemptoris*. Vatican, 1937.

Plato. *Cratylus*. Translated by H. N. Fowler. Cambridge, MA: Harvard University Press, 1926.

———. *Timaeus*. Translated by Benjamin Jowett. Oxford: Clarendon Press, 1953.

Rand, Ayn. *Atlas Shrugged* (1957). New York: Signet, 1997.

———. *The Fountainhead* (1943). New York: Signet, 1952.

———. *The Virtue of Selfishness*. New York: Signet, 1964.

Ratzinger, Joseph. *Introduction to Christianity (Einführing in das Christentum*, 1968). Translated by J. R. Foster. San Francisco: Ignatius Press, 1990.

Rodrik, Dani. *The Globalization Paradox*. Oxford: Oxford University Press, 2011.

Roman Catechism. Translated by J. Donovan. Baltimore, MD: Fielding Lucas, 1829.

Rothbard, Murray N. *For a New Liberty* (1973). Auburn, AL: The Ludwig von Mises Institute, 2006.

———. "Myth and Truth about Libertarians." *Modern Age* (Winter 1980).

Rougeau, Vincent D. "Just Contracts and Catholic Social Teaching." Chap. 5 in *The True Wealth of Nations*, edited by Daniel K. Finn. Oxford: Oxford University Press, 2010.

Sacks, Jonathan. *The Politics of Hope*. London: Vintage, 2000.

Samuelson, Paul A. *The Collected Scientific Papers of Paul A. Samuelson*. Edited by Kate Crowley. Cambridge, MA: Massachusetts Institute of Technology Press, 1986.

Schmoller, Gustav. *Grundriss der allgemeinen Volkswirtschaftslehre (Principles of Political Economy)*. Leipzig: Duncker & Humblot, 1900/1904.

Schumacher, E. F. *Small is Beautiful*. London: Sphere Books, 1974.

Sedlacek, Thomas. *Economics of Good and Evil (Ekonomie dobra a zla*, 2009). Translated by Douglas Arellanes. Oxford: Oxford University Press, 2011.

Sen, Amartya. *L'économie est une science morale*. Paris: La Découverte, 1999.

————. *On Ethics and Economics*. Oxford: Blackwell, 1987.

Shain, Barry. *The Myth of American Individualism*. Princeton, NJ: Princeton University Press, 1994.

Sibley, Angus. "The Hyperthyroid Economy." *Journal of the Royal Society of Medicine*, June 1995.

Simon, Julian. *The Ultimate Resource*. 2nd ed. Princeton, NJ: Princeton University Press, 2006.

Smith, Adam. "History of Astronomy." In *Essays on Philosophical Subjects*, edited by W. P. D. Wightman and J. C. Bryce. Oxford: Clarendon Press, 1980.

————. *An Inquiry into the Nature and Causes of The Wealth of Nations*. London, 1776.

————. *The Theory of Moral Sentiments*. Edinburgh, 1759.

Southern, Richard. *The Making of the Middle Ages*. New Haven, CT: Yale University Press, 1953.

Stiglitz, Joseph. *The Roaring Nineties*. 2nd ed. New York: Norton, 2004.

Sumner, William G. *What the Social Classes Owe to Each Other* (1883). Salem, NH: Ayer, 1987.

Taylor, Charles. *The Ethics of Authenticity*. Cambridge, MA: Harvard University Press, 1991.

Thomas Aquinas. *De Regno*. Translated by Gerald B. Phelan. Toronto: Institute of Medieval Studies, 1949.

————. *Sententia libri Ethicorum* (commentary on Aristotle's Nicomachean Ethics). Translated by Charles I. Litzinger. South Bend, IN: Dumb Ox Books, 1993.

————. *Summa Theologiae*. Translated by the Fathers of the English Dominican Province. Cincinnati, OH: Benzinger Bros., 1917.

Thucydides. *History of the Pelopennesian War*. Translated by Benjamin Jowett. Oxford: Clarendon Press, 1881.

Tocqueville, Alexis de. *Democracy in America* (*La Démocratie en Amérique*, 1835). Translated by Arthur Goldhammer. New York: Library of America, 2004.

Ton, Zeynep. *The Good Jobs Strategy*. Seattle: Lake Union, 2014.

Treanor, William M. "The Origins and Original Significance of the Just Compensation Clause of the Fifth Amendment." *Yale Law Journal* 94 (1985).

Tugwell, Rexford G. *The Democratic Roosevelt*. Garden City, NY: Doubleday, 1957.

Ullmann, Walter. *The Individual and Society in the Middle Ages*. Baltimore, MD: The Johns Hopkins Press, 1966.

Vatican Council II. Pastoral Constitution *Gaudium et Spes*. Vatican, 1965.

Vitousek, Peter, et al. "Human Appropriation of the Products of Photosynthesis." *Bioscience* 36 (1986).

Walras, Léon. *Elements d'économie pure* (4th ed., 1900). Paris: Economica, 1988.

Walzer, Michael. *Spheres of Justice*. Oxford: Blackwell, 1993.

Weiler, Paul C. *Governing the Workplace*. Cambridge, MA: Harvard University Press, 1990.

Wheeler, Hoyt N. *The Future of the American Labor Movement*. Cambridge, UK: Cambridge University Press, 2002.

WWF International. *Living Planet Report 2012*. Gland, Switzerland: WWF International, 2012.

Zamagni, Stefano. "Catholic Social Thought, Civil Economy and the Spirit of Capitalism." In *The True Wealth of Nations*, edited by Daniel Finn. Oxford: Oxford University Press, 2010.

Index